SERVICE-ORIENTED DESIGN WITH RUBY AND RAILS

SERVICE-ORIENTED DESIGN WITH RUBY AND RAILS

Paul Dix

✦✦Addison-Wesley

Upper Saddle River, NJ • Boston • Indianapolis • San Francisco
New York • Toronto • Montreal • London • Munich • Paris • Madrid
Capetown • Sydney • Tokyo • Singapore • Mexico City

Many of the designations used by manufacturers and sellers to distinguish their products are claimed as trademarks. Where those designations appear in this book, and the publisher was aware of a trademark claim, the designations have been printed with initial capital letters or in all capitals.

The author and publisher have taken care in the preparation of this book, but make no expressed or implied warranty of any kind and assume no responsibility for errors or omissions. No liability is assumed for incidental or consequential damages in connection with or arising out of the use of the information or programs contained herein.

The publisher offers excellent discounts on this book when ordered in quantity for bulk purchases or special sales, which may include electronic versions and/or custom covers and content particular to your business, training goals, marketing focus, and branding interests. For more information, please contact:

U.S. Corporate and Government Sales
(800) 382-3419
corpsales@pearsontechgroup.com

For sales outside the United States please contact:

International Sales
international@pearson.com

Visit us on the Web: informit.com/aw

Library of Congress Cataloging-in-Publication Data

Dix, Paul, 1977-
    Service-oriented design with Ruby and Rails / Paul Dix.
        p.   cm.
    Includes bibliographical references and index.
    ISBN 0-321-65936-8 (pbk. : alk. paper) 1. Web services.
2. Service-oriented architecture (Computer science) 3. Web sites—Design.
4. Ruby on rails (Electronic resource) I. Title.
    TK5105.88813.D593 2010
    006.7'8—dc22

                                                              2010021623

ISBN-13: 978-0-321-65936-1
ISBN-10:   0-321-65936-8
Text printed in the United States on recycled paper at Courier in Stoughton, Massachusetts.

First printing, August 2010

Associate Publisher
Mark Taub

Acquisitions Editor
Debra Williams Cauley

Development Editor
Michael Thurston

Managing Editor
John Fuller

Project Editor
Elizabeth Ryan

Copy Editor
Kitty Wilson

Indexer
Jack Lewis

Proofreader
Carol Lallier

Technical Reviewers
Jennifer Lindner,
Trotter Cashion

Cover Designer
Chuti Prasertsith

Compositor
LaserWords

To Pops, for encouraging my weird obsession with computers.

Contents

Foreword

It's an honor for me to present to you this timely new addition to the Professional Ruby Series, one that fills a crucially important gap in the ongoing evolution of all professional Rubyists and couldn't come a moment sooner! It is authored by one of the brightest minds of our international Ruby community, Paul Dix, described as "genius" and "A-list" by his peers. Paul is no stranger to the Ruby world, a fixture at our conferences and involved in some of the earliest Rails project work dating back to 2005. He's also the author of Typhoeus, a successful high-performance HTTP library that is an essential part of the service-oriented ecosystem in Ruby.

Why is this book so timely? Serious Ruby adoption in large companies and project settings inevitably necessitates service-oriented approaches to system design. Properly designed large applications, partitioned into cooperating services, can be far more agile than monolithic applications. Services make it easy to scale team size. As the code base of an application gets larger, it gets harder to introduce new developers to the project. When applications are split into services, developers can be assigned to a specific service or two. They only need to be familiar with their section of the application and the working groups can remain small and nimble.

There's also the fact that we live in the age of The Programmable Web, the boom of web applications, APIs, and innovation over the past few years that is directly attributable to the rise of interoperable web services like those described in this book. Applications that rely on web resources present unique challenges for development teams. Service-oriented traits impact various aspects of how applications should be designed and the level of attention that needs to be paid to how the application performs and behaves if those services are unavailable or otherwise limited.

My own teams at Hashrocket have run into challenges where we could have used the knowledge in this book, both in our Twitter applications as well as our large client projects, some of which we have been working on for years. In a couple of notable cases, we have looked back in regret, wishing we had taken a service-oriented approach sooner. I assure you that this book will be on the required-reading list for all Rocketeers in the future.

Like Hashrocket, many of you buying this book already have big monolithic Rails applications in production. Like us, you might have concerns about how to migrate your existing work to a service-oriented architecture. Paul covers four different strategies for application partitioning in depth: Iteration Speed, Logical Function, Read/Write Frequency, and Join Frequency. Specific examples are used to explore the challenges and benefits of each strategy. The recurring case study is referred to often, to ensure the discussion is grounded in real, not imaginary or irrelevant situations.

Paul doesn't limit himself to theory either, which makes this a well-rounded and practical book. He gives us important facts to consider when running in a production environment, from load balancing and caching to authentication, authorization, and encryption to blocking I/O to parallelism, and how to tackle these problems in Ruby 1.8, 1.9, Rubinius, and JRuby.

Overall, I'm proud to assure you that Paul has given us a very readable and useful book. It is accurate and current, bringing in Rack, Sinatra, and key features of Rails 3, such as its new routing and ActiveModel libraries. At the same time, the book achieves a timeless feeling, via its concise descriptions of service-oriented techniques and broadly applicable sample code that I'm sure will beautifully serve application architects and library authors alike for years to come.

—Obie Fernandez
Author of *The Rails Way*
Series Editor of the Addison-Wesley Professional Ruby Series
CEO & Founder of Hashrocket

Preface

As existing Ruby on Rails deployments grow in size and adoption expands into larger application environments, new methods are required to interface with heterogeneous systems and to operate at scale. While the word *scalability* with respect to Rails has been a hotly debated topic both inside and outside the community, the meaning of the word *scale* in this text is two fold. First, the traditional definition of "handling large numbers of requests" is applicable and something that the service-oriented approach is meant to tackle. Second, *scale* refers to managing code bases and teams that continue to grow in size and complexity. This book presents a service-oriented design approach that offers a solution to deal with both of these cases.

Recent developments in the Ruby community make it an ideal environment for not only creating services but consuming them as well. This book covers technologies and best practices for creating application architectures composed of services. These could be written in Ruby and tied together through a frontend Rails application, or services could be written in any language, with Ruby acting as the glue to combine them into a greater whole. This book covers how to properly design and create services in Ruby and how to consume these and other services from within the Rails environment.

Who This Book Is For

This book is written with web application and infrastructure developers in mind. Specific examples cover technologies in the Ruby programming ecosystem. While the code in this book is aimed at a Ruby audience, the design principles are applicable to environments with multiple programming languages in use. In fact, one of the advantages of the service-oriented approach is that it enables teams to implement pieces of application logic in the programming language best suited for the task at hand. Meanwhile, programmers in any other language can take advantage of these services through a common public interface. Ultimately, Ruby could serve simply at the application level to pull together logic from many services to render web requests through Rails or another preferred web application framework.

If you're reading this book, you should be familiar with web development concepts. Code examples mainly cover the usage of available open source Ruby libraries, such as Ruby on Rails, ActiveRecord, Sinatra, Nokogiri, and Typhoeus. If you are new to Ruby, you should be able to absorb the material as long as you have covered the language basics elsewhere and are generally familiar with web development. While the topic of service-oriented design is usually targeted at application architects, this book aims to present the material for regular web developers to take advantage of service-based approaches.

If you are interested in how Ruby can play a role in combining multiple pieces within an enterprise application stack, you will find many examples in this book to help achieve your goals. Further, if you are a Rails developer looking to expand the possibilities of your environment beyond a single monolithic application, you will see how this is not only possible but desirable. You can create systems where larger teams of developers can operate together and deploy improvements without the problem of updating the entire application at large.

The sections on API design, architecture, and data backends examine design principles and best practices for creating services that scale and are easy to interface with for internal and external customers. Sections on connecting to web services and parsing responses provide examples for those looking to write API wrappers around external services such as SimpleDB, CouchDB, or third-party services, in addition to internal services designed by the developer.

What This Book Covers

This book covers Ruby libraries for building and consuming RESTful web services. This generally refers to services that respond to HTTP requests. Further, the APIs of these services are defined by the URIs requested and the method (GET, PUT, POST, DELETE) used. While the focus is on a RESTful approach, some sections deviate from a purist style. In these cases, the goal is to provide clarity for a service API or flexibility in a proposed service.

The primary topics covered in this book are as follows:

- REST, HTTP verbs, and response codes
- API design

- Building services in Ruby
- Connecting to services
- Consuming JSON- and XML-based services
- Architecture design
- Messaging and AMQP
- Securing services

What This Book Doesn't Cover

Service-oriented architectures have been around for over a decade. During this time, many approaches have been taken. These include technologies with acronyms and buzzwords such as SOAP, WSDL, WS-*, and XML-RPC. Generally, these require greater overhead, more configuration, and the creation of complex schema files. Chapter 9, "Parsing XML for Legacy Services," provides brief coverage of consuming XML and SOAP services. However, SOAP, XML-RPC, and related technologies are beyond the scope of this book. The services you'll create in this book are lightweight and flexible, like the Ruby language itself.

This book also does not cover other methods for building complex architectures. For example, it does not cover batch processing frameworks such as MapReduce or communications backends such as Thrift. While these technologies can be used in conjunction with a web services approach, they are not the focus. However, Chapter 11, "Messaging," briefly covers messaging systems and message queues.

Additional Resources

Code examples are used heavily throughout this book. While every effort has been made to keep examples current, the open source world moves fast, so the examples may contain code that is a little out-of-date. The best place to find up-to-date source code is on GitHub, at the following address:

```
http://github.com/pauldix/service-oriented-design-with-ruby
```

In addition, you can subscribe to a mailing list to discuss the code, text, services design, and general questions on the topic of service-oriented design. You can join here:

```
http://groups.google.com/group/service-oriented-design-
  with-ruby
```

Acknowledgments

An unbelievable number of people contributed to this book through writing, editing, conversations about the content, or just moral support, so please forgive me if I leave anyone out. First, I need to thank Lindsey for putting up with my ridiculous schedule while writing this book and working a full-time job. Thanks to Trotter Cashion for writing Chapter 10, "Security"; to Bryan Helmkamp for writing Chapter 8, "Load Balancing and Caching"; and to Jake Howerton for writing Chapter 12, "Web Hooks and External Services." Thanks to Trotter again and Jennifer Linder for providing excellent editing work and making sure that it makes sense. Thanks to Debra, my editor at Addison-Wesley, and to Michael, my development editor at AW. Thanks to the NYC.rb crew for being smart, fun people to hang out and discuss ideas with. Thanks to the entire team at KnowMore for putting up with me while I wrote and helping me refine my thinking. Finally, thanks to my business partner, Vivek, for providing encouragement during the final editing stages.

About the Author

Paul Dix is co-founder and CTO at Market.io. In the past, he has worked at Google, Microsoft, McAfee, Air Force Space Command, and multiple startups, filling positions as a programmer, software tester, and network engineer. He has been a speaker at multiple conferences, including RubyConf, Goruco, and Web 2.0 Expo, on the subjects of service-oriented design, event-driven architectures, machine learning, and collaborative filtering. Paul is the author of multiple open source Ruby libraries. He has a degree in computer science from Columbia University.

CHAPTER 1

Implementing and Consuming Your First Service

In the grand tradition of programming books beginning with a "hello, world" example, this book starts off with a simple service. This chapter walks through the creation of a service to store user metadata and manage authentication. This includes building the web service to handle HTTP requests and the client library for interacting with the service.

What's a Service?

In this book, *service* generally refers to a system that responds to HTTP requests. Such HTTP requests are usually to write, retrieve, or modify data. Examples of public-facing HTTP services include Twitter's API (http://apiwiki.twitter.com), the Amazon S3 service (http://aws.amazon.com/s3/), the Delicious API (http://delicious.com/help/api), the Digg API (http://apidoc.digg.com), and the New York Times APIs (http://developer .nytimes.com/docs). Internally, services could exist to contain pieces of data and business logic that are used by one or more applications.

Using a broader scope of definition, *service* can refer to a system that provides functionality through a standard interface. Working at this level of abstraction are services such as relational databases (for example, MySQL), Memcached servers, message queues (for example, RabbitMQ), and other types of data stores, such as Cassandra (http://incubator.apache.org/cassandra/).

1

While this book touches on the broader definition of *service* in a few places, the majority of the material focuses on HTTP-based services. More specifically, this book focuses on services that are designed to roughly follow a RESTful paradigm, as described in the appendix, "RESTful Primer." Further, this book focuses on using services within an organization and infrastructure to build out applications. These services may or may not be public facing, like the previous examples.

The details of why, when, and how to use services are covered throughout the course of the book. For now the goal is to implement a simple service.

Service Requirements

A simple user management system is an example of something that can be pulled out as a service. After implementation, this service could be used across multiple applications within an organization as a single sign-on point. The goals and requirements of the service are fairly simple:

- Store user metadata, including name, email address, password, and bio.
- Support the full range of CRUD (create, update, delete) operations for user objects.
- Verify a user login by name and password.

In later versions of the user service, features could map which users work with each other, which user each user reports to, and which groups a user is a member of. For now, the basic feature set provides enough to work on.

The Ruby Tool Set

Ruby provides many tools to build both the service and client sides of services. However, this book heavily favors some specific tools due to their aesthetics or performance characteristics. The following libraries appear often throughout this book.

Sinatra

Sinatra is a lightweight framework for creating web applications. It can be described as a domain-specific language for web applications and web services. Built on top of Rack, Sinatra is perfectly suited for creating small web services like the example in this chapter. In addition to encouraging an elegant code style, Sinatra has fewer than 2,000 lines of code. With this small and readable code base, it's easy to dig through the internals to get a more specific idea of what's going on under the hood.

Sinatra was originally written by Blake Mizerany, and continued development is supported by Heroku. The official web site is http://www.sinatrarb.com, and the code repository is on GitHub, at http://github.com/sinatra/sinatra. Chapter 4, "Service and API Design," provides more in-depth coverage of Sinatra. For now, Sinatra can be installed to work through the example in this chapter using the gem command on the command line, like this:

```
gem install sinatra
```

ActiveRecord

ActiveRecord is the well-known object/relational mapper (ORM) that is an integral part of Ruby on Rails. It provides a simple interface for mapping Ruby objects to the MySQL, PostgreSQL, or SQLite relational databases. Since most readers are probably familiar with ActiveRecord, the choice to use it as the data library was easy. However, the focus of this book is on creating service interfaces, creating clients, and organizing service interactions. Which data store or library to use is beyond the scope of this book. Readers experienced with alternative data stores are welcome to use them in place of ActiveRecord.

ActiveRecord was originally developed by David Heinemeier Hansson as a part of Ruby on Rails. It is an implementation of the ActiveRecord design pattern by Martin Fowler (http://www.martinfowler.com/eaaCatalog/activeRecord.html). The documentation can be found at http://ar.rubyonrails.org, and the source code is part of the Rails repository on GitHub, at http://github.com/rails/rails/tree/master/activerecord/. ActiveRecord can be installed using the gem command on the command line, like this:

```
gem install activerecord
```

JSON

The representation of resources from HTTP services can be in any of a number of formats. HTML, XML, and JSON are the most common. JSON is quickly becoming a favorite choice because of its speed and simplicity as well as the availability of quality parsers in most languages. JSON includes built-in types such as strings, integers, floats, objects (such as Ruby hashes), and arrays. Most complex data types can be represented fairly easily and succinctly by using these basic data structures.

There is no shortage of available JSON parsers for Ruby. The most popular option is the JSON Ruby implementation found at http://flori.github.com/json/. However, Brian Marino's Ruby bindings to YAJL (yet another JSON library) look like a very solid option that can provide some performance increases. Marino's code can be found at http://github.com/brianmario/yajl-ruby, and the YAJL code can be found at http://lloyd.github.com/yajl/. For simplicity, the service example in this chapter uses the JSON Ruby implementation, which can be installed using the gem command on the command line, like this:

```
gem install json
```

Typhoeus

The client libraries for services must use an HTTP library to connect to the server. Typhoeus is an HTTP library specifically designed for high-speed parallel access to services. Being able to run requests in parallel becomes very important when connecting to multiple services. Typhoeus includes classes to wrap requests and response logic as well as a connection manager to run requests in parallel. It also includes raw bindings to the libcurl and libcurl-multi libraries that make up its core functionality.

Typhoeus was originally written by me, and ongoing support is provided at http://KnowMore.com. The code and documentation can be found at http://github.com/pauldix/typhoeus/, and the support mailing list is at http://groups .google.com/group/typhoeus. Typhoeus is covered in greater detail in Chapter 6. "Connecting to Services." For now, it can be install using the gem command line, like this:

```
gem install typhoeus
```

Rspec

Testing should be an integral part of any programming effort. This book uses Rspec as its preferred testing library. It provides a clean, readable domain-specific language for writing tests.

Rspec is written and maintained by the core team of Dave Astels, Steven Baker, David Chemlimsky, Aslak Hellesøy, Pat Maddox, Dan North, and Brian Takita. Coverage of Rspec is beyond the scope of this book. However, detailed documentation and examples can be found on the Rspec site, at http://rspec.info. Rspec can be installed using the gem command on the command line, like this:

```
gem install rspec
```

The User Service Implementation

With the list of tools to build the service and client libraries chosen, you're ready to implement the service. The server side of the system is the first part to build. Remember that this is a Sinatra application. Unlike Rails, Sinatra doesn't come with generators to start new projects, so you have to lay out the application yourself. The basic directory structure and necessary files should look something like the following:

```
/user-service
  /config.ru
  /config
    database.yml
  /db
    /migrate
  /models
  /spec
  Rakefile
```

The user-service directory is the top level of the service. The config directory contains database.yml, which ActiveRecord uses to make a database connection. config.ru is a configuration file that Rack uses to start the service. The db directory contains the migrate scripts for models. The models directory contains any ActiveRecord models. Rakefile contains a few tasks for migrating the database.

The database.yml file looks like a standard Rails database configuration file:

```
development:
  adapter: sqlite3
  database: db/development.sqlite3

test:
  adapter: sqlite3
  database: db/test.sqlite3
```

Rakefile contains the task to migrate the database after you've created the user migration:

```
require 'rubygems'
require 'active_record'
require 'yaml'
```

```ruby
desc "Load the environment"
task :environment do
  env = ENV["SINATRA_ENV"] || "development"
  databases = YAML.load_file("config/database.yml")
  ActiveRecord::Base.establish_connection(databases[env])
end

namespace :db do
  desc "Migrate the database"
  task(:migrate => :environment) do
    ActiveRecord::Base.logger = Logger.new(STDOUT)
    ActiveRecord::Migration.verbose = true
    ActiveRecord::Migrator.migrate("db/migrate")
  end
end
```

First, the dependencies are loaded. Then the :environment task is created. This makes a connection to the database based on what environment is being requested. Finally, the :db namespace is defined with the :migrate task. The migrate task calls the migrate method on Migrator, pointing it to the directory the database migrations are in.

With all the basic file and directory scaffolding out of the way, you can now spec and create the service. The specs for the service define the behavior for expected interactions and a few of the possible error conditions. The specs described here are by no means complete, but they cover the primary cases.

Using GET

The most basic use case for the server is to return the data about a single user. The following sections outline the behavior with specs before starting the implementation.

Spec'ing GET User

To get the specs started, you create a file in the /spec directory called service_spec.rb. The beginning of the file and the user GET specs look like this:

```ruby
require File.dirname(__FILE__) + '/../service'
require 'spec'
require 'spec/interop/test'
require 'rack/test'
```

```ruby
set :environment, :test
Test::Unit::TestCase.send :include, Rack::Test::Methods

def app
  Sinatra::Application
end

describe "service" do
  before(:each) do
    User.delete_all
  end

  describe "GET on /api/v1/users/:id" do
    before(:each) do
      User.create(
        :name => "paul",
        :email => "paul@pauldix.net",
        :password => "strongpass",
        :bio => "rubyist")
    end

    it "should return a user by name" do
      get '/api/v1/users/paul'
      last_response.should be_ok
      attributes = JSON.parse(last_response.body)
      attributes["name"].should == "paul"
    end

    it "should return a user with an email" do
      get '/api/v1/users/paul'
      last_response.should be_ok
      attributes = JSON.parse(last_response.body)
      attributes["email"].should == "paul@pauldix.net"
    end

    it "should not return a user's password" do
      get '/api/v1/users/paul'
      last_response.should be_ok
      attributes = JSON.parse(last_response.body)
      attributes.should_not have_key("password")
    end

    it "should return a user with a bio" do
      get '/api/v1/users/paul'
      last_response.should be_ok
```

```
        attributes = JSON.parse(last_response.body)
        attributes["bio"].should == "rubyist"
      end

    it "should return a 404 for a user that doesn't exist" do
      get '/api/v1/users/foo'
      last_response.status.should == 404
    end
  end
end
```

The first 11 lines of the file set up the basic framework for running specs against a Sinatra service. The details of each are unimportant as you continue with the user specs.

There are a few things to note about the tests in this file. First, only the public interface of the service is being tested. Sinatra provides a convenient way to write tests against HTTP service entry points. These are the most important tests for the service because they represent what consumers see. Tests can be written for the models and code behind the service, but the consumers of the service really only care about its HTTP interface. Testing only at this level also makes the tests less brittle because they aren't tied to the underlying implementation.

That being said, the test still requires a user account to test against. This introduces an implementation dependency in the tests. If the service were later moved from DataMapper to some other data library, it would break the test setup. There are two possible options for dealing with setting up the test data.

First, the service could automatically load a set of fixtures when started in a test environment. Then when the tests are run, it would assume that the necessary fixture data is loaded. However, this would make things a little less readable because the setup of preconditions would be outside the test definitions.

The second option is to use the interface of the service to set up any preconditions. This means that the user `create` functionality would have to work before any of the other tests could be run. This option is a good choice when writing a service where the test data can be set up completely using only the API. Indeed, later tests will use the service interface to verify the results, but for now it's easier to work with the user model directly to create test data.

Each of the successful test cases expects the response to contain a JSON hash with the attributes of the user. With the exception of the "user not found" test, the tests verify that the individual attributes of the user are returned. Notice that each attribute is verified in its own test. This style is common in test code despite its verbosity. When a failure occurs, the test shows exactly which attribute is missing.

The spec can be run from the command line. While in the `user-service` directory, you run the following command:

```
spec spec/service_spec.rb
```

As expected, the spec fails to run correctly before it even gets to the specs section. To get that far, the user model file and the basic service have to be created.

Creating a User Model

To create the user model, a migration file and a model file need to be created. You create a file named `001_create_users.rb` in the `/db/migrate` directory:

```ruby
class CreateUsers < ActiveRecord::Migration
def self.up
    create_table :users do |t|
        t.string :name
        t.string :email
        t.string :password
        t.string :bio

        t.timestamps
    end
  end

  def self.down
    drop_table :users
  end
end
```

The file contains the ActiveRecord migration logic to set up the users table. The fields for the name, email address, password, and bio fields are all there as string types.

When the migration is done, you can add the user model. You create a file called `user.rb` in the `/models` directory:

```ruby
class User < ActiveRecord::Base
  validates_uniqueness_of :name, :email
```

```
  def to_json
    super(:except => :password)
  end
end
```

The model contains only a few lines. There is a validation to ensure that the name and email address of the user are unique. The to_json method, which will be used in the implementation, has been overridden to exclude the password attribute. This user model stores the password as a regular string to keep the example simple. Ordinarily, a better solution would be to use Ben Johnson's Authlogic (http://github.com/binarylogic/authlogic). The primary benefit of Authlogic in this case is its built-in ability to store a salted hash of the user password. It is a big security risk to directly store user passwords, and using a popular tested library reduces the number of potential security holes in an application.

Implementing GET User

With the model created, the next step is to create the service and start wiring up the public API. The interface of a service is created through its HTTP entry points. These represent the implementation of the testable public interface.

In the main user-service directory, you create a file named service.rb that will contain the entire service:

```
require 'rubygems'
require 'activerecord'
require 'sinatra'
require 'models/user'

# setting up the environment
env_index = ARGV.index("-e")
env_arg = ARGV[env_index + 1] if env_index
env = env_arg || ENV["SINATRA_ENV"] || "development"
databases = YAML.load_file("config/database.yml")
ActiveRecord::Base.establish_connection(databases[env])

# HTTP entry points
# get a user by name
get '/api/v1/users/:name' do
  user = User.find_by_name(params[:name])
  if user
```

```
      user.to_json
    else
      error 404, {:error => "user not found"}.to_json
    end
  end
```

The beginning lines in `service.rb` load requirements and set up the environment. The environment loading pulls an optional environment argument from the command line.

The implementation for the GET user is simple. It opens up with a call to the Sinatra domain-specific language with the line `get '/api/v1/users/:name' do`, which is a call on the method `get` that passes in a string and a block. The string specifies the path or URL pattern to match against. This specifies that it should use this block for paths matching `/api/v1/users/`, followed by some string of characters. This will be checked against only if the incoming request is a GET.

Inside the block lies the implementation of the `get` method. Sinatra also provides `post`, `put`, and `delete` methods, which you'll use in a bit. Note here that `params` is a hash that is automatically populated. It stores the request body, if provided, and maps the symbol arguments in the URL match string. In this specific case, the mapping would be `{:name => "paul"}` if the request URL were `/api/v1/users/paul`.

The body of the method uses the `params` hash to attempt to find the user. If the user is found, it is returned as serialized JSON. The `to_json` call is the last statement executed in the block, so it is the return value. Sinatra puts this value in the response body with a status code of 200.

Finally, the error condition of not matching the user must be gracefully handled. Sinatra provides another method, called `error`, that is used for returning error conditions. If the user isn't found, the service returns a 404 error with a JSON error message.

At this point, the service spec can be rerun, and everything should pass. To run the service locally for additional testing, you can run the service regularly as a script, like this:

```
ruby service.rb -p 3000
```

The service will be started on the localhost at port 3000.

POSTing a User

Now that the basic case of finding a user has been covered, the service should be able to create a user. The service will follow the standard Rails conventions and make the call to create a user a POST.

Spec'ing **POST** User

Within the `describe` block for the service in `spec/service_spec.rb`, you add another `describe` block:

```
describe "POST on /api/v1/users" do
    it "should create a user" do
        post '/api/v1/users', {
            :name     => "trotter",
            :email    => "no spam",
            :password => "whatever",
            :bio      => "southern belle"}.to_json
        last_response.should be_ok
        get '/api/v1/users/trotter'
        attributes = JSON.parse(last_response.body)
        attributes["name"].should  == "trotter"
        attributes["email"].should == "no spam"
        attributes["bio"].should   == "southern belle"
    end
end
```

The spec sends a POST to the /api/v1/users entry point. The second argument to post is a string that is sent as the request body. To make things a little easier and more readable, this code uses a hash and converts it to JSON. The service should be able to read this JSON hash and create a user. The expected response is a 200 error message with the newly created user as the body.

This spec now shows using the service interface to confirm the success of the user create. Another GET is issued for the user that was just created. It is checked to make sure that all of the POSTed data is the same.

Implementing **POST** User

With the specs written, the POST user implementation can be put into the service. You add the following code to `service.rb` after the GET interface:

```
# create a new user
post '/api/v1/users' do
  begin
```

```
      user = User.create(JSON.parse(request.body.read))
      if user.valid?
        user.to_json
      else
        error 400, user.errors.to_json
      end
    rescue => e
      error 400, e.message.to_json
    end
end
```

The Sinatra domain-specific language offers a method for defining HTTP POST endpoints to the service. The string matches against a specific URL. The service expects a JSON attributes hash to be in the body of the request. Sinatra exposes a request object with an assessor to the body. It is a StringIO object that has to be read in.

Once the body is read, it can be parsed by JSON and handed to the user create method to create a new user in the database. If the create fails, the errors object is serialized as JSON and returned in the body of a 400 response.

PUTing a User

The service uses HTTP PUT to perform updates to existing users.

Spec'ing PUT User

Within the describe block for the service in service_spec.rb, you add an additional describe block to specify the behavior of user updates:

```
describe "PUT on /api/v1/users/:id" do
it "should update a user" do
      User.create(
        :name => "bryan",
        :email => "no spam",
        :password => "whatever",
        :bio => "rspec master")
      put '/api/v1/users/bryan', {
        :bio => "testing freak"}.to_json
      last_response.should be_ok
      get '/api/v1/users/bryan'
```

```
      attributes = JSON.parse(last_response.body)
      attributes["bio"].should == "testing freak"
    end
  end
```

First, a user is created that can be updated through the service interface. The spec then sends a PUT request to /api/v1/users/bryan, with a body that contains an attributes hash converted to JSON. Once again, the service interface is used to test whether the user has been updated. The check verifies that the passed-in attribute has been updated.

Implementing PUT User

With the specs written, the PUT user implementation can be put into the service. You add the following code to service.rb after the POST interface:

```
# update an existing user
put '/api/v1/users/:name' do
  user = User.find_by_name(params[:name])
  if user
    begin
      if user.update_attributes(JSON.parse(request.body.read))
        user.to_json
      else
        error 400, user.errors.to_json
      end
    rescue => e
      error 400, e.message.to_json
    end
  else
    error 404, {:error => "user not found"}.to_json
  end
end
```

Sinatra provides a put method to match up with the HTTP method of the same name. The matcher looks for the /api/v1/users/ followed by a string of characters that are parsed as the name. First, the user is found from the database. Then the attributes are parsed from the request body and the user is updated.

Much of the code in the PUT method is for handling errors. The code accounts for three possible error conditions: attempts to update a user that doesn't exist, data validation errors when update attributes are called, and JSON parse errors with the body.

Deleting a User

To support full user CRUD, the service must be able to delete users. The HTTP DELETE method is the perfect choice.

Spec'ing DELETE User

Within the describe block for the service in service_spec.rb, you add another describe block to specify the behavior of user deletions:

```
describe "DELETE on /api/v1/users/:id" do
  it "should delete a user" do
    User.create(
       :name      => "francis",
       :email     => "no spam",
       :password  => "whatever",
       :bio       => "williamsburg hipster")
    delete '/api/v1/users/francis'
    last_response.should be_ok
    get '/api/v1/users/francis'
    last_response.status.should == 404
  end
end
```

The delete action only cares that the service response is a 200 error. The service is used to test the deletion by trying to perform a GET on that user. The expected result is a 404 ("not found") error for the recently deleted user. Having well-defined behavior for the GET error condition makes it easy to verify that DELETE actually worked.

Implementing DELETE User

With the specs written, the DELETE user implementation can be put into the service. You add the following code to service.rb after the PUT interface:

```
# destroy an existing user
delete '/api/v1/users/:name' do
```

```ruby
  user = User.find_by_name(params[:name])
  if user
    user.destroy
    user.to_json
  else
    error 404, {:error => "user not found"}.to_json
  end
end
```

Sinatra also provides a `delete` method to match the HTTP method of the same name. The matcher for `delete` looks exactly like the `PUT` matcher. The user is found and deleted from the database. If the user isn't found, a 404 error is returned.

Verifying a User

The final requirement for the service is the ability to verify a user's credentials based on the user's name and password.

Spec'ing User Verification

Within the `describe` block for the service in `service_spec.rb`, you add another `describe` block to specify the behavior of user verification:

```ruby
describe "POST on /api/v1/users/:id/sessions" do
  before(:all) do
    User.create(:name => "josh", :password => "nyc.rb rules")
  end

  it "should return the user object on valid credentials" do
    post '/api/v1/users/josh/sessions', {
      :password => "nyc.rb rules"}.to_json
    last_response.should be_ok
    attributes = JSON.parse(last_response.body)
    attributes["name"].should == "josh"
  end
```

```
    it "should fail on invalid credentials" do
      post '/api/v1/users/josh/sessions', {
        :password => "wrong"}.to_json
      last_response.status.should == 400
    end
  end
```

The service follows the pattern of creating a session. This makes the choice of which URI to use fairly simple. The URI could easily be /api/v1/users/:id/login. However, if you want to do finer-grained session management later, it helps to think of the session as a completely separate resource. Having the session as a resource also falls more closely in line with the general RESTful style.

You need to test for two basic cases: valid credentials and invalid credentials. The body of the request is a JSON hash that has only the password. The name of the user is pulled directly from the URI.

For invalid user name and password combinations, the service should return a 400 HTTP status code, which means that the server received a "bad request." The service could also use the 401 ("unauthorized") response code, but that code specifies that authentication credentials need to be in the request header, which is not quite what is required.

Implementing User Verification

The final piece of the service is ready to be implemented. You now add the following code to the end of service.rb:

```
# verify a user name and password
post '/api/v1/users/:name/sessions' do
  begin
    attributes = JSON.parse(request.body.read)
    user = User.find_by_name_and_password(
      params[:name], attributes["password"])
    if user
      user.to_json
    else
      error 400, {:error => "invalid login
        credentials"}.to_json
    end
```

```
  rescue => e
    error 400, e.message.to_json
  end
end
```

The request to create a session is an HTTP POST. The user name is pulled from the matcher, and the password is in the request body. These are both passed to the finder. If a user matching the two is found, the user object is returned. In a more complete implementation, a session object would probably be created and returned. Finally, the error condition of an invalid login is handled, with a 400 return code.

Implementing the Client Library

A client library must be written to access the service functions from the outside. The goal of the client is to provide a lightweight wrapper to the service that will handle making requests and dealing with error conditions. Chapter 7, "Developing Service Client Libraries," goes into greater depth on cleanly separating request and parsing logic, but for now we'll keep things simple and make this client library very lightweight.

Finding a User

First, the client library should be able to call to the service to look up a user. The file for the library can sit in the same directory as the service, and the spec for the client library can go in the spec directory.

Spec'ing `User.find`

The specs for the client will test end-to-end interaction with the service. This means that the service will have to be running locally in order to run the client-side specs. Many programmers would prefer to mock in their client library specs, but doing so could result in the service and client passing all specs with hidden failures. These tests will serve to make sure that the actual service responses reflect what the client expects.

It's useful to note that when using the client library in other applications, the remote calls should be mocked out. At this point, the library has been fully tested and there's no need to run all the way to the service itself.

As with the service-side tests, there is the problem of how to handle fixture data. The problem is especially tricky when writing the client tests because they shouldn't have direct access to the service database. The first option is to enable the service to start up in a test environment. If it is running in that environment, it should load fixture data. The second option is to use the service API to create fixture data. This chapter uses the first approach. You add the following lines just after line 10 in service.rb:

```ruby
if env == "test"
  puts "starting in test mode"
  User.destroy_all
  User.create(:name => "paul", :email =>
"paul@pauldix.net",
      :bio => "rubyist")
end
```

With these additional lines, you can start the service in test mode before running the client specs by first running the database migrations and then running the service from the command line, like this:

```
rake db:migrate RAILS_ENV=test
ruby service.rb -p 3000 -e test
```

Now that the service is running in test mode, the client and specs can be created. In the spec directory, you create a file named client_spec.rb and copy in the following lines of code:

```ruby
describe "client" do
  before(:each) do
    User.base_uri = "http://localhost:3000"
  end

  it "should get a user" do
    user = User.find_by_name("paul")
    user["name"].should  == "paul"
    user["email"].should == "paul@pauldix.net"
    user["bio"].should  == "rubyist"
  end
  it "should return nil for a user not found" do
    User.find_by_name("gosling").should be_nil
  end
end
```

The setup of the test sets a base_uri on the User class. This tells the service client where the service lives. The two it blocks test the basic find functionality. First, the service should find a user that exists (remember that this user was created when the service was started). Second, it should return nil for a user that doesn't exist. Notice that both tests work with raw JSON responses from the service.

Implementing User.find

Find user is the first method that the client library should implement. In the main service directory, you create a file called client.rb and copy in the following code:

```
require 'rubygems'
require 'typhoeus'
require 'json'

class User
  class << self; attr_accessor :base_uri end

  def self.find_by_name(name)
    response = Typhoeus::Request.get(
      "#{base_uri}/api/v1/users/#{name}")
    if response.code == 200
      JSON.parse(response.body)
    elsif response.code == 404
      nil
    else
      raise response.body
    end
  end
end
```

First, all the library dependencies are loaded and the class is declared. Then the base_uri accessor is created on the class. Finally, the find_by_name class method is declared. The implementation uses a shortcut method provided by the Typhoeus Request class. An HTTP GET is made to the service at the proper endpoint, /api/v1/users/:name. This simple example uses only the basic Typhoeus functionality.

To handle both of the test cases, the response code must be checked. If it is 200, you parse the response body and return it. If the response code is 404, the library should return a nil. Finally, if some other response is encountered, you raise an exception.

> **Ruby HTTP Libraries**
>
> There are many different libraries in Ruby for making HTTP calls. A more detailed discussion of these options appears in Chapter 6, "Connecting to Services." However, it's worth noting that installing Typhoeus may take a little more effort. For this reason, this example uses only the basic HTTP functionality in the library. This should make it an easy adjustment to use Net::HTTP, HTTParty, Patron, Curb, or any other library.

Creating a User

The next step in wiring up the service functionality is to enable the client library to create a user.

Spec'ing User.create

In the client_spec.rb file, you add the following it block right after the "user not found" test:

```
it "should create a user" do
  user = User.create({
    :name => "trotter",
    :email => "no spam",
    :password => "whatev"})
  user["name"].should  == "trotter"
  user["email"].should == "no spam"
  User.find_by_name("trotter").should == user
end
```

This user creation test actually checks for two things. First, it confirms that when a call is made to User.create, the test returns the user hash. Then the final line confirms that the user was actually created in the service. Notice that the previously implemented find_by_name functionality is in use. The call verifies that the server understands the create call the client sent, and it ensures that there is end-to-end coverage with the client and service.

Implementing **User.create**

Now you can wire up user creation. After the find_by_name method, you add the following code:

```
def self.create(attributes)
  response = Typhoeus::Request.post(
    "#{base_uri}/api/v1/users",
    :body => attributes.to_json)
  if response.code == 200
    JSON.parse(response.body)
  else
    raise response.body
  end
end
```

The implementation is very simple. The attributes are passed in as a hash. A POST is made to the service, with the attribute's hash serialized as JSON in the body. This is slightly different from a regular POST request because it doesn't use form variables. The service expects a JSON hash in the body.

Notice that no validation occurs in the client library. The server is able to perform that validation and return errors. This example handles only successful responses gracefully. In a more fully featured client library, the errors should also be handled.

Because create user is running against a locally running service, the first time the spec is run, the user is created. Remember that the service startup clears out the test database. This means that between each full run of the client specs, the local test service needs to be restarted. Chapter 7, "Developing Service Client Libraries," explores other methods for client library testing.

Updating a User

The next step in writing the client is to wire up the functionality to update a user.

Spec'ing `User.update`

The user update test looks very similar to the user creation test. You add the following code after the create user test:

```
it "should update a user" do
  user = User.update("paul", {:bio => "rubyist and author"})
  user["name"].should == "paul"
  user["bio"].should  == "rubyist and author"
  User.find_by_name("paul").should == user
End
```

The test verifies that the user model has a class method called `update`. It takes the user name as the first argument and the attribute's hash as the second. Further, this method should return the full user attribute's hash. Finally, the test verifies that the user has actually been updated.

Implementing `User.update`

With the spec written, the update user method can be added to `client.rb`. After the create method, you add the following code:

```
def self.update(name, attributes)
  response = Typhoeus::Request.put(
      "#{base_uri}/api/v1/users/#{name}",
      :body => attributes.to_json)
  if response.code == 200
    JSON.parse(response.body)
  else
    raise reponse.body
  end
end
```

Here, an HTTP PUT request is made to the service to update the specific resource of the user with the passed-in name. Just as with user creation, the JSON serialized attribute's hash is passed in the request body. It should be noted that a PUT with this service works as it does in Rails. That is, the attributes that are in the hash are updated, while the omitted attributes remain the same. The service should be restarted between each run of the client specs.

Destroying a User

The final step in wiring up full CRUD functionality is enabling deletion of a user.

Spec'ing `User.destroy`

The destroy user spec is fairly simple. However, for the spec to run, a little bit of setup needs to occur in the `service.rb` file. In the test environment setup block, you add the following line to create a user that can be deleted:

```
User.create(:name => "bryan", :email => "no spam")
```

Now that the test data is in the service, the spec can be written. You add the following `it` block after the update spec:

```
it "should destroy a user" do
  User.destroy("bryan").should == true
  User.find_by_name("bryan").should be_nil
end
```

The `User.destroy` spec verifies that the return value for the destroy call is true. Finally, it uses the find functionality to verify that the user was deleted on the service side. Once again, this ensures end-to-end coverage of the client and service.

Implementing `User.destroy`

After the update method in `client.rb`, you add the following method:

```
def self.destroy(name)
  Typhoeus::Request.delete(
    "#{base_uri}/api/v1/users/#{name}").code == 200
end
```

This simple method makes an HTTP DELETE call to the service to delete the specific user resource. The method simply checks that the response code is 200 ("success").

Verifying a User

The final part of the service functionality that needs to be written is the verification of user credentials.

Spec'ing `User.login`

At a minimum, there should be two tests to check that our user verification works as expected. The first test verifies valid credentials, and the second verifies disapproval of invalid credentials:

```
it "should verify login credentials" do
  user = User.login("paul", "strongpass")
  user["name"].should == "paul"
end

it "should return nil with invalid credentials" do
  User.login("paul", "wrongpassword").should be_nil
end
end
```

The tests are fairly simple. Both run against the user paul that is already set up. The first test makes sure that the login method returns the user hash when successful. The second test shows that if login is unsuccessful, the test returns nil.

Implementing `User.login`

After the delete method in client.rb, you add the following for the login functionality:

```
def self.login(name, password)
  response = Typhoeus::Request.post(
    "#{base_uri}/api/v1/users/#{name}/sessions",
    :body => {:password => password}.to_json)
  if response.code == 200
    JSON.parse(response.body)
  elsif response.code == 400
    nil
  else
    raise response.body
  end
end
```

The client makes a simple HTTP POST to the service, with the password in a JSON object in the body. If the request is successful, the response body is parsed. If a

400 code is returned, this means the credentials were invalid and a nil should be returned. Finally, if some other error occurs, an exception is raised.

Putting It All Together

Now that the service and client have been fully written, they're ready for a full test. You start up the service in test mode and run the client-side specs. Because the client specs hit the running service, doing this actually tests both the service side and the client side. When these specs pass, you can be sure that the service works end-to-end.

Having the client specs hit the running service may seem like overkill. In fact, there is a bit of coverage overlap between the server-side specs and the client-side specs. Indeed, the client specs alone are enough to test the service in this case. While this may seem like an appealing shortcut, it's worth having the client and service separate. As more logic is added to both the client and service, it will become important to run tests against underlying methods that aren't part of the public interface. So despite the service's current simplicity, later you'll appreciate having both client- and service-side specs.

Conclusion

This chapter provides a quick introduction to creating a simple service. It may seem like a lot of work, but as you will see throughout this book, the effort can pay off in the long run. For now, this implementation represents the basic functionality of a user service that can be used by many applications.

While most of the effort involved here has to do with creating a simple HTTP-based data store for user accounts, services can be used to contain business logic behind their interfaces. The upcoming chapters look at design considerations, complexity, and configurations for writing services and client libraries. Much of this is done with an eye toward integrating these services into a fully featured Rails application.

CHAPTER 2

An Introduction to Service-Oriented Design

Service-oriented design is about creating systems that group functionality around logical function and business practices. Services should be designed to be interoperable and reusable. The goal of service-oriented design is to split up the parts of an application or system into components that can be iterated on, improved, and fixed without having to test and verify all the other components when an individual is updated. Achieving these goals usually entails a trade-off between complexity and iteration speed. However, large and mature applications are ill-served when built in Rails monolithic style. It is necessary to segment complex or large applications into parts that can be tested and deployed separately. This chapter explores the basic goals of service-oriented design and design guidelines for splitting applications into separate services.

Use of Service-Oriented Design in the Wild

Organizations such as eBay, Amazon, LinkedIn, and other large web-based companies use layers of services to bring their applications together. While many of these environments are based in Java, the advantages that come from their approaches to architecture design can be applied to web applications and systems written in Ruby.

The architecture of Amazon most exemplifies the advantages of good service-oriented design. In May 2006 the Association for Computing Machinery (ACM) published an interview between Jim Gray and Amazon CTO Werner Vogels titled

"A Conversation with Werner Vogels."[1] In the interview Mr. Vogels states that when a user goes to the Amazon.com home page, the application calls out to more than 100 services to construct the page.

Mr. Vogels goes on to say that the move from a monolithic two-tier (database and web application) architecture to a service-oriented approach provides many advantages. These include improvements such as scalability, isolation, and developer ownership of production systems. Further, Vogels states that this has led to improved processes and increased organizational agility to develop new services and features. Amazon's service-oriented architecture has enabled the introduction of new applications and services without requiring reconfiguration of the entire system.

Amazon's approach to its internal systems has driven and informed the development of the Amazon Web Services (AWS) platforms. Every piece of the AWS architecture is exposed as a web service. Here's a breakdown of Amazon's current services:

- **S3 (Simple Storage Service)**—A service for storing files.
- **SQS (Simple Queue Service)**—A service-based messaging queue.
- **SimpleDB**—A scalable service-based database.
- **CloudFront**—A service-based content delivery network.
- **EC2 (Elastic Compute Cloud)**—A service for provisioning virtual private servers.

The AWS platform represents an example of low-level system components exposed through a services layer. A service-oriented design can take advantage of these types of lower-level components as well as services that operate a little further up the stack that provide functionality for a specific application. Higher-level services might include a user system, a comments service, a video transcoding service, and many others.

Service-Oriented Design Versus Service-Oriented Architecture Versus RESTful-Oriented Architecture

There are many approaches to designing a service-oriented application. This book takes an approach slightly different than those espoused in Java books on service-oriented architecture (SOA) or even other books that focus on REST. Within the community of professionals building service-based systems there is a bit of debate about the proper use of terminology and what qualifies as best practices.

---

[1] O'Hanlon, Charlene. "A Conversation with Werner Vogels." *ACM Queue.* Volume 4, Issue 4, May 2006, pp. 14–22. http://queue.acm.org/detail.cfm?id=1142065.

SOA has become a loaded term. To many people, it implies the use of tools such as SOAP, WSDL, WS-*, or XML-RPC. This implication is why the title of this book uses the word *design* as opposed to *architecture*. Even so, this book does focus on architecture. The real goal of service-oriented design is to create simple and agile services layers that can be consumed without the use of generators or strict schemas. In this regard, the style in this book is more in line with REST-based web services than with SOA.

In the book *RESTful Web Services*,[2] Leonard Richardson and Sam Ruby discuss the details for a concept they call resource-oriented architecture (ROA). ROA represents their approach for HTTP-based RESTful design and architecture. Richardson and Ruby lay out the concepts of resources, URIs, representations, and links. They also state that ROA has properties of addressability, statelessness, and connectedness, as well as a uniform interface. When it comes to the design of specific services, this book follows Richardson and Ruby's guidelines. (The appendix, "RESTful Primer," provides an overview of REST.)

The real difference between the focus of this book and that of *RESTful Web Services* lies in the interaction points—that is, how services interact with each other to create a complete working application. The focus of this book is on internal services instead of external ones. While some of an application's services can be exposed to external consumers, their real purpose is to serve other developers working within a single organization. In this regard, this book has more similarity to what one would commonly refer to as SOA. This book also includes a more specific focus on deploying and developing with Rails, Sinatra, and other Ruby libraries and tools.

Of course, SOA, ROA, and RESTful are all meant as guidelines. In the real world, it makes sense to flex a design with the needs of the application rather than adhere to the dogma of a prescribed approach such as REST or SOA. This book takes a pragmatist's view and focuses on what these things mean for a Ruby environment that uses services as part of the core infrastructure for delivering an application or a web page to a user.

Making the Case for Service-Oriented Design

Service-oriented design can appear daunting and complex. It requires more thought up front and decisions about how to separate logic and data in an application. For Rails developers, the idea of designing a complex system ahead of development may

---

[2] Richardson, Leonard, and Ruby, Sam. *RESTful Web Services*. Sebastopol, CA: O'Reilly, 2007.

seem like heresy. One of the biggest advantages of Rails is the ability to quickly add a few models to an application and see results immediately. The Rails development style is all about quick iterations.

However, there's more to the story. Up-front design and services give developers the ability to build apps that support greater complexity and larger team sizes. Service-oriented systems sacrifice iteration speed for stability, reuse, and robustness. The key to pairing Rails applications with services is to use Rails for its strengths and switch over to services when a more stable approach is required. A perfect example of this involves creating a new application. Most new applications have many unknowns in terms of exactly what features will be supported and how popular portions of the application will be (thus informing their need for scale). In the early stages, it is best to use the normal Rails tool set. However, as parts of an application mature, their interfaces and requirements become more concrete. These are the sections that can gain the most from services. Utilizing services is best for sections of an application that have stable, well-defined, and well-understood requirements. The following sections discuss the advantages of using services rather than using a typical monolithic application.

Isolation

Many of the benefits of a service-oriented design stem from the concept of isolation. Isolation makes a service much easier to manage and optimize. Isolated components can be tested separately from other parts of an application. Using isolated components provides an easy way of organizing larger teams. Developers can focus on isolated components. Optimally, this refers to a service running on its own systems, with self-contained business logic and a self-contained data store. The separation of a service from other areas of an application enables increased testability and code reuse. There are multiple levels of isolation, including business logic, shared system, and full isolation.

Business Logic Isolation

Services that isolate based on business logic generally have their own application code, with a shared data store and shared systems. From an organizational perspective, this can be advantageous because the business logic for parts of the system is contained in one place, without leaking into other sections of the application code base. Separation of business logic makes it easier to segment a larger group of workers into teams that can work separately. Services isolated on business logic can share data sources with other systems. Generally, this is more common within a legacy system where multiple services must interface with the same database.

Figure 2.1 shows what business logic isolation might look like for the interactions between separate components. The application servers would probably reside on the same physical server, with the database on another. To achieve true business logic

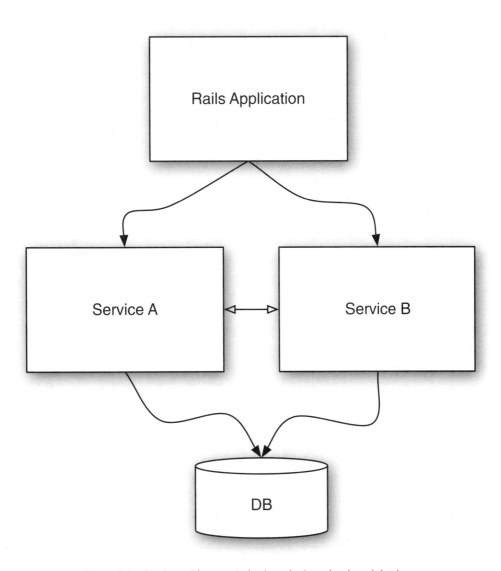

Figure 2.1   Services with separate business logic and a shared database.

isolation, the two services should have separate code bases. Further, they should not communicate with each other through the database. It's too easy to bleed business logic from the two services together through the shared database. Ideally, using services would achieve better isolation. However, for the purposes of migrating existing Rails applications to services, the shared database approach may be necessary in the early stages.

The business logic can be isolated through the use of two services, which share a database. The Rails application can still sit on top of those services. In the Rails MVC view of the world, these services occupy the Model level of the stack. The controllers and views can still be contained within the Rails application.

Shared System Isolation

Shared system isolation refers to separate services running inside their own application instances. This is like multiple Rails applications or Sinatra services running in Passenger or multiple Mongrels on the same system. Each would have its own databases, but they would be running on the same hardware. This type of system provides clean separation of business logic and data layers that is ideal. However, it changes your scaling strategy because of the shared system resources.

Figure 2.2 shows the interaction for two services that implement a shared system level of isolation. The difference between this separation and the business logic isolation just discussed is the separation of the databases. Now, each of the services communicates only with its own database and the external interface of the other service. A typical configuration would have the two databases actually residing on the same database server and the two services running on the same application server. A shared hosting environment is an example of this kind of setup. However, with shared hosting, the two services are actually two different customer applications that have nothing to do with each other.

The disadvantage with shared system isolation is that shared system resources can be tricky to manage. Further, shared system isolation adds complexity with upgrading libraries or running other system-level applications. Thus, improvements to shared system services require testing against other services when making system changes.

Full Isolation

Ideally, services should run in full isolation. With full isolation, they have their own server or virtual private server instances, completely separate code bases and repositories, and their own data stores. Over time, a system could phase from one form of

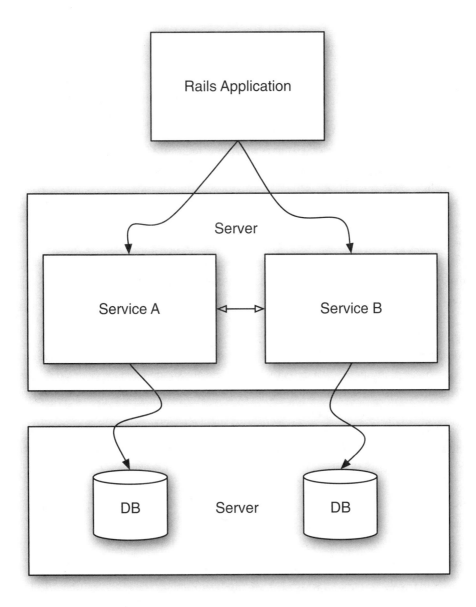

Figure 2.2   Shared systems with isolated services.

isolation to another. Migrating from a typical monolithic Rails application could start with a migration to a shared database and systems, then to isolated databases, and finally to completely isolated systems.

Testing in Isolation

Within the framework of testing, isolation provides the advantage of having a single testable interface. A public service API can be checked and agreed upon. Changes within the service need not affect how the API responds to commands. The testing of a service's interface is very much like unit or model testing within a Rails application. The only difference is that the callable methods are HTTP methods that can be called by any application. All the details of the business logic and how data is stored or optimized are hidden behind the service interface.

The big advantage isolation provides with regard to testing is in the time required to run the test suite. Rails developers working on mature projects with large code bases routinely have to wait longer than 15 minutes for their test suites to run to completion. In fact, it's not entirely uncommon for some teams to work with large code bases that take longer than 40 minutes to run their entire suite of tests. This becomes a major problem when you want to change something small. After even a small change, the full suite of tests must be run to ensure that the change didn't break anything.

With isolated application components, testing to make sure other parts of an application are functioning properly becomes a much smaller problem. For example, consider an application code base that takes 20 minutes to run the full suite of tests. Then break that application into four fairly evenly sized, separate, isolated components. Now the test time for a single change to one of these components is cut down to one-fourth of what was previously needed. If a change is made to one of the new components, it isn't necessary to run the test suite for everything. Only the tests for the single component need to be run, and in this example, that would take roughly 5 minutes rather than 20. As long as the public-facing interface for the component is well tested, changes can be deployed without concern that the other three-fourths of the application still works. Of course, if the API of a service changes, then each consumer must be tested to ensure proper operation.

Robustness

Services that are well designed provide an application with a robust architecture. That is, the architecture is able to withstand stress on the system and changes in the operating environment without loss of functionality. The underlying environment in which services run can change while a service continues to operate without the service consumers having any knowledge of these changes.

For those familiar with object-oriented design, the robustness advantages of services may sound similar to the advantages of encapsulation. Indeed, with services, the aim is to achieve encapsulation for entire sections of an application. In object-oriented design, encapsulation means that the underlying implementation can be changed without the API consumer's knowledge. For services, such changes can include code changes and more drastic changes, such as moving to a different type of database.

For example, consider a user management service. To start with, it includes only basic functionality, such as a user model, authentication, profile data, and a lightweight social network (where people can be friend each other). The initial implementation could use ActiveRecord and a MySQL database. As the load on the service picks up, it starts to outgrow the limits of the regular SQL solution. Because there is a clearly defined services interface, this can be modified without a single change to the rest of the application.

Switching underlying data stores could go something like this: After some hand wringing and careful research, you might decide to move the user data to some NoSQL data store, such as CouchDB, Redis, or MongoDB. First, you would update the implementation to use the new data store, along with migration scripts to move the data from MySQL to the new NoSQL database. Once a new server or two or three have been set up, you could migrate the code and data. When this migration is complete, the other sections of the application are still able to access the user management service without ever knowing about the complete change of the underlying data store.

Scalability

Experienced Rails developers tend to roll their eyes when people mention scalability. People outside the Rails community advise against using Rails because they say it isn't scalable. Meanwhile, Rails developers know that Rails itself isn't the problem. While it's true that scalability in general is difficult, the problem usually comes down to the database. A services approach provides more tools and ability to deal with scaling. Specifically, using services makes it easy to scale portions of an application individually. Data can be split across services, and the performance under load can be optimized for each service.

A partitioned data strategy is part of service-oriented system design. When fully isolating services, you need to make decisions about putting data in one service or another. Once data has been partitioned, changes can be made to the individual services based on their scaling needs. While one service may need to optimize for data writes, another may optimize for many reads. The advantage of a good service design is that these needs can be handled on a case-by-case basis instead of requiring optimization of a single database for all cases.

Services also make it easier to scale team size. When a programming team is larger than six people, it gets hard to coordinate changes in an application. One developer's change may step on another's. Further, as the code base of the application gets larger, it gets harder to introduce new developers to the system as a whole. When an application is split into services, developers can be assigned to a specific service or two. Thus, they need to be familiar only with their section of the application, and the working groups can remain small.

Finally, using services makes it easier to scale the absolute size of an application in terms of the code base. Larger applications have too much code for anyone to be familiar with it all at any given time. In addition, their tests take longer to run. For example, when developing Rails applications, a developer doesn't usually have to dig into the Rails code base. Rails provides a layer of abstraction that doesn't often need to be penetrated. Services can provide this same layer of abstraction for code and for actual production systems.

Agility

When thinking about complex architectures, *agility* is not the word that comes to mind. However, properly designed services can be far more agile than monolithic applications. Changes to the underlying nature of the services can be made without concern for the rest of the application. The pains of deployment can also be eased because deployments don't require the entire application to be updated with each change.

The ability to change underlying service implementations without affecting the rest of the application provides implementation agility. Switching databases or changing message queues or even changing languages can be done without worrying about the rest of the system. This kind of agility is often overlooked in the Rails community, but it becomes a huge asset to applications that mature over a period of years. Using services allows for changing or updating underlying libraries without having to dig through every part of the application code base to make sure everything is still working as expected.

In the Ruby community, a good example of an advantage offered by services is the planning for migration to Ruby 1.9. Services provide greater agility in making these kinds of updates. Services can be upgraded to 1.9 as the libraries they use are confirmed to work. Thus, services can take a phased approach to upgrading to use Ruby 1.9 and take advantage of its features.

One of the keys to maintaining agility in a service environment is proper versioning. Each service interface should be versioned when an update includes a breaking change. As long as the design includes the ability to run multiple versions of a service simultaneously, it's possible to keep somewhat agile with respect to interface changes. If an update to the service API is additive—that is, it doesn't change existing calls and only adds new functionality—the service can remain at the same version.

Interoperability

For large heterogeneous environments, interoperability is an important requirement. When working with multiple languages or interface with legacy databases, legacy systems, or external vendors, using services is a great way to connect with these systems. Web-based interfaces to these systems can provide the ability to flex with changes without breaking sections of an application. The HTTP interface also prevents being tied to a specific messaging implementation that might otherwise be used to communicate with these systems. Services ease interoperation with internal and external systems and with systems written in languages other than Ruby.

Internal interoperability refers to interfacing with systems written in different languages within an environment. Some of these systems already expose their functionality through a web API. Apache Solr, a Java-based indexing and search server, is a great example of a system that provides a service interface. By interacting with this interface, Ruby developers can take advantage of all the work done on this project without having to call into the Java code directly by using something like JRuby. The Solr interface is usually called by other services and applications within an environment.

External interoperability refers to the need to interface with external systems such as those from vendors. Many external services also provide a web-based interface for their customers. Examples include SimpleDB, SQS, SalesForce, Github, Lighthouse, Twitter, Facebook, and countless others. Writing clean, performant Ruby client libraries is key to bringing these services into an application. Writing client libraries is covered in detail in Chapter 6, "Connecting to Services," and Chapter 7, "Developing Service Client Libraries."

Environments with multiple languages in use benefit from the use of HTTP-based services. While Ruby is a great programming language, it isn't always the best tool for every job. If a section of an application would benefit from being implemented in Erlang, Scala, or even Java, HTTP services can provide the message bus for interaction between these disparate setups.

Reuse

After a service has been developed and deployed, it can be reused across the entire system. The argument for reuse is strongest in environments where multiple applications have common shared functionality, such as consultancies and large corporate environments that develop multiple internal applications for different users.

Consultancies that develop and host applications for their clients could reuse services. Currently, the most common model of code reuse across these applications is through the development of plug-ins or gems. Specific examples include user authentication, tagging systems, commenting systems, and searching. However, many of these could be developed and deployed as services. One of the possible gains to taking the service approach is the reuse of system resources across all clients. For example, a user management system could be implemented as a service (as in the example in Chapter 1, "Implementing and Consuming Your First Service"). This system could then be used across all client systems. If this is repeated for other shared functionality, new applications will have to implement and deploy only anything that is custom to their environment.

Providing public-facing APIs is another area where the services used to build a system internally can be reused. If services are created for internal use, they can be exposed later for general use. The popularity of the Twitter API shows that it can be advantageous to expose parts of an application through a RESTful HTTP interface. With the services approach, exposing application functionality to the outside world becomes as easy as simply opening up an already existing internal API to the public.

Conclusion

Hopefully, this introduction has whetted your appetite for exploring the service-oriented approach covered in this book. The extra design work and communication overhead of creating and using multiple services takes a little more effort than creating a typical Rails application. However, the benefits of a service-oriented design can far outweigh the costs associated with inter service communication and more up-front design.

Here's a quick recap of the benefits of service-oriented design:

- **Isolation**—Robustness, scalability, and improved testing strategies all stem from the concept of isolation. Isolation gives an application architecture many of the advantages that encapsulation provides in object-oriented design.

- **Robustness**—Services are robust because their underlying implementation can change with shifting load requirements, libraries, and languages without detriment to the rest of the application.
- **Scalability**—When using services, you need to think up front about how to separate data and manage interaction. This partitioning of logic and data provides the ability to scale the size of the code base and team in addition to the number of requests to process.
- **Agility**—Upgrades to underlying system components are easier with services. Further, new versions of existing services and completely new services can be implemented outside the full architecture. This can provide much-needed agility for mature code bases where changes are typically expensive to verify with the rest of an app.
- **Interoperability**—Using HTTP-based services is a great way to expose the functionality of legacy applications or external vendors.
- **Reuse**—Service-oriented design enables reuse of components across multiple applications or clients.

CHAPTER 3

Case Study: Social Feed Reader

Throughout this book, specific examples are used to explore the challenges and benefits of designing service-oriented applications. The case study presented in this chapter provides a basis for the discussion in the rest of this book. This chapter doesn't implement and discuss every service that this application could contain, but it gives some good areas to focus on. Exploring how an existing application is set up highlights the shortcomings of a typical Rails stack and how to overcome those shortcomings through the intelligent use of services.

A Typical Rails Application

A typical Rails application starts out simple. You develop everything in a single code base, write tests (hopefully), and use a single database. In the beginning, it is likely to take up only two servers—the web and application server and the database—as shown in Figure 3.1.

Simply setting up a few servers can get you pretty far with Rails. However, the complexity builds quickly. In a Rails application, you need to be able to run background tasks. For example, if a user takes an action that triggers sending an email message out to another user, you want the email to be sent in the background instead of during a request that is being made by a waiting user. For that, the

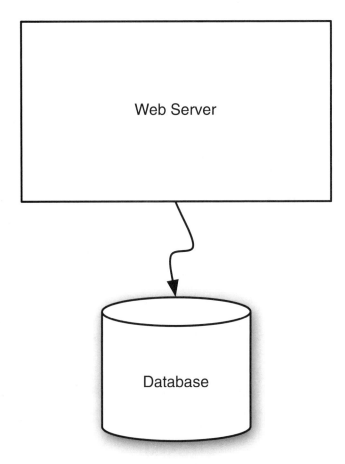

Figure 3.1   A simple Rails deployment.

application needs to be running additional background processes, as shown in Figure 3.2.

The background processing code is typically run on application servers. With a simple background processing system such as Delayed Job, the tasks to be performed are stored in the database in their own table. This means that the background job processing is fully integrated with the database and the Rails application code base (specifically, the models). If the logic for processing these jobs needs to be updated, the application code base must be changed and tested, and the full application must be redeployed.

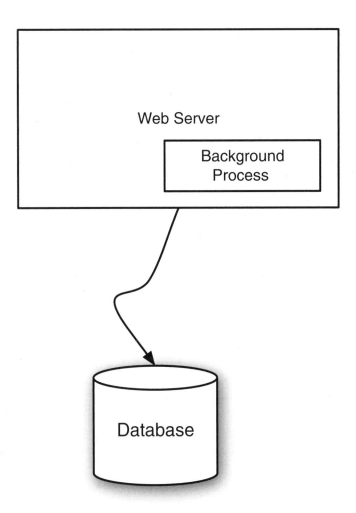

Figure 3.2   A simple Rails deployment with background processing.

Background Processing and Delayed Job

Delayed Job is a library for doing background processing in Rails applications. The code can be found at http://github .com/tobi/delayed_job, and John Nunemaker has written a good tutorial at http://railstips.org/2008/11/19/delayed-gratification-with-rails. There has been plenty written about background processing in Rails applications. Other libraries include Background Job, Async Observer, Spawn, Workling, BackgroundFu, and many others. Some of these run using only the database, while others require external messaging systems. Covering all of them is beyond the scope of this book, but all these libraries have the same general goal: to put a message on a work queue to be handled later by a process running outside the web application. You want the processes to run outside the application in order to return a response to client requests as quickly as possible.

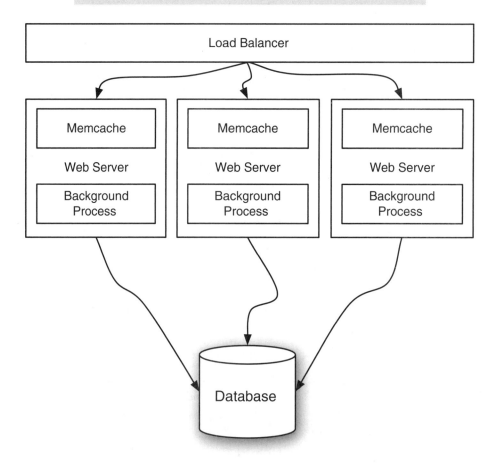

Figure 3.3   A full Rails deployment with background processing.

At this point, the application isn't terribly complex. Only a few things run in the background, and the number of models is manageable. The next steps that are usually taken might include adding Memcached and adding more web servers to handle more requests, as shown in Figure 3.3.

Many Rails deployments look something like the one shown in Figure 3.3. The number of application servers may be greater or lower, but the general look is the same. There is a database server, the Rails application, and some background processing that is tightly integrated with the application. From there, the development proceeds and the application is built and iterated on.

While this setup is quite powerful, one of the problems that might be encountered is what to do when the database is unable to keep up with the number of requests. Typical approaches include performance logging to find spots to optimize queries, getting more powerful hardware for the database server, and splitting out reads and writes to separate replicated servers. What to do in this situation is the typical dilemma that people think of when they think of scaling. It's also one of the issues that service-oriented design tackles.

The other scaling problem isn't often discussed: scaling the team and the size of the project. As the application is improved and iterated, its code gets ever more complex. The project grows larger and has more lines of code added every day. While development continues, the application gains more models, controllers, views, and tests. This means longer times for the test suite to run and more code that each developer needs to be cognizant of while making updates. Taking a service-oriented approach also helps address this scaling problem.

Let's now move from a generic Rails application to a more specific app.

The Rails Social Feed Reader Application

Many Rails developers have had to build some sort of social network at one point or another. These days, most web applications have at least a lightweight social network on top of them. This example considers a feed reader with a social network built on top in order to look at some of the advantages of services. Because most readers already have Rails applications in production, the concerns of migrating an existing application to services are very important. As this case study comes up throughout the book, it provides material for how you might perform the migration to services.

Features

For the sake of brevity, the feed reader needs to be fairly simple. Here is a high-level overview of the features of the current Rails social feed reader:

- **User Profiles and Following**—This includes basic profile information, user name, password, and which users are following each other.
- **Activity Streams**—This refers to the Facebook style of stream. Each user has a stream of activity from the people they follow. In addition, each user has a stream of activity for his or her profile that others can see. Activity can be either subscribing to a feed, commenting on an entry, or voting up or down on an entry.
- **Feeds and Feed Entries**—The system keeps track of which feeds need to be updated and the entries for each of these feeds.
- **Feed Subscriptions**—The system keeps track of which feeds a user is subscribed to.
- **Votes**—The system keeps track of all of the votes, up or down, a user casts on specific feed entries.
- **Comments**—Users can comment on any story they read from their feeds. These comments show up in the stream of any follower. The comments also show up on any entry when a user is reading through his or her list of feeds.
- **Email Notifications**—The system sends email notifications to users for account modifications or when other users start following them.

Current Setup

The current setup for the feed reader application looks like the typical Rails deployment mentioned earlier. There is an application server with background processing. The logic for sending out emails and performing updates of feeds occurs in these background jobs. Everything is tied together fairly tightly. There are separate models for the emails and the feeds, but the logic of actually running these tasks is held within a single process.

The code in the social reader application looks like a regular Rails application. There are models, controllers, and views. When looking at services, most of what gets pulled into a service is the code and logic that lies at the model level. It helps to have in mind what the model schema and relationships for the data look like. The following sections outline the models in the application. Each one is annotated with its database schema using the annotate models gem (see http://github.com/ctran/annotate_models/tree/master).

The User Model

The user model is the common starting place for most applications. Many of the other models are tied in some way to the user model, and the social feed reader application is no different. Every model can be reached through an association on the user model. When breaking up the data into services, some of these associations will have to cross service boundaries. The user model looks as follows:

```
class User < ActiveRecord::Base
  has_many :follows
  has_many :followed_users, :through => :follows
  has_many :followings, :class_name => "Follow",
    :foreign_key => :followed_user_id
  has_many :followers, :through => :followings,
    :source => :user
  has_many :comments
  has_many :votes
  has_many :subscriptions
  has_many :feeds, :through => :subscriptions
  has_many :activities,
    :conditions => ["activities.following_user_id IS NULL"]
  has_many :followed_activities, :class_name => "Activity",
    :foreign_key => :following_user_id
end

# == Schema Information
#
# Table name: users
#
#  id         :integer          not null, primary key
#  name       :string(255)
#  email      :string(255)
#  bio        :string(255)
#  created_at :datetime
#  updated_at :datetime
```

This example shows only the associations, which happen to add the finders that are needed for the application. There are a few has_many :through associations. Users can access their followers, who they are following, the comments they have made, the feeds they are subscribed to, the activities they have performed in the system, and the activities of the users they are following.

The activities are contained in a single denormalized table. Another option would be to map activities through a polymorphic relationship, but such joins can be expensive. A denormalized structure makes retrieving the activities a quick operation. To get a sense of why the relationship for activities looks the way it does, let's look at the activity model.

The Activity Model

The activity model is for keeping a record of user activity such as following another user, subscribing to a feed, or commenting or voting on an entry. It is a denormalized model, so there is some data duplication with the comment, follow, subscription, and vote models. The activity model looks as follows:

```ruby
class Activity < ActiveRecord::Base
  belongs_to :user

  def self.write(event)
    create(event.attributes)
    event.user.followers.each do |user|
      create(event.attributes.merge(:following_user_id =>
        user.id))
    end
  end
end

class CommentActivity < Activity
end

class SubscriptionActivity < Activity
  belongs_to :feed
end

class VoteActivity < Activity
end
```

```
class FollowActivity < Activity
  belongs_to :followed_user, :class_name => "User"
end

# == Schema Information
#
# Table name: activities
#
#  id                  :integer        not null, primary key
#  user_id             :integer
#  type                :string(255)
#  feed_id             :integer
#  followed_user_id    :integer
#  entry_id            :integer
#  content             :text
#  following_user_id   :integer
#  created_at          :datetime
#  updated_at          :datetime
```

The activity model uses single-table inheritance (STI) to keep each type of activity in the same table. The parent class defines a write method that should be called when a comment, subscription, vote, or follow is created. First, it writes an activity without `followed_user_id`, which is used in the user model to find the activities that the specific user performed. Then `write` creates a new activity for each of the user's followers. This is another instance of data duplication, but it cuts down on the number of joins that must be performed to pull the activity for all the users an individual is following.

The Follow Model

The follow model is the join model that specifies which users are following the others. It looks like this:

```
class Follow < ActiveRecord::Base
  belongs_to :user
  belongs_to :followed_user, :class_name => "User"
```

```
    after_create {|record| FollowActivity.write(record)}
end

# == Schema Information
#
# Table name: follows
#
#  id                 :integer       not null, primary key
#  user_id            :integer
#  followed_user_id   :integer
#  created_at         :datetime
#  updated_at         :datetime
```

The follow model contains only the two user IDs of the follower and followee. The logic for creating activities after `create` is contained in the model.

The Feed Model

The feed model contains the basic data for RSS or Atom feeds in the system. Here's how it looks:

```
class Feed < ActiveRecord::Base
  has_many :entries
  has_many :subscriptions
  has_many :users, :through => :subscriptions
end

# == Schema Information
#
# Table name: feeds
#
#  id         :integer          not null, primary key
#  title      :string(255)
#  url        :string(255)
#  feed_url   :string(255)
#  created_at :datetime
#  updated_at :datetime
```

The relationships for the feed model show that it has many entries (the specific blog posts) and many users through the subscriptions.

The Subscription Model

The subscription model maps users to the feeds they are subscribed to. It looks like this:

```
class Subscription < ActiveRecord::Base
  belongs_to :user
  belongs_to :feed

  after_create {|record| SubscriptionActivity.write(record)}
end

# == Schema Information
#
# Table name: subscriptions
#
#  id         :integer          not null, primary key
#  user_id    :integer
#  feed_id    :integer
#  created_at :datetime
#  updated_at :datetime
```

The subscription model is simple, with only a relationship with the user and the feed. The logic to create subscription activities is in the after create block.

The Entry Model

The entry model contains all the information for a specific article or blog post from a feed. Here's how it looks:

```
class Entry < ActiveRecord::Base
  belongs_to :feed
  has_many :comments
end

# == Schema Information
#
# Table name: entries
#
```

```
#  id                  :integer      not null, primary key
#  feed_id             :integer
#  title               :string(255)
#  url                 :string(255)
#  content             :text
#  published_date      :datetime
#  up_votes_count      :integer
#  down_votes_count    :integer
#  comments_count      :integer
#  created_at          :datetime
#  updated_at          :datetime
```

The entry model has relationships to the feed that it belongs to and the comments associated with it. There are also counters for the number of up votes, down votes, and comments. It could also contain a has-many relationship to those votes, but from the entry's point of view, the only important thing for the application to keep track of is the count of vote types.

The Vote Model

The vote model uses STI to define the two different types of votes, the up and down votes:

```
class Vote < ActiveRecord::Base
  belongs_to :user
end

class UpVote < Vote
  belongs_to :entry, :counter_cache => true

  after_create {|record| VoteActivity.write(record)}
end

class DownVote < Vote
  belongs_to :entry, :counter_cache => true
end
```

```
# == Schema Information
#
# Table name: votes
#
# id          :integer          not null, primary key
# user_id     :integer
# entry_id    :integer
# type        :string(255)
# rating      :integer
# created_at  :datetime
# updated_at  :datetime
```

The parent class vote defines the relationship to user that both the up and down vote classes require. The up and down votes both define their relationships to the entry because of the automatic counter cache. This gets incremented in up_votes_count or down_votes_count on the entry object. Finally, only the up vote writes activity. This is because the users probably don't want to see entries that the people they are following thought were bad.

The Comment Model

The comment model is very basic. It holds only the text of a comment from a user and the associated entry:

```
class Comment < ActiveRecord::Base
  belongs_to :user
  belongs_to :entry, :counter_cache => true

  after_create {|record| CommentActivity.write(record)}
end
```

```
# == Schema Information
#
# Table name: comments
#
# id          :integer          not null, primary key
# user_id     :integer
```

```
#   entry_id    :integer
#   content     :text
#   created_at  :datetime
#   updated_at  :datetime
```

The relationships to the user and entry are here in the comment model. Also, a counter cache is kept up on the entry to store the number of comments. Finally, after creation of a new comment, the activity is written.

Converting to Services

The social feed reader application is fairly basic in terms of the number of models. However, the models are a decent cross-section of the different kinds of complexity found in a typical ActiveRecord-based Rails application. There are counter caches, STI, belongs-to, has-many, and has-many-through relationships. With all these things tied so closely together, it's important to know how you might separate the application into discrete services.

Segmenting into Services

There are many different ways to break up the social feed reader application into services. Some choices are straightforward, while others require a little more thought. Answering the following questions helps determine how to redesign for services:

- Which data has high read and low write frequency?
- Which data has high write or update frequency?
- Which joins occur most frequently?
- Which parts of the application have clearly defined requirements and design?

Answering the first three questions will help determine where models might belong in different services. The last question helps determine whether a portion of the application should remain in a typical Rails environment instead of being split out into services. Typically, only portions of applications that are well defined should be considered for use as services. Chapter 4, "Service and API Design," goes into the details of breaking these models into callable HTTP services.

Breaking Up the Application into Services

Finding the right places to split the Rails model-view-controller (MVC) design pattern can be tricky. For an existing application, the conversion must occur slowly over time, as parts are refactored into their own services. The progression of converting an application could take the form shown in Figure 3.4.

Here, at the starting point, everything is contained in a single application. The first step is to implement services at the model layer, as shown in Figure 3.5.

Some or all of the models could be converted to services. For applications that rely heavily on background processing (for example, the social feed reader), this might be enough. Other applications that have many views and associated tests will benefit from having the controller and view layers broken into services. When the models are accessible as services from any application in the environment, this conversion can take place as shown in Figure 3.6.

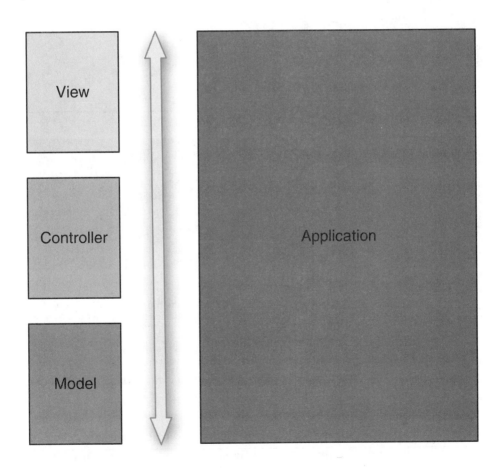

Figure 3.4   A Rails application.

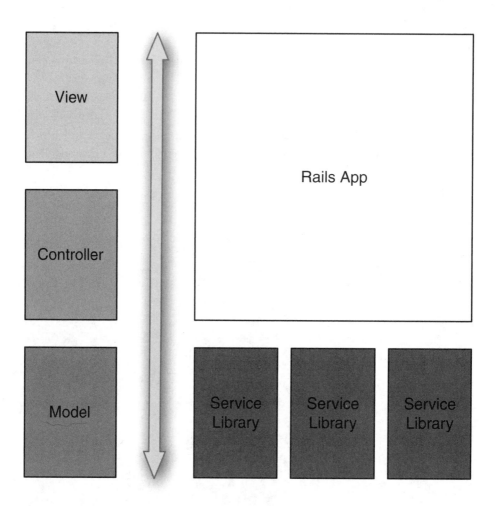

Figure 3.5   A Rails application with services at the model layer.

With the controllers and views broken into separate applications, the Rails application looks less like a regular application. However, the picture in Figure 3.5 isn't yet complete. Once these view services have been made, you can convert the Rails application into nothing more than a proxy route request and stitch all the services together as shown in Figure 3.7.

The final step is to set up the Routing/ESI/Include Module in front of the view services. This has multiple names because it could take one of multiple forms. It could be a small Rails application that handles the routing of requests and builds final pages based on components handed back from services. It could also be an ESI layer that

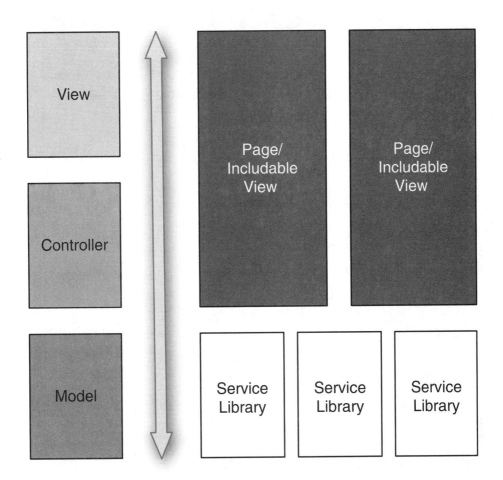

Figure 3.6 A Rails application with services at all layers.

calls out to the services directly. Finally, it could be a Rack application that includes the services as modules. Some of these options are explored later in the book.

Edge Side Includes (ESI)

ESI is a technology that enables building web pages from parts hosted on content-delivery networks or in HTTP caches. For more information, see the formal spec at www.w3.org/TR/esi-lang.

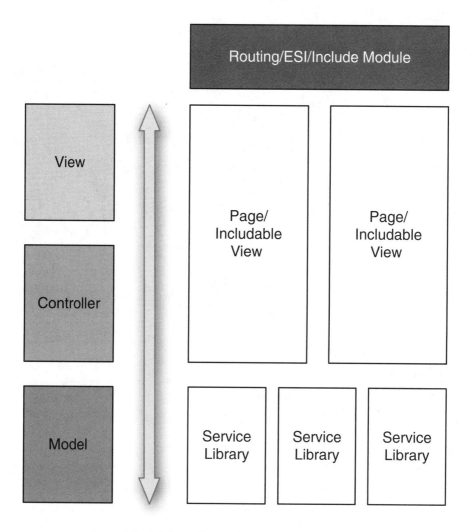

Figure 3.7   A Rails application that connects multiple services.

Conclusion

Ruby on Rails is perfect for quick prototyping, fast iterations, and smaller applications. As your code base, team, and traffic levels grow in volume and size, the complexity can become difficult to manage. This can result in large test suites that take a long time to run or unnecessary cognitive load for developers who have to keep too much of the application in their head. The case study in this chapter provides fodder for specific examples later in the book that illustrate how to convert an application to services and what the trade-offs and concerns are.

CHAPTER 4

Service and API Design

Services require a little more up-front thought than a typical Rails application. Taking the time to think about design decisions before you start creating services can give your application the advantages of flexibility, scalability, and robustness in the long run. One of the keys to ensuring that you reap the benefits of services is proper design.

This chapter covers strategies and examples for designing services. It discusses segmenting functionality into separate services, upgrading and versioning services, and designing APIs that provide sensible and flexible functionality. The goal is to develop services that cover the functionality of the social feed reader described in Chapter 3, "Case Study: Social Feed Reader."

Partitioning Functionality into Separate Services

The first step when considering the design of services is to look at the application as a whole and to make some decisions about how to split up the functionality. This partitioning is one of the toughest design decisions you need to make. The partitioning at this point lies mostly at the model layer of the application. This chapter looks at four different strategies for splitting up the functionality of the models:

- Partitioning on iteration speed
- Partitioning on logical function
- Partitioning on read/write frequency
- Partitioning on join frequency

59

The following sections look at each of these strategies to separate the social feed reader's model layer into services.

Partitioning on Iteration Speed

The services approach works best when you're dealing with well-defined requirements and an API that will remain fairly stable. In these cases, you can design a service and optimize its performance behind the scenes. In cases where things are more dynamic, there is a little extra cost in iterating over a service. This stems from the need to update both the service side and the clients. When developing an application where you're not sure about the stability of the list of features and needs, it might be best to develop a hybrid system.

Existing Rails applications that gradually get converted to services are a perfect example of this type of partitioning. In the beginning, the entire application is built as a single monolithic Rails project. As parts of the application become more mature and stable, they can be refactored out of the app into services.

The social feed reader offers a good example of this type of hybrid approach. A few functions within this application are fairly static. The application needs to consume feeds and store the entries somewhere. Users have reading lists based on subscriptions. These pieces are at the core of the application and will exist regardless of the other iterations that occur around user interaction. A good first step in converting the feed reader application over to services would be to move the storage and updating of feeds and their entries behind a service. This would remove those models, the update logic, and daemon code from the application. More importantly, you could then improve the feed update and storage system without touching the user-facing Rails app.

For sections of the application that may change frequently, it makes more sense to keep them within the standard Rails framework. Features that need quick iterations will have the regular controllers, views, and ActiveRecord models. This might mean keeping users, comments, votes, and their associated data within the standard model. With this type of setup, the feed storage and updating systems can be developed as two separate services. Meanwhile, quick Rails-style iterations can be made over everything else.

The key to this type of partitioning is to identify the parts of the application that are core and unlikely to change. You should avoid the temptation to just stuff everything back into a single monolithic application. With the hybrid approach to the social feed reader, you can make changes to the feed-crawling system without updating the rest of the application. The first version of this service may use a MySQL database to store the feeds. Later, you can change this to a more appropriate document database or key value store without touching any of the other application code. Thus, the application reaps the benefits of services in some areas while still maintaining the flexibility of the Rails rapid development style where appropriate.

Partitioning on Logical Function

Generally, you want to partition services based on their logical function. This means you have to consider each piece of functionality in an application and determine which parts fit logically together. For some boundaries, this is a straightforward decision.

In the social feed reader, one service decision stands out as being driven by logical function: updating feeds. This service really sits apart from the application. Its only purpose is to download XML files, parse them, and insert the new entries into the data store. It doesn't make sense to include this in the application server, user service, or any other service. Even as part of the Rails application, the updating of feeds exists as a process that runs outside the request/response life cycle of the user.

In some cases, a feed update may be triggered by user interaction, while that update still occurs outside the request by getting routed to the Delayed Job queue. Given that this separation already exists, it makes sense to pull the feed updater into its own service so that it can remain isolated. In this way, you can optimize how and when feeds get updated without any other part of the system knowing about these changes. The feed updater service highlights the advantages of isolated testability. When the application is updated, the updater service need not be tested; conversely, when the feed update system is improved or updated, the application layer doesn't need to be redeployed or tested.

The feed and feed entry storage service is also separated logically. Users can subscribe to feeds, but they don't own them. All users of the system share feed and entry data, so this data can be seen as logically separate from users. Other examples of services that are logically separated in applications are those for sending email, monitoring systems, collecting statistics, or connecting with external data entities (such as feed updaters, crawlers, or other external APIs).

Lower-level services are also partitioned based on logical function. As part of your infrastructure, you may decide that a shared key value store is useful for multiple services. Similarly, a shared messaging system or queue system might be useful for many services. These types of services have a single function that they serve that can be shared across all your other services. Amazon provides these in the form of S3 for key value storage and SQS for message queues.

The higher-level parts of an application, such as views and controllers, can also be partitioned based on logical function. For example, a comment thread or discussion could exist across many pages of a site. Instead of using a partial in the application to render HTML, a call could be made to a comment service that renders the full HTML snippet for the comments section of the page. Generally, services are responsible for data and business logic. However, in applications that contain many pages, it may be necessary to split the partial page rendering out into services that can be run and tested independently.

Partitioning on Read/Write Frequencies

Looking at the read and write frequency of the data in an application is another method that can help determine the best way to partition services. There may be data that gets updated very frequently and read less often, while other data may be inserted once and read many times. A good reason to partition along these lines is that different data stores are optimized for different behavior. Ideally, a service will have to work only with a single data store to manage all its data.

Future implementation choices should partly drive your partitioning choices. For data with a high read frequency, the service should optimize a caching strategy. For high-write-frequency data, the service may not want to bother with caching. Splitting these out to different services makes the implementation of each individual service easier later. Instead of having to optimize both reads and writes in a single place, you can simply make one service handle the read case really well while the other service handles the write case.

Handling both reads and writes usually requires a trade-off of some sort. Services that are designed to primarily handle one case need not make this trade-off. The choice is made in advance by designating that data be stored in one location instead of another.

The social feed reader involves data that crosses all ends of the spectrum: high read and low write, high write and low read, and high read and high write. For instance, user metadata would probably not be updated very frequently. Meanwhile, the user reading list, voting information, and social stream all have frequent updates. The reading list is probably the most frequently updated data in the system. As a user reads each entry, it must be removed from his or her list. Further, when each feed is updated, the new entries must be added to every subscriber's reading list.

It could be argued that the reading list belongs in the same service as the user data. It is data owned by the user. Logically, it makes sense to put it with the user data. However, the reading list has a high write frequency, while the other user data probably has different characteristics. Thus, it makes sense to split the reading list out into a separate service that can be run on its own.

It might make sense to keep the vote data with the user data or the entry data. From the perspective of when the data will most likely be read, it might belong with the entry. The list of the user's previous votes also needs to be pulled up later.

There are a few approaches to storing and exposing the vote data. The first is to create a single-purpose service to answer all queries that have to do with votes. This service would be responsible for storing aggregate statistics for entries as well as for individual users. Thus, given a user, it could return the votes. It could also return the aggregate stats for a list of entries. Finally, another service call could be exposed to return the aggregate stats for a list of entries along with the user's vote when given a user ID. This kind of service is very specific but has the advantage of being optimizable. Vote data in this application is an example of high-read and high-write data. Keeping it behind a single service gives you the ability to try out multiple approaches and iterate on the best solution.

The other method is to replicate or duplicate data where it is needed. For example, the entries need to know the aggregate voting statistics. Thus, when a new vote is created, the entry service should be notified of this either through the messaging system or through a direct HTTP call. The vote itself could reside with the regular user data since the individual votes are always pulled up in reference to a specific user. In the old ActiveRecord models, this method was taken through a counter cache. Chapter 11, "Messaging," shows how to enable this kind of cross-service replication with minimal effort and without slowing down the saving of the primary data. Which approach to take really depends on the other needs. Both are legitimate ways to solve the problem.

Partitioning on Join Frequency

One of the most tempting methods of partitioning services is to minimize cross-service joins. For a developer familiar with relational databases, this makes sense. Joins are expensive, and you don't want to have to cross over to another service to join necessary data. You'll make fewer requests if you can perform joins inside a service boundary.

The caveat is that almost all data in an application is joined to something else. So which joins should you minimize? If you took the concept of minimizing joins to its logical conclusion, you'd end up with a single monolithic application. If you're going to separate into services, you need to make some tough decisions about joins.

The previous two ways of partitioning—by read/write frequency and logical separation—are a good starting point. First, data should be grouped together using those criteria. For joins, it is best to consider how often particular joins occur. Take, as an example, the activity stream part of the social feed reader. Whenever a user takes an action such as voting, commenting, or following, all the followers must be notified in the stream. If separate services were created for the activities and the users, the data about which users are following others would need to be accessible from both places. If the "follows" information is not replicated to both places, then it should be put in the single place where it is needed most frequently. Thus, you could minimize the joins that have to occur from the other service.

The other option for minimizing joins is to replicate data across services. In normal relational database jargon, this is referred to as *denormalization*. This is the more sensible course of action when looking at the activity stream and users services. The information about which users are following each other should be replicated to the activity stream service. This data represents a good candidate for replication because it has a much higher read frequency than write frequency. High writes would mean duplicating all those messages and getting little return. However, with a smaller number of writes than reads, the replicated data can make a difference. Further, the write of the follow can be pushed and replicated through a messaging system, and the data will be replicated to both services seamlessly. This method is covered in detail in Chapter 11, "Messaging."

Versioning Services

Services can and should change throughout their lifetimes. In order to keep previous clients functioning and to make upgrades possible, service interfaces must be versioned. To facilitate upgrading services without having to simultaneously upgrade clients, you need to support running a couple versions in parallel. This section looks at two approaches for identifying different versions of services and making them accessible to clients.

Including a Version in URIs

One of the most common methods of indicating service versions is to include a version number in the URI of every service request. Amazon includes service versions as one of the arguments in a query string. The version number can also be made part of the path of a URI. Here are some examples of URIs with versions:

- http://localhost:3000/api/v1/users/1
- http://localhost:3000/users/1?version=1
- http://localhost:3000/api/v2/users/1

These examples show the URI for a specific user object with an ID of 1. The first two URIs refer to the user with an ID of 1 on version 1 of the API. The third example uses version 2 of the API. It's important to note that with different versions of APIs, breaking changes can occur. Possible changes might include the addition or removal of data included in the response or the modification of the underlying business logic that validates requests.

One advantage to putting the version number in the query string is that you can make it an optional parameter. In cases where clients don't specify a version, they could get the latest. However, this also creates a problem because updating your service may break clients that aren't explicitly setting version numbers in their requests.

Ideally, you won't have to run multiple versions for very long. Once a new service version has been deployed and is running, the service clients should be updated quickly to phase out the old version. For external APIs, this may not be a valid option. For example, Amazon has been running multiple versions of the SimpleDB and SQS APIs for a while. Internal APIs may need to run multiple versions only during the time it takes to do a rolling deployment of the service and then the clients. However, it is a good idea to enable a longer lag time between the update of a service and its clients.

REST purists argue that putting the version in the URI is a poor approach. They say this because the URI is ultimately referring to the same resource, regardless of the version. Thus, it should not be a part of the URI. The approach that is generally considered to be RESTful is to use the Accept headers in a request to specify the version of an API. Then the URI of a resource remains the same across versions of an API.

Using Accept Headers for Versioning

In addition to including a version number in URIs, another method for specifying API versions is to include them in the Accept header for each request. This means defining a new MIME type for each version of the API. The following examples show requesting a specific user with either version 1 or version 2.

The following is the HTTP header for requesting the user with the ID 1 accepting version 1 of the API:

```
GET /users/1 HTTP/1.1
Accept: application/vnd.pauldix.chapter5-v1+json
```

The following is the HTTP header for requesting the user with the ID 1 accepting version 2 of the API:

```
GET /users/1 HTTP/1.1
Accept: application/vnd.pauldix.chapter5-v2+json
```

These examples use a MIME type that you define in the vendor tree. There are a few disadvantages to this approach. The first and most important is that not all caching servers look at request headers as part of their caching. Therefore, running multiple versions in parallel may cause unpredictable caching behavior. The only fix is to then turn off caching completely while you're running multiple versions.

> **The Vendor Tree**
>
> The vendor tree is used to define application MIME types for specific vendors. It is an open space that doesn't require registration with the IETF. It is designated by the prefix vnd. in the Accept header. For more information, see http://tools.ietf.org/html/rfc4288#section-3.2.

The second problem with using Accept headers is that many developers aren't comfortable or familiar with the idea of setting headers on their requests. From the standpoint of making an API usable to the outside world, most developers are likely to find a version number in the URI easier to work with. Of course, it is a trade-off. If client developers have to specify the version in the URI, they also probably have to build URIs themselves, which increases the complexity of client libraries slightly.

URIs and Interface Design

Consistency across APIs makes it easier to develop clients for each service. Because URIs represent the public interface of a service, they should be as consistent as possible. The URIs for resources in services should follow a convention that can be programmed against. Rails starts with some conventions that should look familiar. For example, here are some URIs and HTTP methods that you might see in a typical Rails application:

- `GET, POST /users`
- `GET, PUT, DELETE /users/1`
- `GET, POST /users/1/comments`
- `GET, PUT, DELETE /users/1/comments/2`
- `GET, POST /users/1/follows`
- `GET, PUT, DELETE /users/1/follows/23`

The first two examples show the URIs for the typical Rails CRUD (create, update, destroy) style. When combined with the HTTP methods, those two URIs represent the full interface for a basic user. `GET /users` maps to returning a list of all users. `POST /users` maps to creating a new user. `GET /users/1` is the show action for a specific user. `PUT` is an update, and `DELETE` is destroy.

The next two examples show a nested resource. Comments are always attached to a user, so they can be nested within the context of a user. The `GET`, `POST`, `PUT`, and `DELETE` actions all correspond to the CRUD operations for comments.

The final two examples are also for a nested resource called `follows`. These are a little different in that the resource really represents a join to another user. In this case, it is the follows information of one user following another. `GET /users/1/follows/23` would pull back the join information. This might include information about the follows relationship, such as a group the user has been put in or the date of the follow, in addition to the user ID that is following and the user ID that has been followed.

A simple generalization would be to say that these URIs follow a pattern: `/:collection` then an optional `/:id` followed by another collection and ID combo, and so on. In this pattern, `:collection` maps to the plural of an actual model. In the specific examples in the list, `users` maps to the user model, `comments` maps to the comment model, and so on. The `:id` element of the pattern is, of course, the ID for the model. For nested models, the ID of the parent should be contained within the nested model. Thus, a comment should have a user ID associated with it.

This is all fairly standard Rails design, and the convention works for most situations. However, some API elements may not fit in with this kind of resource-based model. Take, as an example, the feed-crawling system in the social feed reader. How could the request to crawl a specific feed be represented as a resource? How would you represent a list of feeds with a specific sort order? How do you represent pagination for long lists? Some of these can be mapped as resources using Rails conventions, while others will have to break convention a little. Here are some examples:

- **GET, POST /feeds/1/crawls**—Returns information about each time a feed has been crawled or posts to request a crawl right away.
- **GET /feeds/1/crawls/last**—Returns the information for the last crawl on a specific feed. This could include information on whether the feed was modified, how many new entries were found, or whether the crawler hit a redirect.
- **GET /feeds?page=2&per_page=20&sort=updated_desc**—Gets a list of feeds, sorted by their updated date in descending order with the requested pagination parameters.

The first example turns crawls into a resource, thereby fitting into the convention. When accessing information about the `last` crawl, this example must depart a little bit from convention because `last` doesn't represent an actual ID. However, it represents a specific singular crawl resource. This means that in the case of using either a real ID or the string `last`, the client can expect a single object to be returned.

The final example shows the request for a collection, with options for sorting and pagination. Here, the query parameters look quite different from other URIs that have been used. This could be changed so that the query parameters are placed in the path of the URI before the query string. However, it's usually easier to manage multiple optional parameters as query parameters. The one concession when using query parameters is that the API should require that they be sorted alphabetically. This can improve the cache hit ratio if caching is employed.

Successful Responses

In addition to standardizing URI design, APIs should also standardize, as much as possible, successful HTTP responses. This section describes some standards that an API may want to include for successful responses.

HTTP Status Codes

RESTful APIs should use the following HTTP status codes to reflect the outcomes of service responses. In the case of successful responses, the first three status codes are the most important and are generally the only ones you need:

- **200 OK**—The request has succeeded. This is the generic success case, and most successful responses use this code.

- **201 Created**—The request has been fulfilled, and the resource has been created. The response can include a URI for the created resource. Further, the server must have actually created the resource.
- **202 Accepted**—The request has been accepted for processing but has not actually been completed. This is a loose response because the actual request may be invalid when the processing occurs. This could be a response from a `POST` that queues up an operation of some kind.
- **304 Not Modified**—The request isn't exactly a success, but it isn't an error either. This could happen when a client requests a resource with an `If-Modified-Since` header. The client should expect that this is a possible response and use a locally cached copy.

HTTP Caching

HTTP caching information should be included in the service's response headers. This caching data can be used not only by services but also by client programs, proxy caching servers, and content delivery networks (CDNs) to speed up the application and reduce the load on your servers. Cache headers can also be used to specify when you don't want a response to be cached. The following are the specific headers that service APIs may want to include:

- `Cache-Control: public`—This header lets your server tell caching proxies and the requesting client whether a response may be cached. A list of directives can be found in the HTTP 1.1 header fields spec at http://www.w3.org/Protocols/rfc2616/rfc2616-sec14.html#sec14.9.
- `ETag: 737060cd8c284d8af7ad3082f209582d`—ETag is an identifier for the resource that also represents a specific version. It is an arbitrary string of characters. It could be something like the ID of an object and its last modified date and time combined into a SHA1 hex digest. This can be sent in later requests to verify that a client's cached version of a resource is current.
- `Expires: Wed, 02 Sep 2009 08:37:12 GMT`—This header gives the date and time after which the cached resource is considered stale. This allows clients and proxies to forgo requests for which their cached resources are still fresh. After the expired time, a new request can be issued to refresh the cached resource.
- `Last-Modified: Mon, 31 Aug 2009 12:48:02 GMT`—This header specifies the last time the requested resource was modified. Clients issuing requests can send this time to the server to verify whether they have the most up-to-date version of a resource.

Successful Response Bodies

The response bodies hold the actual resource data and, if necessary, pointers to other resources. First, a response format must be selected for the API. JSON is the obvious choice because of its simplicity and ubiquity. Legacy services commonly use XML, but JSON is quickly becoming the standard.

Here is an example of comments resources from the feed reader. Specifically, this example looks at returning a list of comments for a user or a single comment:

```
REQUEST: GET /users/1/comments/1
RESPONSE:
{
   "id" : 1,
   "user_id" : 1,
   "entry_id" : 2,
   "body" : "hey, this blog post is wicked sweet",
   "created_at" : 1252355834,
   "modified_at" : 1252355834
}
```

For a single object, the response body is simple. It consists only of a JSON object (or hash) of the requested comment. The keys are the field names, and the values are the field values. One thing to note is that this model returns only the ID of the associated user and entry. This means that the service client would need to have knowledge of the API to construct URIs to request the associated resources.

From an API standpoint, it makes sense to also give a URI pointer to the user and entry in addition to the raw IDs. Remember that services should avoid having clients construct URIs whenever possible. Here is the comment resource updated with those additional values:

```
{
   "id" : 1,
   "user_id" : 1,
   "entry_id" : 2,
   "body" : "hey, this blog post is wicked sweet",
   "created_at" : 1252355834,
   "modified_at" : 1252355834,
```

```
    "user_uri" : "/users/1",
    "entry_uri" : "/entries/2"
}
```

Now here is an example of a request and response for a collection of comments:

```
REQUEST: GET /users/1/comments
RESPONSE:
[
  {"id" : 1, ... "modified_at" : 1252355834},
  {"id" : 2, ... "modified_at" : 1252356789}
]
```

Most of the fields of the individual comments are excluded here for brevity. The fields should be the same as those used previously for a single comment resource. For retrieving all the comments from a user, this works well. However, in most cases when requesting a list, only a page of the list should be returned. This means that the API needs to include pagination links in the response. The service should not require the client program to construct URIs for pagination.

Here's what that list response looks like:

```
{
  "previous" : "/users/1/comments?page=1",
  "next" : "/users/1/comments?page=3,
  "collection" : [ ... ]
}
```

The pagination links are in the "previous" and "next" values. In cases where there are no previous or next pages, either those keys could be excluded or their values could be set to null. The ellipsis in between the brackets is where the comment objects for the response would go. Other options not listed that the API may want to include are the total number of comments or the number of pages. By responding to a collection request with a hash that contains the collection, the API can add more information for the service clients to use besides the raw collection itself.

Error Responses

Service APIs should standardize on how error conditions are conveyed. Some error responses could indicate problems with the server. Other responses could indicate validation errors on a model or permissions restrictions.

HTTP Status Codes

Service APIs should use some standard HTTP status codes:

- **400 Bad Request**—Used as a general catchall for bad requests. For example, if there is a validation error on a model, a service could respond with a 400 error and a response body that indicates what validations failed.
- **401 Unauthorized**—Used when a resource is requested that requires authentication.
- **404 Not Found**—Used when requesting a resource that the server doesn't know about.
- **405 Method Not Allowed**—Used when a client attempts to perform an operation on a resource that it doesn't support (for example, performing a GET on a resource that requires a POST).
- **406 Not Acceptable**—Used when the request is not acceptable according to the Accept headers in the request (for example, if the service uses the Accept headers to indicate a requested API version and a client requests a version that is no longer supported).
- **409 Conflict**—Used when a client attempts to update a resource that has an edit conflict. For example, say that two clients request a blog post at the same time. One client makes changes and submits the post. The second client also makes changes and submits the post, but the server has found that the second client's copy is now out of date. The second client should request the resource again and inform the user of the now-updated post, allowing the user to make changes.

Error Response Bodies

The response bodies for error conditions should be fairly simple. The 400 responses represent the most complex and overloaded error conditions. These errors should include more application-specific error codes and a human-readable error message. These responses also include data validation errors. The following example shows the response body for a request to create a user:

```
{
    "message" : "failed validation",
    "error_codes" : [1, 2, 3],
```

```
  "errors" : [
    ["username", "has already been taken"],
    ["password", "can't be blank"],
    ["email", "can't be blank"]]
}
```

The validation errors show that the user name in the request already exists, the email was blank, and the password was blank. All three failed validation, so the user was not created. Notice also that error codes are contained in the response. These application-specific codes are chosen when designing the API. They make it easier for client library authors to catch specific errors. For example, if you change the user name error to read "user already exists," it shouldn't break properly authored client libraries.

For error conditions other than the application-specific 400 codes, the response bodies are generally blank.

Handling Joins

Joins across services are sometimes a necessary evil. You need to consider a few issues when designing the set of services that make up an entire application. First, the API design must account for how to store references to joined data. Second, the API design determines when and where joins should occur. Third, the overall design should not create the need for too many nested joins.

Storing References

In a typical Rails database, the reference to a joined model consists of the model name followed by an underscore and ID. So a comment in the feed reader is joined to a user through the user_id field. The value is the integer ID of the user. With services, the references can be stored in a similar way. If the ID of the joined model is stored, the responsibility of resolving the join is left to the service client.

In an ideal REST system, the client libraries do not have to construct URIs for resources. If a client sends a request for a comment, the client should also be able to request the user the comment belongs to without having knowledge of how to construct a user URI. One solution is to contain this logic within the comment service. The underlying database model can store only the user_id field. The comment service then needs to ensure that every time a comment resource is returned, it returns the user_uri field in addition to the user_id field.

This puts the responsibility for constructing URIs to joined data inside each service. It's a slight departure from REST because the service is not storing the actual URI. However, it enables easy updates for resources that put version numbers in the URI. When the user service updates its version, the comment service has to update its URI generation logic. Of course, the update to the user system should allow the upgrade of the comment service to happen over time rather than having to update both systems in lock step.

Still another argument can be made for passing raw IDs in the responses. With some services, it makes sense to have the client contain business logic that wraps the data instead of just passing the raw data to the service. A pure RESTful approach assumes that no business logic will be written around the responses. Take basic data validation as an example. When attempting to create a user, you may want to ensure that the email address is in the proper form, the user name isn't blank, and the password isn't blank. With a pure RESTful approach, these validations would occur only in the service. However, if a service client wraps the data with a little bit of business logic, it can perform these kinds of data validations before sending to the service. So if you're already writing clients with business logic, it isn't that much of a stretch to have a client also be responsible for URI construction.

Joining at the Highest Level

The *highest level* for a join is the place in the service call stack where joins should occur. For example, with the social feed reader, consider a service that returns the five most recent reading items for a user. The application server will probably make calls to the user service for the basic user data, the subscription service for the list of reading items in a specific user's list, the feed entry service for the actual entries, and the ratings service for ratings on the list of entries. There are many places where the joins of all this data could possibly occur.

The subscriptions and ratings services both store references to feed entries and users. One method would be to perform the joins within each service. However, doing so would result in redundant calls to multiple services. The ratings and reading lists would both request specific entries and the user. To avoid these redundant calls, the joins on data should occur at the level of the application server instead of within the service.

There are two additional reasons that joins should be performed at the application server. The first is that it makes data caching easier. Services should have to cache data only from their own data stores. The application server can cache data from any service. Splitting up caching responsibility makes the overall caching strategy simpler and leads to more cache hits. The second reason is that some service calls may not need all the join data. Keeping the join logic in the application server makes it easier to perform joins on only the data needed.

Beware of Call Depth

Call depth refers to the number of nested joins that must be performed to service a request. For example, the request to bring back the reading list of a user would have to call out to the user, subscription, feed storage, and ratings services. The call chain takes the following steps:

1. It makes simultaneous requests to the user and subscription services.

2. It uses the results of the subscription service to make simultaneous requests to the feed storage and ratings services.

This example has a call depth of two. There are calls that have to wait for a response from the subscription service before they can start. This means that if the subscription service takes 50 milliseconds to respond and the entry and ratings services complete their calls in 50 milliseconds, a total time of 100 milliseconds is needed to pull together all the data needed to service the request.

As the call depth increases, the services involved must respond faster in order to keep the total request time within a reasonable limit. It's a good idea to think about how many sequential service calls have to be made when designing the overall service architecture. If there is a request with a call depth of seven, the design should be restructured so that the data is stored in closer proximity.

API Complexity

Service APIs can be designed to be as specific or as general as needed. As an API gets more specific, it generally needs to include more entry points and calls, raising the overall complexity. In the beginning, it's a good idea to design for the general case. As users of a service request more specific functionality, the service can be built up. APIs that take into account the most general cases with calls that contain the simplest business logic are said to be *atomic*. More complicated APIs may enable the retrieval of multiple IDs in a single call (multi-gets) or the retrieval or updating of multiple models within a single service call.

Atomic APIs

The initial version of an API should be atomic. That is, it should expose only basic functions that can be used to compose more advanced functionality. For example, an API that has a single GET that returns the data for different models would not be considered atomic. The atomic version of the API would return only a single type of model in each GET request and force the client to make additional requests for other related models. However, as an API matures, it makes sense to include convenience methods that include more data and functionality.

However, simple atomic APIs can be taken too far. For example, the interface for retrieving the list of comments for a single user in the social feed reader is non-atomic. It returns the actual comments in the response. A more atomic version of the API would return only the comment IDs and the URIs to get each comment. The expectation is that the client will get the comments it needs. As long as these GETs can be done in parallel, it doesn't matter that you have to do many to get a full list of comments.

In theory, the parallel request model works. However, in practice it's more convenient to just return the list of comments in the actual request. It makes the most sense for clients because in almost all cases, they want the full comments instead of just the IDs.

Atomicity is about returning only the data that a client needs and not stuffing the response with other objects. This is similar to performing joins at the highest level. As you develop an application and services, it may make sense to have special-case requests that return more data. In the beginning, it pays to make only the simplest API and expand as you find you need to.

Multi-Gets

You might want to provide a multi-get API when you commonly have to request multiple single resources at one time. You provide a list of IDs and get a response with those objects. For example, the social feed reader application should have multi-get functionality to return a list of feed entry objects, given a list of IDs. Here is an example of a request/response:

```
REQUEST GET /api/v1/feed_entries?ids=1,2
RESPONSE:
[{
   "id" : 1,
   "feed_id" : 45,
```

```
   "title" : "an entry",
   "content" : "this is an entry",
   "url" : "http://pauldix.net/1"},
  {"id" : 2,
   "feed_id" : 78,
   "title" : "another",
   "content" : "another entry",
   "url" : "http://pauldix.net/2"}
]
```

For service clients, the advantage of using this approach is that the clients are able to get all the entries with a single request. However, there are potential disadvantages. First, how do you deal with error conditions? What if one of the requested IDs was not present in the system? One solution is to return a hash with the requested IDs as the keys and have the values look the same as they would if they were responses from a single resource request.

The second possible disadvantage is that it may complicate caching logic for the service. Take, for example, a service that runs on multiple servers. To ensure a high cache hit ratio, you have a load balancer in front of these servers that routes requests based on the URL. This ensures that a request for a single resource will always go to the same server. With multi-get requests, the resources being requested may not be cached on the server the request gets routed to. At that point, you either have to make a request to the server that has the cached item or store another copy. The workaround for this is to have the servers within a service communicate to all of the service's caching servers.

Multiple Models

A multiple-model API call is a single call that returns the data for multiple models in the response. An API that represents a basic social network with a user model and a follows model is a good example that shows where this would be useful. The follows model contains information about which user is the follower, which user is being followed, when the follow occurred, and so on. To retrieve a user's full information, the atomic API would require two requests: one to get the user data and one to get all the follows data for that user. A multiple-model API could reduce that to a single request that includes data from both the user and follows models.

Multiple-model APIs are very similar to multi-gets in that they reduce the number of requests that a client needs to make to get data. Multiple-model APIs are usually best left for later-stage development. You should take the step of including multiple models within the API only when you're optimizing calls that are made very frequently or when there is a pressing need. Otherwise, your API can quickly become very complex.

Conclusion

When designing an overall services architecture, you need to make some decisions up front about the services and their APIs. First, the functionality of the application must be partitioned into services. Second, standards should be developed that dictate how to make requests to service APIs and what those responses should look like. Third, the design should account for how many joins have to occur across services. Finally, the APIs should provide a consistent level of functionality.

APIs should take into account the partitioning of the application, consistency in their design, and versioning. Strategies for partitioning application into services include partitioning based on iteration speed, on logical function, on read/write frequency, and on join frequency. Developing standards in the URI design and service responses makes it easier to develop client libraries to access all services. The service APIs should aim for consistency to make URI and response parsing easier to extract into shared libraries for use by everyone. Services should be versioned and be able run multiple versions in parallel. This gives service clients time to upgrade rather than having to upgrade both client and server in lock step.

CHAPTER 5

Implementing Services

This chapter explores a few of the options in Ruby for implementing services. Specifically, in this chapter, you will implement a service from the social feed reader application with Rails, Sinatra, and as a basic Rack application. Implementing the same functionality in all these frameworks will help reveal the differences in these choices and the possible strengths and weaknesses of each.

The Rails framework provides an option that most readers are familiar with for complete web applications. Rails supplies a lot of innate functionality, but at the cost of speed and extra code and complexity that isn't necessary in smaller services. Rails is a good place to start, but you should examine other frameworks to see other ways of organizing logic for handling requests. Sinatra is part of the newest generation of Ruby frameworks that diverge from Rails in design. Rack is the basic web server interface that both Rails and Sinatra are built on.

The Vote Service

The service this chapter focuses on is the vote system from the social feed reader application. Basically, the vote service should provide a way to let users give a "thumbs up" or "thumbs down" to a feed entry. It should also provide different ways to retrieve previous vote data. In addition, the service should provide the following specific features:

- **Vote an entry "up" or "down"**—The service should provide an API call to rate an entry. This call should require a user ID, an entry ID, and whether the vote is up or down. Further, a user should be able to have only a single vote per entry. The user should be able to change a vote from up to down, but the service should make sure the user can't continually vote the same way on an entry.

- **Get the entry IDs voted on by a user**—Given a user ID, the service should return the list of entry IDs that a user has voted up or down. This list should be in date descending order (by when votes were created), and the API should provide a method to retrieve the list with pagination options.
- **Get the vote totals for an entry**—Given an entry ID, the service should return the total up and total down votes for an entry.
- **Get the vote totals for a list of entries**—Given a list of entry IDs, the service should return the total up and down votes for each entry in the list.
- **Get the vote for an entry and user**—Given an entry ID and a user ID, the service should return the vote information for that user and entry.
- **Get the vote information for a list of entries for a user**—Given a list of entry IDs and a single user ID, the service should return the vote information for the entries in the list the user has voted on.
- **Get the vote totals for a user**—Given a user ID, the service should return the total number of entries voted up and down.

When you look at this list of requirements, you should notice that there is only a single call that writes data to the service: when a user votes on an entry. The rest of the API calls are for returning data based on those votes. With so many different read-based calls, this service could be optimized for those reads. The single write could be routed through a messaging system instead of through a RESTful interface. Chapter 11, "Messaging," covers how to write highly scalable write interfaces using messaging. For now, the full API will be exposed through REST.

You need to make a few design choices with respect to the API. The JSON data format has already been selected. Now you must make decisions for the URI design and how the API should behave. For instance, how are the user's vote totals exposed? One way would be to return totals when getting the votes themselves. The URI and response might look something like the following:

```
REQUEST GET /api/v1/votes/users/1/up
RESPONSE:
{
    "total" : 78,
```

```
    "entry_ids" : [2, 6, 23, 1, 9],
    "next_page" : "/api/v1/votes/users/1/up?page=2&per_page=5"
}
```

Two additional calls would be available in connection with the preceding method of returning up votes: Return all votes for a user and return the down votes. Having the total in the votes API calls fulfills the final requirement of retrieving totals for a user. However, it probably makes sense to include an extra call to retrieve just the numbers.

A Multi-Get Interface

One of the important design choices to be made is how to expose a multi-get interface. *Multi-get* refers to the ability to retrieve information for multiple IDs at once. Specifically, the API must be able to retrieve the votes for a list of entry IDs. Multi-gets are often exposed as either a GET or a POST call. The requests for each might look as follows:

```
REQUEST GET /api/v1/votes/entries?ids=1,2,3,4,5
REQUEST POST /api/v1/votes/entries
REQUEST BODY (option 1):
[1,2,3,4,5]
REQUEST BODY (option 2):
ids=1,2,3,4,5
```

The GET request includes everything the service needs in the URI. The POST request shows two options for the request body. The first is to make the request body a simple JSON array of entry IDs. The second is a standard "form variables"–style POST request. This is what the request body for a POST from an HTML form would look like. With the second option, the logic for pulling out the IDs in Rails or Sinatra would look exactly as it looks when the IDs are pulled from the GET request. That is, ids is accessible through the params hash, like this: params[:ids].

Exposing the multiple get as a GET request is appealing because it aligns closely with the idea of REST. It is a read request on a resource. The specific list of IDs represents the resource. Further, always sorting the IDs in the same order before the request is made ensures that repeated requests for the same set of IDs will be a cache hit. This is important if lists of the same IDs are regularly requested.

The disadvantage of using GET is the limitation on URI length. If the entry IDs are UUIDs or something similar, each ID will use 36 characters. While these types of IDs are not common in normal Rails applications, UUIDs are used very often in distributed systems. In fact, the vote system should probably not enforce that an entry ID be an integer. It should be up to the entry system to decide whether it will use integer or string IDs.

URI length limits vary, depending on clients, servers, and proxies that exist between them. Browsers often have the strictest limitations on URI length. Internet Explorer has a limit of around 2 KB, while Firefox has a limit of 65 KB. However, these service APIs will be used by other libraries and not in a browser address bar, so the GET request can be used with larger limits.

For the purposes of Ruby services, it makes sense to look at the settings for the two most popular web servers: Nginx and Apache. Nginx has a default URI length limit that depends on the platform it is built on. It is either 4 KB for 32-bit systems or 8 KB for 64-bit systems. The default setting can be increased through the `large_client_header_buffers` setting (see http://wiki.nginx.org/NginxHttpCoreModule#large_client_header_buffers). Apache has a default URI length of 8190 bytes. This default can be increased through the `LimitRequestLine` directive (see http://httpd.apache.org/docs/2.2/mod/core.html#limitrequestline). The potential limitations are worth keeping in mind if the API is expected to handle many IDs in a single request.

The API should be able to return the vote values for a single entry and for a single entry and user (in addition to the multi-get versions). Instead of implementing separate calls for the single gets, the multi-get interface can be reused. The request will simply have a list containing only one ID, and the response will have a list of results with only one element. Limiting the total number of endpoints in an API will make it easier to program against, test, and modify.

Responses for an API should follow a predictable convention. There are many different ways to return responses to multi-get requests. One response format could return a JSON array of objects where the order is the same as the IDs requested. The other option is to return a JSON hash with the ID as a key and the response as a value. The latter option is a little more verbose, but it's more explicit and easier to handle in the client code.

The Vote Interface

The final API decision to be made is what the interface for creating a vote should look like. There are many valid ways to expose this functionality. The only requirement is that the back-end server logic enforce the "one vote per entry per user" rule.

The data that must be conveyed is the entry ID, the user ID, and the vote value (up or down).

There aren't any hard rules for the interface. The decision really boils down to aesthetics. Let's explore some of the possible interfaces to see which might be the most sensible:

```
Option 1:
REQUEST POST /api/v1/votes
REQUEST BODY:
{
   "user_id" : 3,
   "entry_id" : 45,
   "vote" : 1
}


Option 2:
REQUEST POST /api/v1/votes/entries/45
REQUEST BODY:
{
   "user_id" : 3,
   "vote" : "up"
}


Option 3:
REQUEST POST /api/v1/votes/entries/45/users/3
REQUEST BODY:
{
   "vote" : -1
}


Option 4:
REQUEST POST /api/v1/votes/entries/45/up
REQUEST BODY:
{
   "user_id" : 3
}
```

```
Option 5:
REQUEST PUT /api/v1/votes/entries/45/users/3/vote_up

Option 6:
REQUEST PUT /api/v1/votes/entries/45/users/3
REQUEST BODY:
{
   "value":  "up"
}

Option 7:
REQUEST POST /api/v1/votes/entries/45
REQUEST BODY:
{
   "user_id" : 3,
   "value"  : "up"
}
```

Each of these options uses a different combination of specifying the data in the URI and in the request body. The options also use different HTTP methods and values for the vote. The options highlight the three decisions that must be made when designing the vote interface:

- How should the vote value be represented?
- What data should be specified in the URI or the request body?
- Which HTTP method should be used?

The vote value could be represented as a string of "up" or "down," or it could be represented as an integer value of 1 or −1. From a math perspective, the 1 and −1 values are appealing. They can be added together, and they use fewer characters for transmitting the actual vote value. The "up" and "down" values provide a little more readability. The words also have symmetry. It's intuitive that if you see "up" as a vote value, you can assume that "down" is the other one. With a value of 1 you might wonder if 0, −1, or any other integer values are valid. Finally, using "up" or "down" keeps you from attempting to add the values passed in from the API call, which could introduce bugs. What if someone posts a vote value of 100? The server will have to make sure to bounds check the values. When you use "up" and "down," it's already known that the server will have to check which of those the value is. It keeps you from attempting something clever like using integer values for votes and adding them to totals, which is where you might introduce bugs. However, it is important to note that the server has to ignore case on the value.

The choice of which URI to use is another place where API design has a large amount of flexibility. The seven options take various approaches in how to divide the data. The vote information can be transmitted in the URI or in the request body. One option shows all the data conveyed in the request body, while another has a completely empty request body with a fully descriptive URI.

The best choice for URI can be narrowed down by considering how RESTful the interface is and what the requirements are. Specifically, one requirement is that a user can have one vote per entry. This makes options that don't expose the vote as a specific resource less appealing (for example, the calls to vote_up as a remote procedure call).

Considering REST design goals helps determine whether to use PUT or POST for the interface. Notice that the options that expose the vote as a specific resource both use PUT, while all the others use POST. This makes sense because specific resources should be put while the others represent an append to a list or an RPC-style API call.

API Design Guidelines

The following guidelines help determine which API makes the most sense:

- **URIs should be descriptive**—For submitting a vote, the URI should at least contain the word *vote* or *votes*.
- **When possible, API endpoints should be exposed as resources**—Preference is given to the resource and RESTful style. Avoid constructing APIs that look like remote procedure calls (for example, XML-RPC). Examples such as those with vote_up in the URI can be ruled out based on this guideline.
- **Data should be descriptive**—Ideally, the data being transmitted should be human readable. It should be clear what the intention is by reading the URI and the request body. Vote values of integers leave a bit of guesswork. While they may be more efficient, they aren't as descriptive.

These criteria can help you narrow down your choice to option 6 or option 7. Either one of these seems like a decent choice. However, option 6 is a little more appealing because it is more specific. Option 7 has the vote appended to the list of votes on an entry. Meanwhile, option 6 is a PUT to specify the value of the vote for a given entry and user. This gives the most descriptive URI and fits quite nicely with REST principles. The call is setting the value of the vote resource.

Models

Before you get to the HTTP service interface, you need to create the data models. The same ActiveRecord models can be used across all services. This will help highlight how the HTTP service interface portion differs among frameworks. When it comes to the service design, the underlying model shouldn't be very important. It can have performance implications for later, but the underlying model can be changed later with ease because of the service-layer abstraction.

The implementation example uses the simplest data structure to store everything. In fact, the data for this entire service can be encapsulated in the following model (which is based on ActiveRecord 2.3):

```
class Vote < ActiveRecord::Base
  validates_inclusion_of :value, :in => %w[up down]
  validates_uniqueness_of :user_id, :scope => :entry_id
  validates_presence_of :entry_id
  validates_presence_of :user_id

  named_scope :up,   :conditions => ["value = ?", "up"]
  named_scope :down, :conditions => ["value = ?", "down"]
  named_scope :user_id, lambda {|user_id|
    {:conditions => ["user_id = ?", user_id]}}
  named_scope :entry_id, lambda {|entry_id|
    {:conditions => ["entry_id = ?", entry_id]}}

  def self.create_or_update(attributes)
    vote = Vote.find_by_entry_id_and_user_id(
      attributes[:entry_id],
      attributes[:user_id])
    if vote
      vote.value = attributes[:value]
      vote.save
      vote
```

```
      else
        Vote.create(attributes)
      end
    end

    def self.voted_down_for_user_id(user_id, page, per_page = 25)
      entry_ids_for_user(user_id, "down", page, per_page)
    end

    def self.voted_up_for_user_id(user_id, page, per_page = 25)
      entry_ids_for_user(user_id, "up", page, per_page)
    end

    def self.entry_ids_for_user(user_id, value, page, per_page)
      votes = paginate_by_user_id_and_value(
        user_id, value, :page => page, :per_page => per_page)
      votes.map {|vote| vote.entry_id}
    end
  end
```

The first four lines of this model provide the necessary validations. The vote value may only be an "up" or a "down," each user may have only one vote per entry ID, and an entry ID and user ID are required. If a validation error occurs, the service responds with a 400 error and the JSON representation of the ActiveRecord errors.

The named scopes provide the finders that will be used in the various service API calls. They provide calls to to find up votes, down votes, votes by user ID, and votes by entry ID. The remaining methods wrap up the logic that the service will provide. The API needs to create a vote or update its vote value through the create_or_update method. The remaining methods return only the data needed for service responses. Note that the entry_ids_for_user method uses the Will Paginate gem (http://wiki.github.com/mislav/will_paginate) to provide pagination.

This model is a very simple representation for the functionality needed by the vote service. For example, it's not storing any aggregate stats. Instead, everything is calculated on the fly. In order to get the service up quickly, this is fine, but over time it will most likely migrate to a more denormalized design. This could include additional tables or indexes for looking up votes by either user or entry or counter caches to store totals.

Remember that one of the big advantages of using services is encapsulation. These kinds of changes can be made to the underlying models over time, with the service consumers remaining blissfully ignorant. In a standard Rails application, this is much more difficult because there may be many more points of entry directly to the vote model. With the vote service, the only thing that touches the model is the service layer itself.

Rails

A full Rails application can be created to serve up the vote service. To start it off, you have to go through the regular steps to create the Rails application, the vote model, and the vote controller:

```
rails votes-service
./script/generate model vote entry_id:string \
   user_id:string value:string
./script/generate controller votes
```

The three commands shown here create the basic structures for the Rails service. The following sections show examples for both Rails 2.3 and Rails 3. Many readers may still be running Rails 2.3, but feel free to skip to the next section if you've already upgraded to Rails 3.

Rails 2.3 Routes

You need to define the service entry points in the routes. The following section covers how to use routes in Rails 2.3 to specify the HTTP entry points. You edit the routes to create the public entry points for the service. These declarations in routes.rb represent the entire public interface for the vote service:

```
map.connect 'api/v1/votes/entries/:entry_id/users/:user_id',
   :controller => "votes", :action => "create", :method => :put
map.user_up_votes 'api/v1/votes/users/:user_id/up',
   :controller => "votes",
   :action => "entry_ids_voted_up_for_user"
map.user_down_votes 'api/v1/votes/users/:user_id/down',
   :controller => "votes",
   :action => "entry_ids_voted_down_for_user"
```

```
map.entry_totals 'api/v1/votes/entries/totals',
  :controller => "votes", :action => "totals_for_entries"
map.user_votes 'api/v1/votes/users/:user_id/votes',
  :controller => "votes", :action => "votes_for_users"
map.user_totals 'api/v1/votes/users/:user_id/totals',
  :controller => "votes", :action => "totals_for_user"
```

As you can see, this interface doesn't use routes in the standard RESTful resources style. The first route specifies the controller and action for creating a vote. The following named routes show how votes and the aggregate totals can be retrieved. Now the actions must be created in the vote controller to handle each public API call.

Rails 3 Routes

Rails 3 features a new router that gives it some additional functionality and introduces a new domain-specific language for defining routes. The syntax for defining the routes for the service make it a bit cleaner and even makes it possible to specify the API version in the HTTP header:

```
VoteService::Application.routes.draw do |map|
  scope "/api/ratings" do
    constraints(:accept =>
      "application/vnd.pauldix.voteservice-v1+json") do

      controller :votes do
        put "/entries/:entry_id/users/:user_id/vote",
          :to => "create"

        get "/users/:user_id/up",
          :to => "entry_ids_voted_up_for_user"

        get "/users/:user_id/down",
          :to => "entry_ids_voted_down_for_user"

        get "/entries/totals",
          :to => "totals_for_entries"
```

```
get "/users/:user_id/votes",
  :to => "votes_for_users"

get "/users/:user_id/totals",
  :to => "totals_for_user"
    end
  end
end
end
```

The Rails 3 example removes the version from the URI. The scope block at the beginning tells the Rails router to look only for incoming requests that start with /api/ratings. The constraints block shows the version check. It states that the request header must contain Accept: application/vnd.pauldix.voteservice-v1+json. For some APIs, it may be preferable to default to the latest version of the API if no Accept header is present to request a specific version. Thus, only requests for older versions of the API would require the header. The section after the constraints shows the matching of the URI entry points to the vote controller.

The Rails Controller

The Rails controller code can be used in either the Rails 2.3 or Rails 3 API. It maps the incoming requests to the appropriate model logic for storing and retrieving votes:

```
class VotesController < ApplicationController
  # create a new vote
  # /api/v1/votes/entries/:entry_id/users/:user_id
  def create
    begin
      json = Yajl::Parser.parse(request.body.read)

      vote = Vote.create_or_update(
        :user_id => params["user_id"],
        :entry_id => params["entry_id"],
        :value => json["value"])
```

```
      if vote.valid?
        render :json => vote.to_json
      else
        render :json => vote.errors.to_json, :status => 400
      end
    rescue => e
      # log it and return an error
      render :json => e.message.to_json, :status => 500
    end
  end

  # GET /api/v1/votes/users/:user_id/up
  def entry_ids_voted_up_for_user
    page      = (params[:page] || 1).to_i
    per_page  = (params[:per_page] || 25).to_i
    user_id   = params[:user_id]
    count     = Vote.up.user_id(user_id).count
    entry_ids = Vote.voted_up_for_user_id(user_id, page,
      per_page)

    data = {
      :total    => count,
      :entries  => entry_ids
    }

    data[:previous_page] = user_up_votes_url(
      :user_id => user_id,
      :page => page - 1,
      :per_page => per_page) if page > 1

    data[:next_page] = user_up_votes_url(
      :user_id => user_id,
      :page => page + 1,
      :per_page => per_page) if (page*per_page) < count

    render :json => data.to_json
  end
```

```ruby
# GET /api/v1/votes/users/:user_id/down
def entry_ids_voted_down_for_user
  page     = (params[:page] || 1).to_i
  per_page = (params[:per_page] || 25).to_i
  user_id  = params[:user_id]
  count    = Vote.down.user_id(user_id).count
  entry_ids = Vote.voted_down_for_user_id(user_id, page,
    per_page)

  data = {
    :total    => count,
    :entries  => entry_ids
  }

  data[:previous_page] = user_down_votes_url(
    :user_id => user_id,
    :page => page - 1,
    :per_page => per_page) if page > 1

  data[:next_page] = user_down_votes_url(
    :user_id => user_id,
    :page => page + 1,
    :per_page => per_page) if (page*per_page) < count

  render :json => data.to_json
end

# GET /api/v1/votes/entries/totals?ids=1,2
def totals_for_entries
  entry_ids = params["ids"].split(",")

  data = entry_ids.inject({}) do |result, entry_id|
    result.merge!(entry_id => {
      :up   => Vote.up.entry_id(entry_id).count,
      :down => Vote.down.entry_id(entry_id).count
    })
  end
```

```
    render :json => data.to_json
  end

  # GET /api/v1/votes/users/:user_id
  def votes_for_users
    user_id  = params["user_id"]
    entry_ids = params["ids"].split(",")

    data = entry_ids.inject({}) do |result, entry_id|
      vote = Vote.find_by_user_id_and_entry_id(user_id,
        entry_id)
      if vote
        result.merge!(entry_id => vote.value)
      else
        result
      end
    end

    render :json => data.to_json
  end

  # GET /api/v1/votes/users/:user_id/totals
  def totals_for_user
    user_id = params["user_id"]

    data = {
      :up   => Vote.up.user_id(user_id).count,
      :down => Vote.down.user_id(user_id).count
    }

    render :json => data.to_json
  end
end
```

The create method is the action that creates the vote. If there are validation errors, they are converted to JSON and returned with an HTTP response code of 400. There is also a general catchall for unexpected errors that returns with the exception message and an HTTP response code of 500. If all goes well, the API returns a response code of 200 with the vote JSON in the body. To parse the JSON in the request body, the example uses the yajl-ruby library, but you can also use the JSON gem.

JSON Parsing with YAJL Ruby

There are many libraries for parsing JSON. The most commonly used is Florian Frank's JSON library (http://flori .github.com/json/). However, yajl-ruby (http://github .com/brianmario/yajl-ruby) is a more recently developed library that offers incredible performance and a streaming parser. It is a Ruby library that provides bindings to the C JSON library named YAJL (http://lloyd.github.com/yajl/).

Next are the methods for returning user up and down votes. The example keeps all the response assembly code in the controller to keep things visible. As a result, the controller actions have quite a bit of code in them for handling pagination. Another option for organizing this kind of logic is to use a presenter pattern. The important part of these methods is that links are included for previous and next pages, if needed. It's a good idea to include some kind of pagination like this in any API call that can return a list. The API would also want to add limits on the page size later.

The Presenter Pattern

The presenter pattern offers an additional layer of abstraction outside the standard MVC style. This additional abstraction is helpful when managing views based on state. In the case of the vote API, the state and alternate views are based on pagination. For more information on the presenter pattern, see http://blog.jayfields.com/2007/03/rails-presenter-pattern.html.

Finally, APIs return the vote information for a specific list of entry IDs. This example uses the GET method with the single parameter ids. For the response, it builds up a hash of entry ID to the corresponding vote information. Once the hash is built, it is returned as JSON in the response.

The overall structure of this controller jumps out because it doesn't map to the standard Rails RESTful CRUD style of development. These calls are fairly specific, and there are far more GETs than CREATEs. For the most part, the API is simply an HTTP-facing interface for the model object. The only things that lie outside the model have to do with parsing requests and managing URIs.

For the simple needs of the vote service, the entire Rails framework is overkill. It doesn't need any of the view or helper constructs. Further, the way it uses controllers seems a bit off. It doesn't fit with the regular Rails paradigm. Let's take a look at some offerings that are a bit more service focused or modular.

Sinatra

Sinatra is a lightweight web services framework built on top of Rack. It is designed for small, simple web applications and services, so it is a perfect fit for your vote service. You can use the same model as you did with your Rails implementation.

Sinatra doesn't come with any built-in generators, so you have to generate your own application structure. However, the number of directories and the amount of support code needed is minimal. The example has to be able to run ActiveRecord migrations, load an environment, and support the Rack application loading style. The directory structure should like this:

```
votes-service
  config
    database.yml
  config.ru
  db
    migrate
      20090920213313_create_votes.rb
  models
    vote.rb
  Rakefile
  service.rb
```

The setup and required files are very simple. Included are config, db, and models directories. The vote model and its migration have been copied over from the Rails example. The HTTP services interface is defined in service.rb. Finally, the rackup command and other web servers use the config.ru file to load the application.

With the basic structure created, it's time to look at the implementation of the service in service.rb:

```ruby
require 'rubygems'
require 'yajl'
require 'active_record'
require 'action_pack'
require 'will_paginate'
require 'sinatra'
# this line required to enable the pagination
WillPaginate.enable_activerecord

require 'models/vote.rb'

class Service < Sinatra::Base
  configure do
    env = ENV["SINATRA_ENV"] || "development"
    databases = YAML.load_file("config/database.yml")
    ActiveRecord::Base.establish_connection(databases[env])
  end

  mime :json, "application/json"

  before do
    content_type :json
  end

  # create or update a vote
  put '/api/v1/votes/entries/:entry_id/users/:user_id' do
    begin
      json = Yajl::Parser.parse(request.body.read)

      vote = Vote.create_or_update(
        :user_id => params["user_id"],
        :entry_id => params["entry_id"],
        :value => json["value"])
```

```ruby
    if vote.valid?
      return vote.to_json
    else
      error 400, vote.errors.to_json
    end
  rescue => e
    # log it and return an error
    error 500, e.message.to_json
  end
end


# return the entry ids the user voted up on
get '/api/v1/votes/users/:user_id/up' do
  page      = (params[:page] || 1).to_i
  per_page  = (params[:per_page] || 25).to_i
  user_id   = params[:user_id]
  count     = Vote.up.user_id(user_id).count
  entry_ids = Vote.voted_up_for_user_id(user_id, page,
    per_page)

  data = {
    :total     => count,
    :entries   => entry_ids
  }

  if page > 1
    data[:previous_page] =
      "/api/v1/votes/users/#{user_id}/up?page=" +
      "#{page - 1}&per_page=#{per_page}"
  end

  if (page*per_page) < count
    data[:next_page] =
      "/api/v1/votes/users/#{user_id}/up?page=" +
      "#{page + 1}&per_page=#{per_page}"
  end
```

```ruby
  data.to_json
end

# return the entry ids the user voted down on
get '/api/v1/votes/users/:user_id/down' do
  page     = (params[:page] || 1).to_i
  per_page = (params[:per_page] || 25).to_i
  user_id  = params[:user_id]
  count    = Vote.down.user_id(user_id).count
  entry_ids = Vote.voted_down_for_user_id(user_id, page,
    per_page)

  data = {
    :total    => count,
    :entries  => entry_ids
  }

  if page > 1
    data[:previous_page] =
      "/api/v1/votes/users/#{user_id}/down?page=" +
      "#{page - 1}&per_page=#{per_page}"
  end

  if (page*per_page) < count
    data[:next_page] =
      "/api/v1/votes/users/#{user_id}/down?page=" +
      "#{page + 1}&per_page=#{per_page}"
  end

  data.to_json
end

# return the vote totals for a specific list of entries
get '/api/v1/votes/entries/totals' do
  entry_ids = params["ids"].split(",")
```

```ruby
  data = entry_ids.inject({}) do |result, entry_id|
    result.merge!(entry_id => {
      :up   => Vote.up.entry_id(entry_id).count,
      :down => Vote.down.entry_id(entry_id).count
    })
  end

  data.to_json
end

# return the users' vote for a specific list of entries
get '/api/v1/votes/users/:user_id' do
  user_id   = params["user_id"]
  entry_ids = params["ids"].split(",")

  data = entry_ids.inject({}) do |result, entry_id|
    vote = Vote.find_by_user_id_and_entry_id(user_id,
      entry_id)
    if vote
      result.merge!(entry_id => vote.value)
    else
      result
    end
  end

  data.to_json
end

# return the total number of up and down votes for user
get '/api/v1/votes/users/:user_id/totals' do
  user_id = params["user_id"]

  data = {
    :up   => Vote.up.user_id(user_id).count,
    :down => Vote.down.user_id(user_id).count
  }
```

```
        data.to_json
    end
end
```

First, the required libraries for Service are loaded. Inside the Service class itself is a configure block that gets called when the service is initially loaded. It is here that the ActiveRecord connection is set up. The MIME type JSON is then defined so it can be set on every response coming from this service in the before block.

The rest of service.rb is the full API interface. Unlike with Rails, with Sinatra, routes are defined with the implementations of their handlers. For example, line 20 in this example defines the URI for creating a vote. It should be a PUT call that matches the pattern /api/v1/votes/entries/:entry_id/users/:user_id.

There are two major differences between this code and the Rails code. First, the Sinatra service has dropped all the extra baggage around the service. Everything is contained in a single file. Second, the routes reside with the implementation of what those routes do. For a small service like the vote service, this single file can be referenced to get an idea of what the public interface looks like. It's a single point of reference for the service interface.

Rack

This section looks at using the raw Rack interface for implementing the vote service. Rack was designed to wrap HTTP requests and responses in a very simple interface that is modular and versatile. It is on top of this simple unified API that Rails, Sinatra, and many other frameworks are built. In fact, you could build your own simple service framework on top of Rack. The following example works with Rack directly.

As with Sinatra, with Rack there is a simple directory structure to the service. The entire service can be contained within a single file. For pure Rack applications, everything can be contained in a service.ru file. The rackup file becomes the actual service:

```
require 'rubygems'
require 'yajl'
require 'active_record'
require 'action_pack'
require 'will_paginate'
WillPaginate.enable_activerecord
```

```
require 'models/vote.rb'

module Rack
  class VotesService
    def initialize(environment)
      dbs = YAML.load_file("config/database.yml")
      ActiveRecord::Base.establish_connection
        (dbs[environment])
    end

    # every request will enter here
    def call(env)
      request = Rack::Request.new(env)
      path = request.path_info
      begin
        # return the vote totals for a specific list of entries
        if path == "/api/v1/votes/entries/totals"
          ids = ids_from_params(request.params)
          return get_entry_totals(ids)
        # create or update a vote
        elsif path.start_with?("/api/v1/votes/entries") &&
            path.end_with?("vote") && request.put?
          entry_id, user_id = entry_id_and_user_id_from_path
            (path)
          value = Yajl::Parser.parse(request.body.read)
          return process_vote(entry_id, user_id, value)
        # it's a request to get information for a user
        elsif path.start_with? "/api/v1/votes/users"
          # get the users votes on specific entries
          if path.end_with? "votes"
            ids = ids_from_params(request.params)
            return get_user_votes(user_id_from_path(path),
              ids)
          # get the entry ids a user voted down on
          elsif path.end_with? "down"
            return get_down_votes(user_id_from_path(path),
              request.params)
```

```
        # get the entry ids a user voted up on
        elsif path.end_with? "up"
          return get_up_votes(user_id_from_path(path),
            request.params)
        # get the up and down totals for a user
        elsif path.end_with? "totals"
          return get_user_totals(user_id_from_path(path))
        end
      end
    rescue => e
      # log it and return an error
      return [500, { 'Content-Type' => 'application/json' },
        e.message.to_json]
    end

    [404, { 'Content-Type' => 'application/json' },
      "Not Found".to_json]
  end

  def process_vote(entry_id, user_id, value)
    vote = Vote.create_or_update(
      :user_id => user_id,
      :entry_id => entry_id,
      :value => value)

    if vote.valid?
      [200, { 'Content-Type' => 'application/json' },
        vote.to_json]
    else
      [400, { 'Content-Type' => 'application/json' },
        vote.errors.to_json]
    end
  end

  def get_entry_totals(entry_ids)
    data = entry_ids.inject({}) do |result, entry_id|
```

```ruby
    result.merge!(entry_id => {
      :up   => Vote.up.entry_id(entry_id).count,
      :down => Vote.down.entry_id(entry_id).count
    })
  end

  [200, {'Content-Type'=>'application/json'}, data.to_json]
end

def get_up_votes(user_id, params)
  page     = (params[:page] || 1).to_i
  per_page = (params[:per_page] || 25).to_i
  count    = Vote.up.user_id(user_id).count
  entry_ids = Vote.voted_up_for_user_id(user_id, page,
    per_page)

  data = {
    :total   => count,
    :entries => entry_ids
  }

  if page > 1
    data[:previous_page] =
      "/api/v1/votes/users/#{user_id}/up?page=" +
      "#{page - 1}&per_page=#{per_page}"
  end

  if (page*per_page) < count
    data[:next_page] =
      "/api/v1/votes/users/#{user_id}/up?page=" +
      "#{page + 1}&per_page=#{per_page}"
  end

  [200, {'Content-Type'=>'application/json'},
    data.to_json]
end
```

```ruby
def get_down_votes(user_id, params)
  page     = (params[:page] || 1).to_i
  per_page = (params[:per_page] || 25).to_i
  count    = Vote.down.user_id(user_id).count
  entry_ids = Vote.voted_down_for_user_id(user_id, page,
    per_page)

  data = {
    :total    => count,
    :entries  => entry_ids
  }

  if page > 1
    data[:previous_page] =
      "/api/v1/votes/users/#{user_id}/down?page=" +
      "#{page - 1}&per_page=#{per_page}"
  end

  if (page*per_page) < count
    data[:next_page] =
      "/api/v1/votes/users/#{user_id}/down?page=" +
      "#{page + 1}&per_page=#{per_page}"
  end

  [200, {'Content-Type'=>'application/json'}, data.to_json]
end

def get_user_totals(user_id)
  data = {
    :up   => Vote.up.user_id(user_id).count,
    :down => Vote.down.user_id(user_id).count
  }

  [200, {'Content-Type'=>'application/json'}, data.to_json]
end
```

```ruby
  def get_user_votes(user_id, entry_ids)
    data = entry_ids.inject({}) do |result, entry_id|
      vote = Vote.find_by_user_id_and_entry_id(user_id,
        entry_id)
      if vote
        result.merge!(entry_id => vote.value)
      else
        result
      end
    end

    [200, {'Content-Type'=>'application/json'}, data.to_json]
  end

  def user_id_from_path(path)
    path.match(/.*users\/(.*)\/.*/)[1]
  end

  def entry_id_and_user_id_from_path(path)
    matches = path.match(/.*entries\/(.*)\/users\/
      (.*)\/vote/)
    [matches[1], matches[2]]
  end

  def ids_from_params(params)
    params.has_key?("ids") ? params["ids"].split(",") : []
  end
  end
end

environment = ENV["RACK_ENV"] || "development"
service = Rack::VotesService.new(environment)
run service
```

The beginning of the rackup file looks very similar to the Sinatra service, with the same required libraries. The VotesService class is inside the Rack module, but this is only out of convention and not a requirement. The important part of the VotesService class is the `call` method. Every request that comes into Rack will invoke a call and pass in the `env` variable.

The `env` variable consists of the regular CGI environment variables that hold information about the request. Those variables can be accessed through the `env` hash, but it's easier to work with the Rack `Request` wrapper than the environment variables directly. `Request` takes the `env` variables and wraps them in a friendlier interface. The rest of the call method is a series of statements that determine which request is being made to the API.

To make things a little more readable, the implementation of each API entry point is its own method. This means that the entire body of call methods is devoted to resolving a request to a Ruby method. The implementations of these methods are almost identical to the implementations in the Sinatra example.

In normal circumstances, you probably wouldn't want to write Rack code like this. The code inside the call method highlights some of the common things you want out of a service framework: mapping a request URI and HTTP method to a Ruby method (like routes in Rails) and pulling out values from the request path and query string. A more advanced service interface might route based not only on URI and HTTP method but on headers as well. For example, if you were using headers to specify the API version, it would be helpful to route based on that information. The raw Rack implementation shows what common elements Sinatra and Rails provide.

Conclusion

This chapter takes a quick tour of a few of the options for implementing services in Ruby. However, it only scratches the surface. There are many frameworks out there, including Wave, Mack, and several others. However, the three options reviewed in this chapter give a good idea of different ways for structuring the code for a service.

While Rails is probably the most familiar option, it includes extra code and scaffolding that are unnecessary. Sinatra provides a simple, clean interface for mapping requests to blocks of code for their implementation. The common element among most frameworks is Rack. However, while you can write a raw Rack-based service, its implementation is quite messy.

Ultimately, the choice of which framework to use comes down to aesthetics. Most frameworks can accomplish the job. While requests may run a little more slowly through the Rails framework, the service application layer is horizontally scalable. However, services should strive for simplicity. This means keeping the amount of code to a minimum and striving for readability and maintainability throughout.

CHAPTER 6

Connecting to Services

Connecting to services is a fairly easy task, but there are some things to consider when running in a production environment. This chapter discusses blocking I/O, parallelism, and how to tackle these problems in Ruby 1.8, 1.9, and JRuby. It also covers how to gather performance statistics to ensure that service owners are meeting requirements. Finally, examples show how to test and mock service calls and methods for running in development mode.

Blocking I/O, Threading, and Parallelism

One of the core requirements for creating a working services architecture is the ability to run requests in parallel. Without parallelism, you'd be unable to make more than a couple service calls within the client's request/response lifecycle. For instance, consider an example in which each service takes 30 milliseconds to respond. Further assume that it takes 10 service requests to get all the data needed to respond to a single request. When run serially, these requests would take a total of 3 seconds. When run in parallel, it should be only a little over 30 milliseconds, with maybe a few extra milliseconds for actual I/O and overhead.

This example highlights the importance of running requests in parallel. There are two approaches for achieving parallelism with requests: asynchronous and multithreaded I/O. Each of these approaches is a solution to the problem of blocking I/O. That is, when performing I/O operations (such as transferring data over a network), code execution blocks and waits for a response. Let's take a look at how each of these approaches solves this problem.

Asynchronous I/O

Asynchronous I/O is an approach that lets a program continue to execute while waiting for data. In the case of the previous example, with 10 service requests, the first request starts, and execution moves on to starting the other nine before the first request completes. A typical pattern with asynchronous I/O is to create handler code that gets called when each request is done, commonly referred to as a *reactor design pattern*.

Implementations of the reactor design pattern exist for Ruby in the form of the EventMachine (http://rubyeventmachine.com/), Revactor (http://revactor.org), and NeverBlock (http://github.com/oldmoe/neverblock) libraries. The goal of these libraries is to let your program continue to execute while waiting for I/O. Coverage of the specific reactor libraries is beyond the scope of this book. Instead, this chapter covers Typhoeus, which supports asynchronous HTTP calls via libcurl-multi, an asynchronous request library written in C. Another option for performing asynchronous requests is the Curb library, which also includes bindings to libcurl-multi.

Multi-threading

Multi-threaded models are another approach for achieving parallelism for service requests. The goal in a multi-threaded services client is to put each of the blocking I/O calls in a thread of its own. This way, program execution can continue in the primary thread while the worker threads wait for requests to complete. To understand how this works inside Ruby, we need to take quick detour to discuss threading models.

Each of the Ruby implementations takes a slightly different approach to implementing threading. The differences between implementations lie mainly in the types of threads they use. The two kinds of threads are green, or user-level, threads and native, or kernel-level, threads. Kernel-level threads are managed by the underlying operating system. This means that the operating system is responsible for scheduling their execution. If one of the threads is waiting on I/O, the operating system can automatically move over to another thread.

User-level threads rely on the Ruby interpreter to schedule their execution. Multiple user-level threads run within a single kernel-level thread. What this means for service requests is that I/O within user-level threads blocks execution on all other user-level threads. Of course, this defeats the goal of running requests in parallel.

In the Ruby implementations, Ruby 1.8 has a user-level thread implementation. This has a negative impact on the performance of multi-threaded service clients in Ruby 1.8. Ruby 1.9 uses kernel-level threads, but it has a global interpreter lock (GIL). This means that even though the threads are kernel level, only one can run at a time in the interpreter. This can also have a negative impact on performance. JRuby and Rubinius use regular kernel-level threads that are scheduled by the operating system.

The different types of threading in the Ruby implementations means that threaded I/O performance can vary quite a bit from implementation to implementation. Java users are accustomed to using multi-threaded techniques for achieving parallelism, but with Ruby, you have to be a bit more careful. The difference in performance depends on how much data is returned in the service request and the response time of the services being called.

In tests using the different Ruby implementations, asynchronous clients are almost always faster than multi-threaded clients. However, the difference between them can be quite small, depending on the specific case. Testing and benchmarking your approach is always the best way to ensure that you're achieving your desired performance.

Typhoeus

Typhoeus is a Ruby library with native C extensions to libcurl and libcurl-multi. libcurl-multi provides an interface for performing asynchronous requests. This makes Typhoeus an implementation that uses the asynchronous I/O reactor style to achieve parallelism. Typhoeus has been tested with Ruby 1.8.6, 1.8.7, and 1.9.1.

Before you can run through these examples, you first need to install the library. Typhoeus requires a current version of libcurl, which can be found at http://curl .haxx.se/libcurl/. Once libcurl is installed, you can Typhoeus with the following:

```
gem install pauldix-typhoeus --source=http://gems.github.com
```

Making Single Requests

Now that you have Typhoeus installed, you're ready to make some requests. Typhoeus has three classes that manage making HTTP requests: request, response, and hydra. The request class contains all the information about a request, including the URI, the headers, the request body, and other parameters, such as timeout and authentication. The response object holds information about the response, including

the HTTP status code, the headers, the body, and the time taken. hydra is the class
that manages requests and runs them in parallel.

The following is a simple example:

```
require 'rubygems'
require 'typhoeus'

hydra = Typhoeus::Hydra.new
request = Typhoeus::Request.new("http://localhost:3000",
  :timeout => 100)
request.on_complete do |response|
  puts response.code
  puts response.body
end
hydra.queue(request)
hydra.run
```

This example shows how to create a single request to a server running on the local
machine. First, you create the hydra object that will manage requests. Then you create the request object. The example also passes a timeout value that gives the request
100 milliseconds to complete before it times out. At this point, the request has not yet
been run. Before you run it, you assign an on_complete handler. This block of code
is called after the request completes. The block is yielded a response object.

Finally, you queue up the request in the hydra object and run it. run is a blocking call that does not return until all queued requests are called. For a single request,
this looks like a lot of effort compared to a regular Net::HTTP call. Only when you
run more requests do the advantages of this asynchronous style become apparent.

For single requests like the preceding example, Typhoeus has a few shortcut methods to reduce the amount of setup and code required and run them right away:

```
require 'rubygems'
require 'typhoeus'

response = Typhoeus::Request.get("http://localhost:3000",
  :timeout => 100)
puts response.body
```

```
response = Typhoeus::Request.post
  ("http://localhost:3000/posts",:body => "title=foo")
puts response.code

response = Typhoeus::Request.put
  ("http://localhost:3000/posts/1",:body => "title=bar")

response = Typhoeus::Request.delete("http://localhost:3000/
  posts/1")
```

This example shows running GET, PUT, POST, and DELETE requests. The options hash takes all the same options that the Request constructor takes. The request is run immediately and the resulting response object is returned.

Making Simultaneous Requests

Now it's time to look at a more complex example. For this example, you'll return to the social feed reader application and produce a set of requests for a user's reading list. That is, given a user ID, you want to pull the sorted list of feed entries that the user has to read, along with any ratings information for each entry. Calls to multiple services have to be made to get this data. First, you call the feed subscriptions service to get a list of entries for a user's reading list. Once that list is returned, you make calls to the entry service to pull back the data for each entry. Finally, you make a call to the ratings service to get the ratings for each of the entries in this list.

The following example shows how you would make those calls using Typhoeus:

```
require 'rubygems'
require 'typhoeus'
require 'json'

hydra = Typhoeus::Hydra.new
ratings  = {}
entries  = {}
entry_id = []

entry_list_request = Typhoeus::Request.new(
  "http://localhost:3000/api/v1/reading_lists/paul")
```

```ruby
entry_list_request.on_complete do |response|
  entry_ids = JSON.parse(response.body)

  ratings_request = Typhoeus::Request.new(
    "http://localhost:3000/api/v1/ratings/entries",
    :params => {:ids => entry_ids.join(",")})

  ratings_request.on_complete do |response|
    ratings = JSON.parse(response.body)
  end
  hydra.queue(ratings_request)

  entry_request
  entry_request = Typhoeus::Request.new(
    "http://localhost:3000/api/v1/entries",
    :params => {:ids => entry_ids.join(",")})

  entry_request.on_complete do |response|
    entries = JSON.parse(response.body)
  end
  hydra.queue(request)
end

hydra.queue(entry_list_request)
hydra.run
```

This code example is a bit messy because it keeps everything in one place, but this makes it easier to see exactly what is happening. (Chapter 7, "Developing Service Client Libraries," covers how to write clean libraries with code reuse of parsing logic.) Now it's time to examine what is going on in the example.

First, you initialize the variables that will be accessed from the completion handlers of the requests. Then you create the GET request for the reading list. The handler for the reading list request is the interesting part. First, you parse the response. As with the collection-based requests in the previous chapter, you can assume that the body is a hash with an element called entries that contains the entry IDs. This is the only part of the response needed to make the other requests.

Once the entry IDs have been returned in the first request, you can build requests to the entry and ratings services. The ratings service request gives the ratings of the entry IDs that are passed in the `params` hash. The `on_complete` handler assigns the parsed response to be used later. The same is done with the request to the entry service (which returns the full entry). Each of these requests is added to the `hydra` queue.

Finally, the fully built `entry_list_request` is added to the `hydra` queue and a blocking call is made to run. Let's take a look at how the call to run `hydra` proceeds. First, the entry list request is run. The `on_complete` handler is called when it is complete. The ratings and entry requests are added to the queue, and the `on_complete` block returns. At this point, `hydra` picks back up and runs the two requests in parallel. When either one finishes, its `on_complete` block is run.

The important thing to take note of is that the `on_complete` handlers for the ratings and entry requests are not guaranteed to run in any particular order. The entry request could complete and run its `on_complete` block before the ratings request, despite the fact that they appear in opposite order in code. Given the way the example is structured, this isn't a concern. However, if you had built in some code on the entry request `on_complete` handler which assumed that the ratings request `on_complete` handler had already been run, you'd have a problem.

This section is meant to serve merely as an introduction to Typhoeus and the common asynchronous programming style used in other reactor libraries. Many event-driven libraries include the idea of completion handlers or callbacks that are run on events. Typhoeus is covered in greater detail, along with how to write clean libraries, in Chapter 7, "Developing Service Client Libraries."

Multi-threaded Requests

One option for performing requests in parallel is to run them in multiple threads. However, this isn't as straightforward in Ruby as it is in other languages. Because of the user-level threads in Ruby 1.8 and the global interpreter lock in Ruby 1.9, the performance of threaded requests may not actually reflect true parallelism. Still, there are some performance gains in running multiple requests via threads. Here is an example of using standard `Net::HTTP` in a multi-threaded fashion:

```
require 'thread'
require 'net/http'
```

```
threads = nil
responses = Queue.new

threads = (0..99).map do |i|
  Thread.new do
     url = "http://localhost:3000/api/v1/entries/#{i}"
     body = Net::HTTP.get(URI.parse(url))
     responses.push([url, body])
   end
end
threads.each {|thread| thread.join}

# do something with the responses
```

This example creates a new thread for each request to be run. The responses are
put onto a queue. The use of the queue is important because it is thread-safe. Then it
iterates over the threads and makes sure each one has completed before execution continues. When all requests are complete, it's possible to do some processing with the
responses.

The following example uses a thread pool:

```
require 'thread'
require 'net/http'

url_queue = Queue.new
thread_pool = []
responses = Queue.new

50.times do
   thread_pool << Thread.new do
     loop do
       url = url_queue.pop
       responses.push([url, Net::HTTP.get(URI.parse(url))])
     end
   end
end
```

```
100.times do |i|
  url_queue.push "http://localhost:3000/api/v1/entries/#{i}"
end

responses = []
while responses.size < 99
  responses << @responses.pop
end

# do something with the responses
```

A thread pool is usually more efficient in systems that use native threads because of the higher overhead in setting them up. The thread pool sets up the threads once and reuses them to make connections over time. You'd want to use this method when running Ruby 1.9, MacRuby, Rubinius, or JRuby. Here's what is going on in this example. First, it sets up the variables that the thread pool will be using. Then the threads in the pool are started—in this case, a total of 50 threads. This represents the maximum number of concurrent requests that can be made. Each of these waits for a URI on the queue and runs the request. A more complex example would put full request objects into the queue. Now that the thread pool is running, the script can simply queue up URIs to be requested. Finally, the example pulls responses from the responses queue until all have returned.

The two threaded examples are fairly simple and not entirely complete. A real-world set of service requests would require a bit more complexity. Specifically, it would need to call out to different services after some requests finish. However, these examples show the basics of how to run multi-threaded requests.

JRuby

In JRuby, there are multiple options for running requests in parallel. Because of JRuby's kernel-level threads, parallelism can be achieved through multi-threaded clients. It's possible to use a thread pool model with Net::HTTP as in the previous section, or you can take advantage of some Java libraries. Here is a quick example that uses the built-in Java concurrency library for running requests inside a thread pool:

```
require 'net/http'
include Java
import 'java.util.concurrent.Executors'
```

```
class Request
  include java.util.concurrent.Callable
  def initialize(url)
    @url = url
  end

  def call
    Net::HTTP.get(URI.parse(@url))
  end
end

thread_pool = Executors.new_fixed_thread_pool(50)

futures = []
100.times do |i|
  request = Request.new("http://localhost:3000/entries/#{i}")
  futures << thread_pool.submit(request)
end

results = futures.map {|f| f.get}
# do something with results

thread_pool.shutdown
```

Here is what's going on in this example. First, it brings in the necessary Java libraries to handle the thread pool. The Executors Java class includes a factory to generate a thread pool. In order to use the thread pool, you first need to create a class that implements the Callable interface. This is where the request class comes in. Including the Callable interface in the class translates to telling Java that request implements the interface. It must define the method call to conform to that interface. In the example, call simply runs the request using the JRuby Net::HTTP implementation.

When the request class has been defined, everything is ready to make the necessary calls. First, the example creates the thread pool and specifies that it should run 50 concurrent threads. Now it's ready to submit jobs to the pool for execution. The request objects are initialized and submitted to the thread pool. The submit method returns an instance of the Java Future class. The return value of the request's call method can be accessed through this object. Indeed, that's what is happening later, when looping through `futures` to get the value of each request. Finally, the thread pool has to be shut down for the script to complete and exit.

While the previous example uses `Net::HTTP`, JRuby gives you access to everything in Java, including a solid HTTP client. The Apache Commons HTTPClient (http://hc.apache.org/httpcomponents-client/index.html) is a Java library for performing HTTP requests. It's a mature library that includes a fairly expansive feature set. Specific coverage is beyond the scope of this book, but if you're running on JRuby, it's one of the better options for making HTTP requests.

Logging for Performance

One of the keys to running a reliable architecture is logging. Having consistent client-side logging provides you with the additional information you need to ensure that service operators are fulfilling the overall architecture performance needs. Because you know that you'll want logging across all your service requests, it helps to build it in on some global level.

Typhoeus includes a simple method for adding handlers to every request. Here is an example:

```
require 'logger'

logger = Logger.new("response_times.txt")
hydra = Typhoeus::Hydra.new
hydra.on_complete do |response|
  if response.code >= 200 && response.code < 500
    logger.info(
      "#{response.request.url} in #{response.time} seconds")
  else
    logger.info("#{response.request.url} FAILED")
  end
end
```

The `hydra` object can also take an `on_complete` handler that will be called after each request completes. In the body of this handler, you're checking to make sure the response code is in the 200–500 range. You expect some 400 errors due to data validation problems. You're really only concerned about differentiating regular requests from server errors. Once you've logged the details about the request, `hydra` continues and calls the `request` object's `on_complete` handler.

When you have the request info logged to a file, you can calculate some useful statistics. These are the most important things you'd want to calculate:

- Average response time
- Minimum response time
- Maximum response time
- Number of failures and percentage of requests that fail
- Percentage of requests served within certain time

Tracking these statistics over time gives you an indication of how well services are performing. For production systems, tracking these statistics also gives you indications about when systems are starting to slow down under load. Whether you're using Typhoeus or another library, it's a good idea to log information about every request sent out. Later, you can visit these logs to see how your services are performing.

Handling Error Conditions

It helps to think up front about how your clients will handle error conditions. Some error conditions can be anticipated and programmed against, while others need to be caught and logged for later inspection. Identifying what you want to do for each error condition can be tricky. Let's go through some of the errors you might encounter.

One of the basic error conditions you expect is a general data error. These are the 400 errors that your services are throwing to indicate data validation problems. In this case, you can handle the error and bubble it up to the user like a standard Active-Record data validation.

The other errors are unexpected ones. For some of these, you can log them and continue execution without the response. Consider the previous example involving building a user's reading list. You made three calls to build the list: first to get the entry IDs, second to get the ratings for these entries, and third to get the entries themselves. If the request to get the entry ratings failed, it's still conceivable that you could render the page without ratings. It's not ideal, but it's better than throwing an error to the user.

Finally, there are conditions that are considered unrecoverable. These errors prevent you from continuing. When you face such an error, you might want to retry the request. Typhoeus has built-in retry logic to make this operation easy. You simply pass in the number of retries as an option to the request constructor, like this:

```
request = Typhoeus::Request.new("http://localhost:3000",
   :retry => 1)
```

Note that Typhoeus triggers a retry only if the response code is in the 0–199 or 500+ range. Any response code within 200–499 will not be retried. If you want finer-grained retry logic, it's easy to write your own within the request handler, like this:

```
hydra = Typhoeus::Hydra.new
request = Typhoeus::Request.new("http://localhost:3000/
   fail/1")
request.on_complete do |response|
   if response.code == 500 && request.failures < 3
     hydra.queue(request)
   elsif request.failures >= 3
     # log stuff
   else
     # do stuff
   end
end
hyra.queue(request)
hydra.run
```

With this example we're only retrying if the response code is 500. Also, we're only trying the request again if we've failed less than three times. After three failures we'll log the error and throw an exception.

Testing and Mocking Service Calls

Proper testing is a key component in building a successful application architecture. When writing clients, you need to consider how you want to test the service calls and how you want other libraries that use the clients to mock out their functionality. For testing your service clients, the best option is to mock at the lowest level. That is, you should mock at the level of the HTTP request.

Typhoeus includes functionality for mocking out requests based on the URI and method. The following example shows the usage:

```
require 'rubygems'
require 'typhoeus'

hydra    = Typhoeus::Hydra.new
request  = Typhoeus::Request.new("http://localhost:3000/
   foo")
request.on_complete do |response|
   # do something
end

mock_response = Typhoeus::Response.new(:code => 404,
   :headers => "whatever", :body => "not found", :time => 0.1)
hydra.mock(:get,
   "http://localhost:3000/foo").and_return(mock_response)

hydra.queue(request)
hydra.run
```

You can see that the setup of the request in this example looks just like a regular Typhoeus request. Lines 10–13 set up the mocking portion. First, you create a response object. In this example, you're mocking out a 404 NOT FOUND response. The call to `hydra.mock` tells `hydra` that the mock response should be returned on a GET to http://localhost:3000/foo. When the request is queued up and run, the request's `on_complete` handler is called with the mock response object.

Using mock response objects to test the service client helps to avoid calls to a running service. However, as the example shows, the mock response object is closely tied to the API of the service being called. If at some later time you change the URI or the service response body, this test won't tell you that your client is now broken. Because of this, it's also a good idea to include a full integration test to ensure that the service being called works the way the client expects it to.

If you're not using Typhoeus to make requests, you have a few other options. For `Net::HTTP`, a good option for mocking at the request level is Blaine Cook's FakeWeb (http://fakeweb.rubyforge.org). Another option is to wrap all calls to your HTTP library in a single class that can be mocked.

Requests in Development Environments

In a typical Rails application, a developer can run most of the environment locally on his or her machine. This means that when you're developing, you're able to make calls to the database directly. However, with service-based environments, you probably won't be able to run every service on your development computer. This means you have to think about how development environments connect to services for testing purposes.

The simplest setup for development environments is to have each service running where it is accessible to each developer. Of course, this removes the ability to develop locally without a network connection. Another option is to build a development mode into each service client. Ultimately, running development environments with services can be tricky. Writing solid tests and mocking out the service calls is the cleanest method for developing against services. The next chapter explores how to write clients that include mocking functionality that hides the underlying service details.

Conclusion

This chapter covers the basics of connecting to services. Making requests in parallel is a necessary component of building service clients that perform well enough to be run inside the request/response lifecycle. To achieve this, requests can be run asynchronously or in multiple threads. Generally, asynchronous clients perform a little better than multi-threaded clients, but this may vary depending on the specific environment.

The next chapter goes into the details about how to write fully featured client libraries. The goal is to write clients that are well tested, that support mocking, and that provide simple, readable interfaces.

CHAPTER 7
Developing Service Client Libraries

Client libraries represent the usable interface of services for developers in the rest of an application. That is, services are called through their client-side libraries instead of directly through HTTP. Client libraries provide an additional layer of abstraction that makes working with services easier for front-end application developers. Thus, developing, organizing, and deploying client libraries are key parts of service-oriented design. Good libraries include client-side validation, clear and well-documented APIs, connection and request abstraction, and simple methods for mocking. This chapter covers how to tackle each of these issues and looks at writing client libraries that conform to Rails 3.0's ActiveModel.

Packaging

The first step when designing a new library is to organize the structure of the files and directories. This includes how to package the library for deployment and installation on other computers. RubyGems is the obvious choice for creating and sharing libraries. This is true even for service client libraries that are private and will be shared only by internal services and developers. Gems can be deployed via a private file server, a local gem server, or inside the Bundler cache of an application.

> **Bundler**
>
> Bundler (http://gembundler.com) is a new system of managing an application's packages. It is part of how Rails 3 manages dependencies. The .gem files, which are built gems, can be placed in an application's local Bundler cache so that they can be installed by Bundler without checking a remote gem server. In Rails, the cache is located in the vendor/bundler/ruby/1.8/cache/ directory. In place of 1.8, you substitute the version of Ruby that your application is being developed on.

To create a gem, all that is required is a gemspec. It's possible to create this file manually by using the syntax on the Gem::Specification documentation page (http://rubygems.rubyforge.org/rubygems-update/Gem/Specification.html). However, it can get a bit time-consuming and can cause problems if you forget to update the gemspec with new files. An easier way to get started creating a RubyGems gem is to use a generator such as Jeweler.

Jeweler

Jeweler (http://github.com/technicalpickles/jeweler), created by Josh Nichols, is a generator for starting new gems. It has a convenient command-line interface for starting new gems and comes with built-in rake tasks to handle things like generating the gemspec, building the gem, and pushing to RubyGems (http://rubygems.org). For internal libraries, you'll probably want to skip the last part, but the other conveniences of the library make it worth using even for private gems.

This chapter focuses on building out an example from the social feed reader application. First, you create a library for the entry service. Remember that this service has methods for getting the information on feed entries, given a list of IDs. A larger example might have the service also return entries given a source (such as a feed URL or an ID), but the single list of IDs is enough to highlight the important parts. The second library is for accessing the vote service created in Chapter 5, "Implementing Services." The third library is for accessing the reading list for a user. The simple example in this chapter only returns a list of entry IDs, given the user email. A more complete example would include getting a list of subscriptions and adding and removing feeds from the subscriptions. It is important to make these three separate libraries, one for each service, to ensure that when the service is updated, only its gem has to be updated.

First, you install Jeweler and its dependencies. This requires that you have the `git` and `gemcutter` gems installed in addition to any testing library that you'll use. You also need `git` installed. The Jeweler installation is simple:

```
gem install jeweler
```

Now it's time to create the gems. For organizational purposes, it's easiest to create a single repository that all the gems can be put in. However, in a production environment, it's a good idea to keep each client gem as a directory in the larger structure of the service code. That way, the client can be iterated and improved with the service code.

In the overall gem directory, it's simple to create the skeleton structure of the gems with the following commands:

```
jeweler --rspec pauldix-entries
jeweler --rspec pauldix-readling-list
jeweler --rspec pauldix-ratings
```

These examples use RSpec, but Jeweler includes helpers to generate files for many other testing frameworks. You can use the command `jeweler-help` to see the available options. The gems have my name, `pauldix`, as a prefix to ensure that they won't collide with any public gems. For your gems, you should use the organization name or an abbreviation as a prefix to the gem name. The generator creates a basic directory structure for you, as well as some starting files. Here is the initial list for the `pauldix-entries` gem:

```
pauldix-entries/
  lib/
    pauldix-entries.rb
  LICENCE
  Rakefile
  README.rdoc
  spec/
    pauldix-entries-spec.rb
```

```
spec.opts
spec_heleper.rb
```

There are only a couple more things to set up to get an initial version of the gem built. First, you go into `Rakefile` and make the following changes:

```
# at the top of the file with the other requires
require 'lib/pauldix-entries/version.rb'


    # right after line 14
    gem.version = PauldixEntries::VERSION
    gem.files = FileList['lib/**/*.rb', '[A-Z]*',
       'spec/**/*'].to_a
```

The `require` is a file that sets a version constant that will be shown next. This is useful for other libraries that want to ensure the version of the gem at runtime. The other lines are modifications to the gem specification. The first line sets the gem version from a constant in a module that will be set up next. The second line sets the generator to create a gemspec that includes all `.rb` files from the lib directory and all its subdirectories, pulls in the README and LICENCE files from the root directory, and pulls in all the files from the spec directory and its subdirectories.

Now it's time to create the `lib/pauldix-entries/version.rb` file. You create the directory and make the `version.rb` file look like this:

```
module PauldixEntries
   VERSION = "0.0.0"
end
```

Next, you load the version file in `lib/pauldix-entries.rb`. This file is responsible for loading all the other files and required gems used in the library. To begin, it's only the following single line:

```
require 'pauldix-entries/version.rb'
```

With all this setup out of the way, it's time to generate a gemspec and build the gem. Jeweler includes a few `rake` tasks for getting this done. From the root of the gem directory, you issue the following commands:

```
rake gemspec
rake build
```

The first command generates the gemspec. It's worth taking a quick look at the generated file just to see what the `rake` task has built. The second command generates the gemspec and creates the gem file `pkg/pauldix-entries-0.0.0.gem`. This file can be used to install the gem. You need to take the same steps to get the vote service gem ready to go. Later sections fill out the files in these gems and make them functionally complete.

Building and Deploying a Library

Part of packaging a library is building and deploying it. With RubyGems, this is simple. Once the gemspec is written or generated, you can build the gem file with a single command. Deployment then consists of getting this single gem file to the target servers and getting it installed. It's possible to run your own gem server so that you can issue the `gem install` command with the —source flag, but that's more than is necessary.

With RubyGems, it's possible to install using only the gem file. You simply issue the following command:

```
gem install pauldix-entries-0.0.0.gem
```

Because the gem installation is completely contained in the single gem file, deployment to a server is as simple as copying the file to the server. If you're using Capistrano for deployment, it is a good idea to include a task that builds the gem and copies it up to the target servers. It's also possible to use a shared file service such as S3 as the source. Or you may just want to check the gem files into the repository and install from there. Whatever your choice, it should come down to running a single command to get the new client library gem deployed to your servers.

Parsing Logic

The first chapter of this book briefly introduces JSON in an example that creates a user service. In that example, the user objects are serialized as JSON and parsed in the client. Because of JSON's simple format, the example presents much of what you need to know.

The form that JSON takes can be summarized in a few sentences. First, you start with an array or an object. An array consists of ordered values, while an object is an unordered set of name/value pairs (like a Ruby hash). The mapping of JSON's object to Ruby hashes is part of what makes JSON so easy to work with. The names in an object are strings, while the values in an array or an object can be either a number, a string, an array, or an object. So arrays and objects can contain more arrays and objects. This small and simple grammar makes it easy to write a JSON parser and even easier to use one.

There are more than a few options for parsing JSON in Ruby, but this section focuses on only two: the JSON gem and yajl-ruby. The following examples use this as input to the JSON parser:

```
{
  "results" : [{"name" : "geoffrey"}, {"name" : "gail"}],
  "total" : 2,
  "uri" : "http://pauldix.net"
}
```

This sample JSON is used in this chapter to show how to access objects, arrays, and the different kinds of values.

The JSON Gem

The JSON gem is the de facto standard for parsing JSON in Ruby. It has both a pure Ruby implementation and a native C implementation. The C implementation offers speed improvements, while the pure Ruby version may be easier to install. Installation on Ruby 1.8, or 1.9 can be done via the following command:

```
gem install json
```

Installation on JRuby must be done via the `jgem` command. The gem also has a different name on JRuby. It can be installed with the following command:

```
jgem install json-jruby
```

Now that the gem is installed, it's ready for use:

```
require 'rubygems'
require 'json'
```

```
# input corresponds to the example JSON shown earlier
parsed = JSON.parse(input)
results = parsed["results"]

puts results.size          # => 2
puts results[0].inspect    # => {"name" => "geoffrey"}
puts parsed["total"]       # => 2
puts parsed["uri"]         # => "http://pauldix.net"
```

The parsing logic is contained in a single line: the call to JSON.parse. From there, the parsed input can be manipulated through standard Ruby objects. The object is parsed as a Hash, the array as an Array, the number as a Fixnum, and the string as a String. The hash keys are strings, as shown on the line that assigns the results value.

YAJL Ruby

YAJL (yet another JSON library) is a streaming JSON library written in C. "Streaming" refers to the library's ability to parse JSON as the document comes in. This can be quite handy when you're working with large files that may be difficult to keep in memory or when you're parsing JSON as it comes in from an HTTP response. yajl-ruby is a Ruby library written by Brian Lopez that has bindings to YAJL.

The yajl-ruby project page (http://github.com/brianmario/yajl-ruby) boasts that it offers speed improvements over the standard JSON gem for both generating and parsing JSON. Due to its reliance on C libraries, it is available only in Ruby 1.8 and 1.9. The following command installs the gem:

```
gem install yajl-ruby
```

When the gem is installed, it's ready for use:

```
require 'rubygems'
require 'yajl'

parsed = Yajl::Parser.parse(input)
results = parsed["results"]

puts results.size          # => 2
puts results[0].inspect    # => {"name" => "geoffrey"}
```

```
puts parsed["total"]     # => 2
puts parsed["uri"]       # => "http://pauldix.net"
```

Nearly everything is the same in this example as in the previous one. The only difference is the `require` to `yajl` and the use of `Yajl::Parser` instead of `JSON`. However, this example could have kept the parsing line the same by using yajl-ruby's built-in JSON compatibility API. You simply need to require that instead of `yajl`, like this:

```
require 'yajl/json_gem'
```

With the built-in compatibility, the yajl-ruby gem is the best option available for users of native libraries. It's also worth noting that using this won't automatically force use of YAJL in Rails 2.3 applications. For that, the `yajl-ruby` plugin written by Rick Olson should be used (http://github.com/technoweenie/yajl-rails). In Rails 3, YAJL is used by default if it is installed.

Wrapping Parsed Results

Wrapping parsed results is a good idea to keep code easier to read and maintain. While parsed JSON provides native Ruby data types, it's still a good idea to wrap that data in a class. This provides more clarity about the data that the results could return. The wrapper classes for the input you worked with before and the JSON parsed results might look like this:

```
class ResultSet
  attr_reader :uri, :total, :people

  def initialize(attributes)
    @people = attributes[:people]
    @total  = attributes[:total]
    @uri    = attributes[:uri]
  end

  def self.from_json(json_string)
    parsed = JSON.parse(json_string)
```

```ruby
      people = parsed["results"].map do |item|
        Person.new(item)
      end

      new(
        :people => people,
        :total  => parsed["total"],
        :uri    => parsed["uri"])
    end
  end

  class Person
    attr_reader :name

    def initialize(attributes)
      @name = attributes["name"]
    end
  end

  results = ResultSet.from_json(input)
```

There is a clear separation between where the parsing happens and where the regular Ruby object code exists. This is a part of solid object-oriented design called *encapsulation*. Further, data elements of the object are clearly defined in the beginning of the class. This is very helpful for other developers who look at the code and need to know what data is available. As any developer who has put comments at the top of ActiveRecord models about what fields exist in the database can tell you, having that documentation helps with understandability later.

The class method `ResultSet.parse` contains the JSON parsing logic and the logic to set up each object. The `results` array in the parsed JSON is looped through to build `Person` objects. Finally, a new `ResultSet` object is returned.

Much of the code in the wrapper classes is boilerplate. While the classes give clarity about what data they store and how the parsing works, there is clearly room for simplification. Fortunately, there are already some tools built to simplify the creation of model classes, as discussed in the next section.

ActiveModel

ActiveModel is one of the building blocks of Rails 3.0. It is a library that makes the creation of classes that represent data models easier. It includes modules for validation, serialization, and other well-known features of ActiveRecord. These modules can be used to help write client libraries for services. The validations are particularly useful because they can be used to avoid unnecessary calls to a service to verify the validity of a new model.

Validations

A client library for the vote service from Chapter 5, "Implementing Services," shows the use of some of ActiveModel's features. That service has only one endpoint to post new data: the request to create a new rating or vote. Remember that a rating has an associated user ID and entry ID, as well as the type of vote it is (up or down).

In the `pauldix-ratings` gem that was generated earlier, a file can be added in `lib/pauldix-ratings/rating.rb`. The start of the ratings file that includes validations looks like this:

```
class PauldixRatings::Rating
  include ActiveModel::Validations

  attr_accessor :user_id, :entry_id, :vote

  validates_presence_of :user_id, :entry_id
  validates_inclusion_of :vote, :in => %w[up down]

  def initialize(attributes)
    @entry_id = @attributes[:entry_id]
    @user_id = @attributes[:user_id]
    @vote = @attributes[:vote]
  end

  def read_attribute_for_validation(key)
    send(key)
  end
end
```

The `Rating` class is namespaced by the module `PauldixRatings`. The first line includes the `Validations` module in ActiveModel. A `require` should be added to the `lib/pauldix-ratings.rb` file for ActiveModel. The next line defines the attributes that a rating has: `user_id`, `entry_id`, and `vote`.

The validations look exactly like normal ActiveRecord validations. They are verifying that `user_id` and `entry_id` are present and that the vote value is either up or down. The `read_attribute_for_validation` method is required for validations to work properly. It takes a key, which is an attribute name, and returns that attribute's value.

The final part of code is the `initialize` method. It contains the assignments for the attributes. A common shortcut for this kind of variable assignment is to do something like this:

```
@attributes.each_pair {|k, v| send("#{k}=", v)}
```

This shortcut is definitely more succinct than explicitly assigning each attribute. However, it may not be understandable to other developers looking at this code. One of the first questions another developer is likely to ask when using this library is "What values can go in the attributes?" It's trivial for a small file like this `Rating` class, but as the class gets larger, with more `attr_accessors` and method definitions, it becomes less simple to determine.

The validation code in the `Rating` class now enables calls like this:

```
rating = PauldixRatings::Rating.new(:entry_id => "entry1",
  :vote => "up")
rating.valid? # => false
rating.errors # => :user_id => ["must be present"]
```

Here, a new rating is created, and its validity is checked afterward. After `valid?` has been called, the `errors` object is populated with any of the associated errors. Validation in the client gem like this can save a round trip to the service to check whether a newly created model will be able to save. If the client library and server API versions are kept in sync, this validation should hold when posting to the server.

ActiveModel includes built-in validations for the following:

- `validates_confirmation_of`—Used for attributes such as the validation of a password or an email with confirmation.
- `validates_acceptance_of`—Used for attributes such as check boxes for accepting the terms of service.

- `validates_exclusion_of`—Ensures that an attribute is not an excluded value given in an enumerable.
- `validates_format_of`—Ensures that an attribute matches a given regular expression pattern.
- `validates_inclusion_of`—Ensures that an attribute has a value in a given enumerable.
- `validates_length_of`—Ensures that an attribute is within the bounds of length restrictions. Restrictions include minimum, maximum, is, and within.
- `validates_numericality_of`—Ensures that an attribute is a number that can be represented by a float. Additional checks include `greater_than`, `greater_than_or_equal_to`, `less_than`, `less_than_or_equal_to`, and `equal_to`.
- `validates_presence_of`—Ensures that an attribute is not blank or nil.
- `validates_with`—Ensures that an attribute passes a custom validation. `with` refers to the validator that is used.

One validation that is noticeably absent from this list is `validates_uniqueness_of`, which ensures that a value is unique in the table (for example, a user email address). That's because it's not built into ActiveModel. It makes sense when you think about what is required for this validation to work. It's very implementation specific. For example, with MySQL, that validation would work if a request were made to the database to obtain a lock on that value and then write afterward. Uniqueness is a requirement that cannot be validated on the client side alone. It requires integration with a specific data store. With the other validations, the client has everything on hand it needs to validate the data.

The preceding list represents all the validators that are built into ActiveModel. For more detailed coverage about the use of each, the best place to refer to is the API documentation (http://api.rubyonrails.org).

Serialization

ActiveModel includes a module to help with serialization for both XML and JSON. This section covers only JSON. The JSON serialization module in ActiveModel calls out to the serialization library that is set in ActiveSupport. At the time of this writing, the ActiveSupport library includes built-in support (in order of preference) for YAJL, JSONGem, and Yaml. The serialization module requires that the two methods `attributes=` and `attributes` be defined on the model. Further, the `attributes` method should return all of the model's attribute names as string keys in the hash (even if they are not set).

Modifying the Rating class to use the serialization module is a little tricky. The following code is the new Rating class with support for validations and serialization:

```ruby
class PauldixRatings::Rating
  include ActiveModel::Serializers::JSON
  include ActiveModel::Validations

  ATTRIBUTES = [:user_id, :entry_id, :vote]
  attr_accessor *ATTRIBUTES

  validates_presence_of :user_id, :entry_id
  validates_inclusion_of :vote, :in => %w[up down]

  def initialize(attributes = {})
    self.attributes = attributes
  end

  def attributes
    ATTRIBUTES.inject(
      ActiveSupport::HashWithIndifferentAccess.new
      ) do |result, key|
      result[key] = read_attribute_for_validation(key)
      result
    end
  end

  def attributes=(attrs)
    attrs.each_pair {|k, v| send("#{k}=", v)}
  end

  def read_attribute_for_validation(key)
    send(key)
  end
end
```

The requirement to have an attributes setter and getter motivate the changes in the Rating class. The initialize method has been simplified with a simple call to the attributes= method. Readability in the class is maintained by specifying at the

top in the ATTRIBUTES constant what attributes the model has. The attributes=
method loops through the key/value pairs and assigns each value to the key's attribute.
This is identical to the shortcut mentioned earlier.

The validation logic remains exactly as it was before. The serialization module has
now given the Rating class the ability to marshal from JSON or to convert a rating
object to JSON:

```
rating = PauldixRatings::Rating.new(
  :user_id => "paul", :entry_id => "entry1", :vote => "up")
json = rating.to_json # => outputs json string with attributes

rating = PauldixRatings::Rating.new.from_json(json)
```

The first example shows how to convert a rating to JSON. The JSON is simply
the attributes hash converted to a JSON object. The next example shows how to
marshal a rating from JSON. You simply create a new rating object and call
from_json and pass in the string. The from_json call actually modifies the rating it is
called on. Finally, it returns a reference to that same rating.

Connection and Request Logic

Now that the parsing and validation of the models has been handled, logic for connecting to services can be pulled into the library. The key to managing request logic is to
ensure proper handling of errors and to make sure that joins are done in a performant
manner. The examples for these libraries omit much of the error handling for brevity.
However, any possible return code should be accounted for in a production library.

Data Reads

Logic for reading data is handled a little differently than the logic for writing data. Remember that when reading data, the ideal is to run requests in parallel. This ensures that calls
can be made to multiple services in the minimum amount of time. Enabling this kind of
behavior requires that the objects that hold data (in a way similar to ActiveRecord models)
should never actually make requests themselves. They can build request objects, but it is
the responsibility of a controller outside the data object to manage those requests. This is
very different from ActiveRecord, which makes connections within the data object.

A detailed example shows the issues you need to consider when performing data
reads. This example considers a user's reading list from the social feed reader application.

The example assumes that there is a service that stores specific blog entries, another service that stores ratings data for each entry, and another service that returns a reading list for a specific user.

In the beginning of this chapter, you set up a gem for each of these services. The full code for these libraries is available at http://github.com/pauldix/service-oriented-design-with-ruby/tree/master/chapter_08/. The following sections show only the most important parts of it.

First, it's worth talking about how to handle joins. In this example, there are three separate gems (`PauldixEntries`, `PauldixRatings`, and `PauldixReadingList`). An entry can have many ratings and a ratings total (aggregate statistics). A rating and a ratings total belong to an entry. A reading list has many entries. These joins represent a fairly complex relationship to model across gem boundaries. If each one referenced the other, it would lead to circular gem dependencies, where the entries gem requires the ratings gem and vice versa.

To avoid circular dependencies, it's a good idea to have at most one library that joins the gems together. This could happen in the Rails or Ruby application that references these gems, or it could occur in one gem that ties them all together. For this example, the `PauldixReadingList` gem performs the joins. Thus, it includes the `requires` for the `PauldixEntries` and `PauldixRatings` gems.

The reading list gem should have an object that stores configuration. This is necessary for setting up development, testing, and production environments:

```
class PauldixReadingList::Config
  class << self; attr_accessor :host, :hydra; end
end
```

The `config` object has class accessors to store a `host` object and a `hydra` object. Remember from the previous chapter that a `hydra` object is the connection manager object that Typhoeus uses to queue and run HTTP requests. This will be used later to queue up requests while in the `ReadingList` class. The `host` object is simply the host for the HTTP service of the reading list.

Before looking at `ReadingList`, it's worth taking a look at how it is used. The following example contains three sections, each of which would be placed in different parts of a Rails application:

```
# this would go in a service initializer in config/initializers/
HYDRA = Typhoeus::Hydra.new
```

```
PauldixEntries::Config.hydra = HYDRA
PauldixRatings::Config.hydra = HYDRA
PauldixReadingList::Config.hydra = HYDRA

# this would go in config/environments/development.rb
host = "localhost:3000"
PauldixEntries::Config.host = host
PauldixRatings::Config.host = host
PauldixReadingList::Config.host = host

# code in a controller or presenter or non-ActiveRecord model
reading_list = nil
PauldixReadingList::ReadingList.for_user("paul",
  :include => [:entry, :rating_total]) do |list|

  reading_list = list
end

HYDRA.run

# now the data can be used
entry = reading_list.entries.first
entry.title
entry.body
entry.author
entry.published_date
```

The first section of this example initializes the configuration objects for the three gems with the same hydra object. This means that any requests that the three libraries queue up will be run by the same connection manager. The second section sets the host that each service can be found on. This is usually an environment-specific setting that depends on whether it is being run in development, testing, staging, or production.

The final section shows how the reading list can be used to get a list of entries for a specific user. The call to get the list for a user takes two arguments: the user name and the include options. This specific call tells the reading list to include the entries and the rating totals for those entries. Finally, the call to get a list for a user requires a block to be passed in. This is because of the evented programming style of Typhoeus. The block is called when the request has completed.

Finally, a call is made to `hydra` to run all queued requests. The important thing to note about the example so far is that the request is not run by the reading list gem. The request is queued up by the reading list gem, but it is run outside this gem. This ensures that the `hydra` manager is able to run requests in parallel. A close look at the `ReadingList` class shows how this works:

```ruby
class PauldixReadingList::ReadingList
  attr_accessor :entry_ids, :previous_page, :next_page

  def initialize(json, options = {})
    json = Yajl::Parser.parse(json)
    @next_page = json["next_page"]
    @entry_ids = json["entry_ids"]
    @previous_page = json["previous_page"]
    @includes = options[:include]
  end

  def self.for_user(user_id, options = {}, &block)
    includes = options[:include] || []

    request = Typhoeus::Request.new(get_by_id_uri
      (user_id))
    request.on_complete do |response|
      list = new(response.body, options)

      list.request_entries if includes.include?(:entry)
      list.request_rating_totals if includes.include?
        (:rating_total)

      block.call(list)
    end

    PauldixReadingList::Config.hydra.queue(request)
  end

  def self.get_by_id_uri(user_id)
```

```
    "http://#{PauldixReadingList::Config.host}/api/v1/
      reading_list/users/#{user_id}"
    end

    def request_entries
      PauldixEntries::Entry.get_ids(entry_ids) do |entries|
        @entries = entries
      end
    end

    def request_rating_totals
      PauldixRatings::RatingTotal.get_ids(entry_ids) do |ratings|
        @rating_totals = ratings
      end
    end
  end
```

The reading list contains three pieces of data: a URI for the previous page in the list, the next page, and an array of the entry IDs of the current page. This previous- and next-page functionality is exactly like the design of the vote service in Chapter 5, "Implementing Services." The initializer contains logic to parse a JSON string and assign the values.

The for_user method contains the first interesting bit of code. First, a Typhoeus Request object is created. It is a simple GET request. Another small method call is made to construct the URI for the email. This will call to the config object for the host name. The request object's on_complete handler is then set. This isn't called right away. It will be called when the request has completed.

Inside the on_complete handler is where the reading list is instantiated and the joins for entries and ratings occur. The instantiation parses the JSON response from the ReadingList service. The joins are made only if the includes have been specified on the call to for_user. The joins will be addressed in a moment. For now, look at the remainder of the for_user method. The last line in the on_complete block calls the block that was passed in and gives it the newly created list, so these block calls occur only after the requests have completed.

Now it's time to look at the joins. Both are identical, so we'll look only at the join to the entry service. The method shown earlier in the reading list contains a single call to a method on Entry called get_ids. It takes an array of entry IDs and a block. Just like the reading list request `for_user`, the block is run only after the request has been completed. In the completion, the `entries` instance variable is assigned the variable that was yielded to the block.

Finally, here is the associated code in the `Entry` class in `PauldixEntries` that shows the logic for getting and parsing entries:

```
def self.get_ids(ids, &block)
  request = Typhoeus::Request.new(get_ids_uri(ids))

  request.on_complete do |response|
    json = Yajl::Parser.parse(response.body)

    entries = ids.map do |id|
      new(json[id].merge("id" => id))
    end

    block.call(entries)
  end

  PauldixEntries::Config.hydra.queue(request)
end

def self.get_ids_uri(ids)
  "http://#{PauldixEntries::Config.host}/api/v1/
    entries?ids=#{ids.join(",")}"
end
```

The `get_ids` method takes an array of entry IDs and a block. It creates a request object. Just like the `ReadingList` class, it has a method for generating the URI for those IDs. The URI that is generated points to the entry service with a comma-separated list of IDs as a query parameter. The `on_complete` block is then assigned to the request. It parses the response body and creates ID objects. This multi-get call works as the multi-get for ratings works on the vote service created in Chapter 5, "Implementing Services." It is a hash with the entry ID as a key, and the value is the entry JSON. The last line in the `on_complete` block calls the passed-in block with the newly created entry objects. Finally, the `request` object is queued in `hydra`.

The reading list has now set up all the `request` objects for getting the reading list and running the requests for the specific ratings totals and entries in parallel. A single call to `hydra.run` runs all the requests. The final bit of logic is to combine the results into a single collection of entry objects. The following code is in the `ReadingList` class:

```
def entries
  return @entries if @includes_run

  include_rating_total = @includes.include?(:rating_total)

  if @includes.include?(:rating_total)
    @entries.each_with_index do |entry, index|
      entry.rating_total = @rating_totals[index]
    end
  end

  @includes_run = true
  @entries
end
```

The `entries` method assumes that all the requests have already been run. It loops through the entries and assigns them their associated ratings totals. The important thing to take away from this rather long example is that these classes (`ReadingList`, `Entry`, and `Rating`) never make requests. They only create the `request` objects and queue them up. The responsibility for running the requests lies outside these classes. That way, if other requests need to be made for other services, they can be queued up as well.

Data Writes

Data writes can be handled a little differently than data reads. This is because normally data writes do not need to occur in parallel. Usually, a single write is performed, and errors or success status is immediately handed back to the caller. This means that a blocking model where the data object performs the request to update makes more sense. An example with the `Rating` class highlights how this is done. Remember that a rating has an entry ID, a user ID, and a vote (up or down):

```
def save
  return false unless valid?
```

```
request = Typhoeus::Request.new(
  "/api/v1/ratings/entries/#{entry_ids}/users/
    #{user_id}/vote",
  :method => :post,
  :body => {:vote => vote}.to_json)

PauldixRatings.hydra.queue(request)
PauldixRatings.hydra.run

if response.code == 200
  return self
else
  errors.add(:http_code, response.code)
  errors.add(:http_response_body, response.body)
  return nil
end
end
```

The save method makes the request to save a rating. First, it checks that the rating passes all validations. If so, it creates a request object and runs the request. If the response is a 200 code, it returns success. Otherwise, it sets errors on the rating object so that they can be handled by the caller.

Another option for saving ratings is to simply write them to a messaging system to be saved asynchronously. The only validations that must be performed are that an entry ID and a user ID are present. The other validations—that a user only gets one vote on an entry and that the user and actual entry exist—can be validated later. Having the votes go directly into a message queue makes the system very scalable and tolerant of high spikes in vote traffic. Chapter 11, "Messaging," goes into greater detail on how to use messaging systems to create scalable systems that are tolerant of usage spikes.

Mocks, Stubs, and Tests

One of the great things about the Rails and ActiveRecord style of development is that developers can have the database and the models in their development environment. This means that the controllers, the views, and their associated tests can be created and run against only resources on the developer's computer. When working with services, it is much more difficult to have a full environment on every developer's machine. In fact, this works against the service-oriented design goal of isolation.

The best way to design around this is to provide stubs, or mocks, for client libraries that have to call out to services. You can provide a single method that can be called to stub out a client library. That way, it can be set up in the development or test initializer in an application. The following examples show how to stub out service calls for the reading list and entry service libraries.

From the reading list, there is a stub for user IDs and the associated entry IDs they should return:

```
def self.stub_all_user_ids_with_ids(user_ids, ids)
  body = {
    :entry_ids => ids
  }.to_json

  response = Typhoeus::Response.new(
    :code => 200,
    :headers => "",
    :body => body,
    :time => 0.3)

  user_ids.each do |user_id|
    PauldixReadingList::Config.hydra.stub(:get,
      get_by_id_uri(user_id)).and_return(response)
  end
end
```

The `stub` method takes an array of user IDs and entry IDs. First, it creates the body of the response that is being stubbed. Then a `response` object is created that contains that body. Finally, the user IDs are iterated through, with a call to `hydra.stub` for each. This means that any call to `hydra` with a request for one of the associated user reading list URIs returns this response object.

Now a stub for the entry class needs to be created:

```
def self.stub_all_ids(ids)
  body = ids.inject({}) do |result, id|
    result[id] = {
      :title => "test title",
```

```
          :body => "something",
          :author => "whatevs",
          :published_time => Time.now}
      result
    end.to_json

    response = Typhoeus::Response.new(
      :code => 200,
      :headers => "",
      :body => body,
      :time => 0.3)
    PauldixEntries::Config.hydra.stub(:get,
      get_ids_uri(ids)).and_return(response)
  end
```

The `Entry` class stub works in very much the same way as the `ReadinList` stub. It takes a list of IDs that are to be stubbed out. It creates a body that looks exactly like what a real service call would return. Then a response object is created and a call is made to `hydra` to stub out each of the entry ID URIs with the prebuilt response.

Finally, these stubs can be used so that service calls can be avoided but data will be available:

```
# calls to stub out
entry_ids = %w[entry1 entry2 entry3]
PauldixEntries::Entry.stub_all_ids(entry_ids)
PauldixRatings::RatingTotal.stub_all_ids(entry_ids)
PauldixReadingList::ReadingList.stub_all_user_ids_with_ids(
  ["paul"], entry_ids)

# regular calls to service clients
reading_list = nil

PauldixReadingList::ReadingList.for_user("paul",
  :include => [:entry, :rating_total]) do |list|

  reading_list = list
end

HYDRA.run
```

```
# data can be accessed without ever calling out to a service
reading_list.entries
```

The first lines of the example call the stub methods. The entry IDs that are being stubbed out are `entry1`, `entry2`, and `entry3`. The user ID that is being stubbed out is `paul`. The call to configure the clients would still have to have occurred before the calls to `stub`.

After the stubs have been set, the clients can be called. The call to `HYDRA.run` returns the stubs and executes all the client code in the `on_complete` blocks, without ever hitting the network. This example shows very specific stubs, but it's a good idea to have single calls to the clients that will stub out any requests made. That way, the testing and development using these libraries can be done without the actual services running.

The one gotcha with stubbing out service request calls is that the stubs must accurately reflect what the services will return. For this reason, it is a good idea to keep the client libraries with the service code. That way, the client can be fully integration tested against a service when it is updated. A developer updating a service will already have to be able to run it locally. Thus, the developer should also run the client against the service.

Conclusion

Writing client libraries for services is a vital component of creating a successful service-based design. Good client libraries abstract away the complexity of business logic and scaling effort hidden behind a service wall. The key goals with client libraries are readability and ease of use of the API. Further, client libraries should not be responsible for making actual service calls. The best method is to give each client library the logic to form a request and send it off to a connection manager such as `hydra`. That way, other libraries can queue requests at the same time.

Client libraries should be developed in tandem with the services they connect to. Services should be able to run multiple versions in parallel so that other applications that use the clients will not need to be upgraded in lock step. Then the new client libraries can be packaged up and deployed to applications after the services they connect to have been upgraded.

One final point about the client library examples in this chapter is that they have very similar code in their request logic. If services are standardized with conventions for how multi-gets, single requests, and data writes are made, much of this logic can be abstracted into a module that all the client libraries can use. This will cut down on code duplication and make the creation of more services easier.

CHAPTER 8

Load Balancing and Caching

This chapter looks at two important concepts for bringing a service-oriented design to production: load balancing and caching. First, *load balancing* is used to distribute the workload of service requests across multiple processes and servers to increase the reliability and capacity of a system. Second, services apply *caching* strategies, with HTTP headers and Memcached, to improve response times by reducing the amount of work the services have to perform.

Latency and Throughput

Before diving into the details of load balancing and caching, we need to establish the concepts of latency and throughput. *Latency* refers to the elapsed time per request, usually measured in milliseconds. *Throughput* refers to the number of requests a service can process over a period of time, usually measured in requests per second.

The latency of a service is also known as the *response time*, and it is one component of the overall perceived responsiveness of the applications that use the service. If latency is high, the application will feel slow. For this reason, you should monitor the latency of your services from day one, even before you start worrying about scaling your system.

The maximum throughput of a system can be thought of as one measure of its capacity. If a system cannot handle the rate of incoming requests, the response times

147

will degrade, and eventually the service will fail. When latency is at an acceptable level, you spend a lot more time worrying about the throughput of the services as you scale the system to accommodate increasing load.

Under the simplest conditions, with a service that's able to process one request at a time, the throughput is the reciprocal of the latency. For example, if the service can generate responses in 500 milliseconds, the throughput is two requests per second. In real life, services must process multiple requests at the same time, and the relationship between latency and throughput is more complex.

This chapter refers to these concepts often, as they are the building blocks of deploying distributed network services.

Load Balancing

Load balancing is a strategy for distributing requests from a single IP address and port to multiple processes across multiple servers. When it's time to bring a service to production, it provides three essential benefits: failover, scalability, and decreased latency. First, even in the smallest deployment, load balancing ensures that a service remains available when a portion of a Ruby process is unable to process requests (a capability known as *failover*). Second, as you need to handle increased capacity, load balancing allows you to scale by adding processes. Third, with a good algorithm, load balancing helps maintain the best possible latencies in the face of response time variation.

Services can be scaled horizontally or vertically. Vertical scaling works by increasing the resources (memory, CPU, I/O, and so on) of each server so each server can do more work. Horizontal scaling, on the other hand, means increasing capacity by adding more servers. Services are well suited to horizontal scaling; therefore, balancing the load across multiple servers is particularly important. In a service-oriented design, the load balancer sits between the application processes and the service processes. Figure 8.1 illustrates how the different pieces fit together.

Load Balancing Algorithms

As a load balancer receives each request, it must decide which process (or *backend*) should handle the request. The simplest algorithm a load balancer could implement might be to randomly select a known backend, but the result would not be very balanced. Some backends might receive too many requests while others sit idle. Fortunately, there are a number of better load balancing strategies that are easy to use, including round-robin, least-connections, and URI-based load balancing.

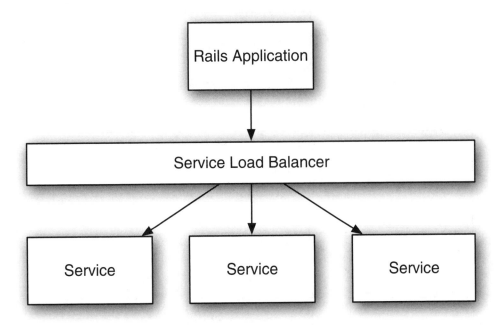

Figure 8.1 Load balancing with a service tier.

Round-Robin Load Balancing

A load balancer operating using a round-robin algorithm keeps an internal counter of which backend was most recently used, and it uses the next choice from a sequential list of all known backends. As each request arrives, the next backend is selected, and the counter is incremented, looping back to the beginning of the list when necessary. If every request requires the same amount of computation to process, the workload is distributed evenly. Figure 8.2 shows how round-robin load balancing works.

Round robin is straightforward and can provide two of the primary benefits of load balancing—horizontal scalability and failover—but it doesn't perform well when there is variability in response times. If a single-threaded Ruby process is processing a slower request and a fast request is distributed to it, the fast request has to wait until the slower request is finished before it can start to be handled. In practice, most web services have some actions that respond much more quickly than others, so an algorithm that is designed to handle such situations gracefully is often preferable. The least-connections algorithm, discussed next, is designed specifically to handle the scenario of variable response times.

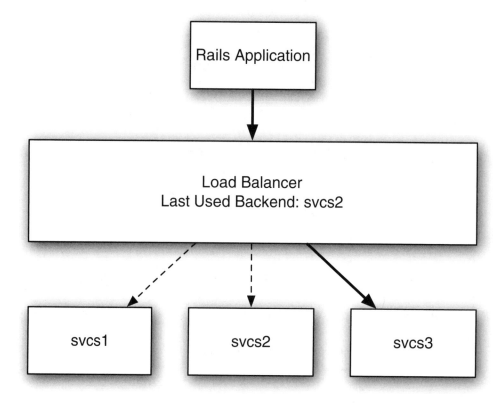

Figure 8.2   A round-robin load balancer.

Least-Connections Load Balancing

With the least-connections algorithm, the load balancer attempts to route requests based on the current amount of load on each backend. It accomplishes this by keeping track of the number of active connections for each backend. A backend's connection counter is incremented as requests are dispatched to it and decremented as they complete. When a request arrives, the load balancer routes it to the backend with the fewest active connections. Figure 8.3 shows the operation of a least-connections load balancer.

Unlike round robin, least-connections algorithms avoid the problem of a request queuing behind another when a backend is available. The requests still take the same amount of time to process in the backend, but the latency, as seen by the service client, is more consistent.

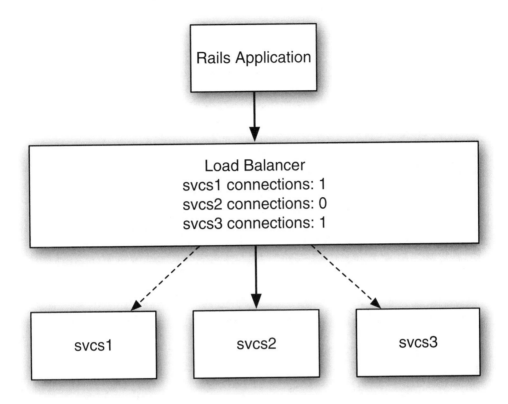

Figure 8.3   A least-connections load balancer.

URI-Based Load Balancing

An alternative approach to load balancing relies on the data in the request rather than the state of the clusters processing the data. URI-based load balancers work by using a hash algorithm to map each path to a backend. In a service-based architecture that leverages REST-style URLs, this means all requests for a piece of data can be routed to the same backend (server) while it's available. If the backend goes down, the load balancer adjusts by routing requests to available backends in the pool. Figure 8.4 shows how a URL-based load balancer distributes load.

The question of why a service implementer would want to load balance based on URL instead of active connections is an interesting one. The answer usually relates to caching. If a given backend can cache the representations of N objects, where N is significantly smaller than the total number of objects in the system, then a URL-based load balancing strategy can significantly increase the number of requests that result in

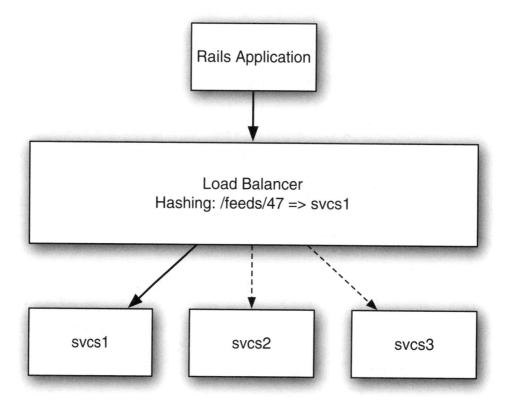

Figure 8.4   A URL-based load balancer.

a cache hit (a metric known as *cache hit ratio*). Sacrificing connection-based load balancing for cache locality is a reasonable approach in some situations, but it is the sort of scaling consideration that should be carefully weighed and measured.

Implementing Load Balancing

Load balancers come in many forms but can be divided into two primary classifications: hardware and software. Hardware load balancers are network appliances that get racked in a data center. Because of their high cost, they are generally found in large-scale deployments. Software load balancers, on the other hand, are quite ubiquitous. A software load balancer may exist as a component of a larger piece of software, such as a web server or an application server, or it may be a proxy specifically designed to serve just that purpose.

Phusion Passenger and Unicorn

Newer Ruby application servers have load balancing baked in. Both Phusion Passenger and Unicorn maintain a pool of worker processes to service incoming requests. When a request comes in, it's routed to the next available process, using a form of a least-connections algorithm. Passenger and Unicorn understand that a single-threaded Ruby process can handle only one request at a time, so they never ask it to process more than that. Additional requests queue outside the worker processes until a new worker becomes available. This provides a good load balancing strategy within an individual server, but it doesn't provide any support for failover when someone invariably kicks out the power cord of an application server.

HAProxy

The HAProxy website describes HAProxy as a "reliable, high-performance TCP/HTTP load balancer," and this praise is well deserved. This is a software-based, open source, and easy-to-configure load balancer. HAProxy also features an informative, web-based user interface for debugging or monitoring the traffic it's handling in real time.

In Ruby service-oriented architectures, HAProxy is usually used one of two ways. If the services are being run with an application server such as Passenger or Unicorn that already handles ensuring that a single worker process receives only one request at a time, using HAProxy is a simple way to balance traffic across multiple hosts. If the services are being run with an application server such as Mongrel or Thin that doesn't implement a worker pool, HAProxy can also be configured to route requests only to available processes.

To get started with HAProxy, you install it on a new server using your system's package management system. Next, you need to find and update the configuration file (often `/etc/haproxy.cfg`). The following is a basic HAProxy configuration file that round-robins traffic received on port 8080 to port 8080 on three servers. It also exposes the HAProxy monitoring interface on port 8100. You would use a configuration like this if the `svcs1-3` servers were running Unicorn or Passenger on port 8080:

```
global
  maxconn 1024
  daemon
  pidfile /var/run/haproxy.pid
  log /var/run/syslog local0
```

```
    user nobody
    group nobody

defaults
  log global
  option httplog
  mode http
  clitimeout 20000
  srvtimeout 20000
  contimeout 4000
  retries 3

listen svcs_proxy :8080
  server svcs1 svcs1:8080 check
  server svcs2 svcs2:8080 check
  server svcs3 svcs3:8080 check

listen admin 127.0.0.1:8100
  stats uri /
```

Now you just start up HAProxy and reconfigure your service clients to hit the load balancer. HAProxy balances traffic evenly across the three hosts and ensures that if one of the hosts goes down, it stops receiving traffic. The Passenger or Unicorn servers on the svcs hosts take care of making sure requests are never sent to a worker process that is already busy. Figure 8.5 shows the operation of HAProxy in front of Unicorn.

The other common way to use HAProxy in a service-oriented architecture is to place it in front of Mongrel or Thin processes that can handle only one request at a time. In this configuration, HAProxy handles failover if a Ruby process or host goes down. HAProxy also makes sure that requests are routed only to available backends. The key to this configuration is the maxconn 1 option, specified at the server level, which tells HAProxy to never allow more than one active connection to Mongrel or Thin at a time. Here is how the previous configuration could be updated to balance across two svcs hosts, each running Mongrels on ports 9001 and 9002:

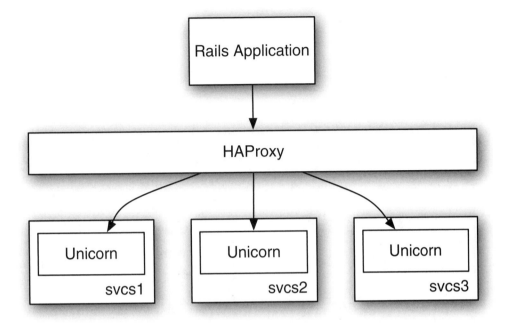

Figure 8.5   HAProxy in front of Unicorn.

```
listen svcs_proxy :8080
    server svcs1_9001 svcs1:9001 maxconn 1 check
    server svcs1_9002 svcs1:9002 maxconn 1 check
    server svcs2_9001 svcs2:9001 maxconn 1 check
    server svcs2_9002 svcs2:9002 maxconn 1 check
```

Figure 8.6 shows the operation of HAProxy with Mongrel.

Caching with Memcached

Caching, the act of storing the result of a computation for faster access later, can dramatically decrease a service's latency and increase throughput while keeping the underlying code maintainable and clean. Broadly, services can cache two ways. They can implement caching *internally* by storing results in the Ruby processes memory or in Memcached. They can also leverage the caching support in the HTTP specification to cache data *externally*. In a service-oriented design under high scalability demands, it's likely that the services would leverage both approaches.

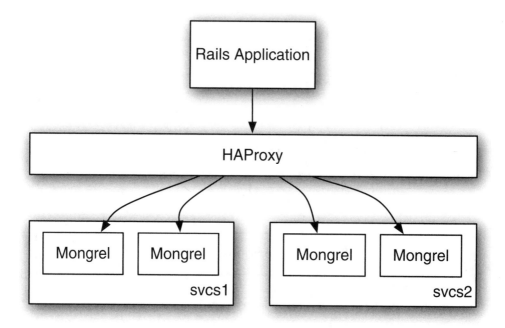

Figure 8.6   HAProxy in front of Mongrel.

Memcached is a scalable, open source system for caching objects in memory. It's one of the simplest and fastest forms of a broader group of data storage implementations known as key/value stores. At its core, the Memcached daemon process provides a well-defined interface for reading and writing to memory from other processes, with a bit of caching-oriented convenience such as time-based expiration and least-recently used (LRU) eviction layered in (covered in the following sections). It's completely temporal—no data will survive a server failure—but that's just fine in most caching use cases where the source data is stored in a more durable data store. For these reasons, it's a good first choice for implementing internal caching in a Ruby-based service.

The Memcached Client and ActiveRecord

A handful of Memcached clients are implemented for Ruby. The memcache-client library maintained by Mike Perham is the easiest to get started with and also the most popular, in part because it's the default Memcached client used by ActiveSupport in Rails. It can be installed with RubyGems, using the following command:

```
$ gem install memcache-client
```

Once the memcache-client library is installed, you can create a connection to a local or remote Memcached process by instantiating the `MemCache` class. By default, Memcached runs on port 11211:

```
require "memcache"

$memcache = MemCache.new("localhost:11211")
```

With a connection established and stored in a global variable, the cache can be used from anywhere in the service. The general pattern followed when implementing Memcached is to first check the cache for the desired value. If the value is present, return it; otherwise, compute the result and store it in Memcached so it's available the next time it's needed. Here's how this might look in an ActiveRecord class:

```
class Employee < ActiveRecord::Base

  def year_to_date_pay
    pay = $memcache.get("User:#{id}:ytd_pay")

    if pay.nil?
      pay = calculate_year_to_date_pay # Expensive call
      $memcache.set("User:#{id}:ytd_pay")
    end

    pay
  end

private

  def calculate_year_to_date_pay
    # ...
  end

end
```

Memcached servers are aware of only strings, so a little bit of magic is necessary behind the scenes for them to store other types. The memcache-client library uses Ruby's `Marshal` module to encode the integers returned from the `calculate_year_to_date_pay` method before sending them over the wire. It decodes the strings it receives into their native Ruby types when they are returned from the server. This allows Memcached to store most objects a Ruby process might use, from Booleans all the way up to arrays of Active-Record objects. The caveat is that when values are read from Memcached, the classes must already have been loaded into the Ruby process for `Marshal.load` to succeed. If the objects stored are core Ruby types, this isn't a concern, but if they are application or library classes, they should be eagerly required when the process boots.

The previous example includes boilerplate code for the sake of illustration but can be improved with a simple abstraction. The pattern of computing a result and storing it only if it's not available from the cache can be simplified by using Ruby blocks. The memcache-client library implements a `fetch` method that does just that. Here is how it could be applied to slim down the `Employee` class:

```
class Employee < ActiveRecord::Base

  def year_to_date_pay
    $memcache.fetch("User:#{id}:ytd_pay") do
      calculate_year_to_date_pay # Expensive call
    end
  end

  # ...

end
```

Adding a cache to an object is relatively easy, but cache invalidation can be a much trickier proposition. Fortunately, Memcached provides some tools to help. The simplest of these tools is time-based expiration.

Time-Based Expiration

Whenever a value is stored in Memcached, an expiration is included. The memcache-client library sends an expiration value of 0 by default, which informs Memcached that the key should not be expired after a set amount of time. If a duration (in seconds) is provided as the second argument to the `fetch` method, memcache-client uses it when storing the value on a cache miss, and the Memcached process expires the key after the given number of seconds has passed.

If a service is caching data that can be stale for some amount of time, a time-based expiration might be all that's necessary for cache invalidation. The previous examples omit expirations, so the year-to-date pay data would be cached indefinitely. The following example shows how to set cache values that expire in five minutes:

```
def year_to_date_pay
  $memcache.fetch("User:#{id}:ytd_pay", 5.minutes) do
    calculate_year_to_date_pay # Expensive call
  end
end
```

If a call is made within five minutes of setting the cached value, it will be returned. If a request comes in after five minutes, the Memcached server responds that it doesn't hold that cache key, at which time the calculation needs to be called again. Time-based cache expiration is simple and is automatically handled by the Memcached server, but it is limited in flexibility. For situations that require more control of cache invalidation, other strategies are necessary.

Manual Expiration

Another approach to cache invalidation is for the application code to explicitly delete the relevant keys from the Memcached server when conditions occur that might cause the cached values to be out of date. Building on the previous examples, if an employee's year-to-date pay is modified only when a new paycheck is created, it may make sense to leave off a time-based expiration and delete the cache key in a callback:

```
class Employee < ActiveRecord::Base

  def expire_year_to_date_pay
    $memcache.delete("User:#{id}:year_to_date_pay")
  end

  # ...

end

class Paycheck < ActiveRecord::Base
  belongs_to :employee
```

```ruby
    after_create :expire_employee_pay

    # ...

  private

    def expire_employee_pay
      employee.expire_year_to_date_pay
    end

  end
```

While this is seemingly straightforward, in practice it can be difficult to identify all the events that would cause a given key to be invalid. On the other hand, when an event occurs, it can be similarly difficult to identify all the cache keys that may include the data that has changed. When it's possible to get away with time-based expiration, it should be preferred to manual expiration.

Generational Cache Keys

In many cases, a program can't return out-of-date data from a cache, and manual expiration of cache keys would be cumbersome. Fortunately, there's one last cache invalidation strategy that can help. Generational cache keys leverage an important property of Memcached only briefly mentioned up to this point: the least-recently used eviction algorithm.

Every Memcached server runs with a maximum memory limit that can be specified when it is booted with the –m flag. (The default is 64MB.) Up to that point, Memcached happily stores whatever keys and values are sent to it. Eventually, as the server approaches the limit, it starts to make decisions about which keys to evict. Every time a key is accessed, Memcached keeps track of the time. When it is time to start evicting data, the Memcached server makes an educated guess that dropping the data that was used least recently will yield the best performance. In practice, this means if you store data in Memcached and eventually stop accessing it, it will eventually be dropped from memory in favor of more valuable keys—without any intervention.

A service can implement a form of cache invalidation by changing the cache key based on the data used to compute the value. As the computed cache key changes, Memcached eventually evicts the old keys. As long as the cache key includes representations of all the source data that's represented in the value, the cache will never return out-of-date data. The cache key might be composed of data already readily available to the service, or the service might store denormalized data like a version field on records in order to make computing the cache key as simple as possible later.

Consider again the example of the employee and paycheck models. Suppose the service has to calculate many year-to-date values for each employee. It's possible for the Employee class to expire all those values when a paycheck is created, but it's more complicated than necessary. Instead, you can leverage ActiveRecord's counter cache feature by adding a `paychecks_count` column to the `employees` table and simply including that in all the paycheck-related cache keys:

```ruby
class Employee < ActiveRecord::Base

  def year_to_date_pay
    $memcache.fetch("User:#{id}:#{paychecks_count}:
      ytd_pay") do
      calculate_year_to_date_pay # Expensive call
    end
  end

  def year_to_date_taxes
    $memcache.fetch("User:#{id}:#{paychecks_count}:
      ytd_tax") do
      calculate_year_to_date_taxes # Expensive call
    end
  end

  # ...
end

class Paycheck < ActiveRecord::Base
  belongs_to :employee, :counter_cache  => true

  # ...
end
```

With creatively composed cache keys, generational cache keys can replace manual expiration for most cache invalidation and leave the resulting code more maintainable.

HTTP Caching

The HTTP specification has caching support baked in. With a little extra work, this caching can be leveraged to drastically improve the latency and throughput of a Ruby web service. Most web developers are familiar with browser caches, but two other types of HTTP-based caches can affect the behavior of a given request: proxy caches and gateway caches. Network administrators deploy proxy caches between their users and the Internet, so they aren't relevant to the implementation of web services. Gateway caches, also known as *reverse-proxy caches*, on the other hand, are deployed by application engineers and are quite useful for scaling web services. From the standpoint of a service client, the gateway cache looks like the actual service, and the client can receive the benefits of the cache without any modifications.

Expiration-Based Caching

The HTTP implementation of expiration-based caching is analogous to the time-based expiration functionality of Memcached described earlier. After computing a response, a service adds a `Cache-Control` header that specifies the number of seconds the gateway cache should wait before asking for the same data again. While the cache is valid, the gateway can return responses to the service client immediately. Because it's much faster for the cache to return the response from memory than it is for the service to generate it, latencies and throughputs improve drastically.

Imagine that you are implementing a service that stores data about RSS feeds. Because this data changes infrequently, it might be acceptable to cache responses for one minute. If the service returns an expiration-based caching header and you add a gateway cache between the service clients and the services, an initial request through the stack would still reach the backend, as shown in Figure 8.7.

Because the gateway cache has no stored data for the given URI, it forwards the request. The response comes back from the Ruby process with a max-age caching directive, so the cache stores the response in memory. The benefit of this implementation kicks in with the next request a few seconds later, as shown in Figure 8.8.

This time, the gateway cache sees that it has a cached, fresh response for the given URI. Instead of forwarding the request to the backend, it immediately returns the cached response to the service client. The service client receives its response faster, and the load on the Ruby services is reduced.

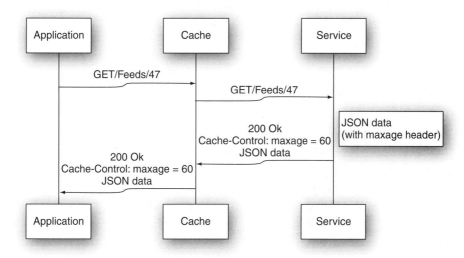

Figure 8.7   A first request in expiration-based HTTP caching.

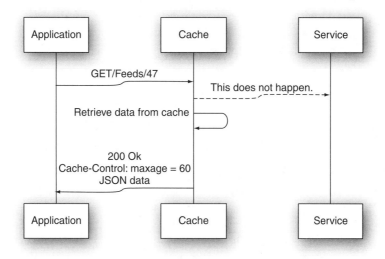

Figure 8.8   A second request in expiration-based HTTP caching.

Validation-Based Caching

For cases in which expiration-based caching won't suffice, HTTP also offers a validation-based caching model based on the Last-Modified and ETag headers. By adding either header to its responses, a service enables support for "conditional GETs" from clients that support it—like gateway caches. In the validation model, the gateway cache still has to forward a request to the backend in order to determine whether its cached response is valid. The efficiencies come when the service is able to identify that the gateway cache has a fresh response. Instead of regenerating the response, the service can respond with a 304 Not Modified status, which saves time and bandwidth.

To see this in action, suppose the RSS feed service from the previous example had to always return up-to-date information. To support this, a developer could add a version number to the feeds table that is incremented every time the RSS data changed. Figure 8.9 shows how the first request would look.

Again, because the gateway cache has no stored representation of the requested resource, the request is forwarded to the Ruby backend. The generated response is stored in the cache and returned to the service client. If the next request for the same feed occurs before the feed is updated, it can leverage the gateway cache as shown in Figure 8.10.

This time, the gateway cache still forwards the request to the service, but the service is able to determine that the cache is fresh. Instead of generating a response body and sending it back upstream, it immediately returns a 304 Not Modified status. As long as the service can determine whether the cache is valid or not in significantly less time than it would take to generate the full response, latencies will be reduced, along with the resources required to run the Ruby service processes.

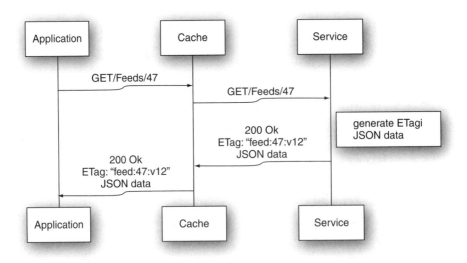

Figure 8.9 A first request in validation-based HTTP caching.

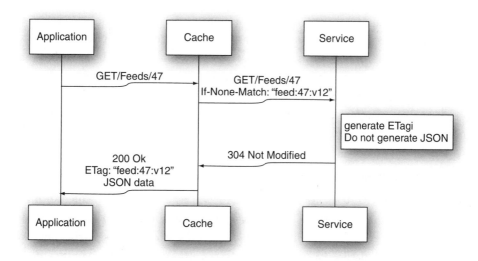

Figure 8.10 A second request in validation-based HTTP caching.

Implementing HTTP Caching

There are a number of open source implementations of HTTP gateway caches to consider when deploying a Ruby web service. Most gateway cache implementations are run as processes between the application servers and a load balancer such as HAProxy. However, Rack-Cache is an interesting Ruby-based alternative that has emerged recently.

Rack-Cache

Rack-Cache is a gateway cache implemented as a Rack middleware. Ryan Tomayko wrote it in order to make it as easy as possible for Ruby developers to experiment with HTTP caching. It's by far the most convenient gateway cache implementation to use when developing locally. To use Rack-Cache, you install the gem and insert it into a service's middleware stack:

```
require 'service'
require 'rack/cache'

use Rack::Cache,
  :verbose      => true,
  :metastore    => 'memcached://localhost:11211/',
  :entitystore  => 'memcached://localhost:11211/'

run Service.new
```

The `metastore` and `entitystore` configuration options tell Rack-Cache where to store the cache metadata and full response bodies, respectively. By default, Rack-Cache uses the heap, but this is just the sort of data that Memcached handles very well. This is all that's necessary for Rack-Cache to start acting like a gateway cache. It supports both the expiration and validation caching models. The Rack-Cache source code is also an informative read for an interested Rubyist looking to better understand the mechanics of how gateway caches work.

Squid and Varnish

Out-of-process gateway caches such as Squid and Varnish are implemented in high-performance languages such as C and work with applications implemented in any language. They can be a bit more difficult to set up properly than Rack-Cache, but they also provide more performance than Rack-Cache in a production environment. By virtue of being around longer and supporting a larger number of users, they are also a bit more flexible and configurable than Rack-Cache. The details of configuring Squid and Varnish are beyond the scope of this book, but these tools are worth taking a look at for production once a service has HTTP caching logic built in and tested using Rack-Cache.

Conclusion

When it's time to bring a service to production, latency and throughput are key concepts. Efficient load balancing enables a service to scale horizontally by adding additional servers to increase throughput (and thus capacity). Caching, both within a process and externally via HTTP headers, is a proven technique to reduce latency and increase throughput while still leaving the underlying code clean and maintainable. As you scale a service, you should regularly test your latency and capacity to ensure that you can meet the requirements of your environment and the demand you expect.

CHAPTER 9

Parsing XML for Legacy Services

Sometimes an application must integrate with legacy services whose design is out of your control. It is common for these services to use XML formats such as SOAP, XML-RPC, or RESTful XML. This chapter covers some of the tools for parsing and working with XML-based services.

XML

Many older (and some newer) services use XML as their serialization format. While JSON is quickly becoming the preferred method of serialization due to its ease of use and simplicity, client libraries must occasionally work with XML. Libraries for parsing XML in Ruby include REXML, Nokogiri, Hpricot, LibXml Ruby, and SimpleXML.

The focus of this section is on parsing responses using REXML and Nokogiri. The reason for the choice of these two libraries is simple. REXML is included with Ruby, and Nokogiri currently has the best performance and is actively being developed and supported. While the other XML libraries are usable, for libraries outside the standard REXML, Nokogiri is currently the leading option.

The services written so far in this book have been JSON based, so this section explores an example outside the services created in previous chapters. The Amazon

EC2 Query API provides a real-world instance where parsing and requesting XML-based services is useful. The next sections look at methods for parsing XML for one of the EC2 requests.

Amazon describes in the EC2 API documentation some common XML data types. These data types include multiple elements, which can be found in the API reference (http://docs.amazonwebservices.com/AWSEC2/latest/APIReference/). The examples for working with XML step through parsing the call to "describe instances." This response gives information about virtual computer instances running in Amazon's Elastic Compute Cloud:

```
<DescribeInstancesResponse
  xmlns="http://ec2.amazonaws.com/doc/2009-08-15/"
  <reservationSet>
    <item>
      <reservationId>r-44a5402d</reservationId>
      <ownerId>UYY3TLBUXIEON5NQVUUX6OMPWBZIQNFM
        </ownerId>
      <groupSet>
        <item>
          <groupId>default</groupId>
        </item>
      </groupSet>
      <instancesSet>
        <item>
          <instanceId>i-28a64341</instanceId>
          <imageId>ami-6ea54007</imageId>
          <instanceState>
            <code>0</code>
            <name>running</name>
          </instanceState>
          <privateDnsName>10-251-50-132.ec2.internal
          </privateDnsName>
          <dnsName>ec2-72-44-33-4.compute-1.amazonaws.com
          </dnsName>
          <keyName>example-key-name</keyName>
          <amiLaunchIndex>23</amiLaunchIndex>
          <productCodesSet>
```

```
            <item><productCode>774F4FF8</productCode>
              </item>
        </productCodesSet>
        <instanceType>m1.large</instanceType>
        <launchTime>2007-08-07T11:54:42.000Z
          </launchTime>
        <placement>
          <availabilityZone>us-east-1b
            </availabilityZone>
        </placement>
        <kernelId>aki-ba3adfd3</kernelId>
        <ramdiskId>ari-badbad00</ramdiskId>
    </item>
    <item>
        <instanceId>i-28a64435</instanceId>
        <imageId>ami-6ea54007</imageId>
        <instanceState>
          <code>0</code>
          <name>running</name>
        </instanceState>
        <privateDnsName>10-251-50-134.ec2.internal
        </privateDnsName>
        <dnsName>ec2-72-44-33-6.compute-1.amazonaws.com
        </dnsName>
        <keyName>example-key-name</keyName>
        <amiLaunchIndex>23</amiLaunchIndex>
        <productCodesSet>
          <item><productCode>774F4FF8</productCode>
            </item>
        </productCodesSet>
        <instanceType>m1.large</instanceType>
        <launchTime>2007-08-07T11:54:42.000Z
          </launchTime>
        <placement>
          <availabilityZone>us-east-1b
            </availabilityZone>
        </placement>
```

```
      <kernelId>aki-ba3adfd3</kernelId>
      <ramdiskId>ari-badbad00</ramdiskId>
    </item>
  </instancesSet>
</item>
</reservationSet>
</DescribeInstancesResponse>
```

The entire response is wrapped in the DescribeInstanceResponse XML element. Within that element is a reservationSet that contains the information for instance reservations. Each instance reservation is contained within item elements. These elements map together instances and their security groups.

The client library should parse out the reservation sets, each of which contains a reservation ID, an owner ID, a security group, and the collection of instances. Each of the instances contains an instance ID, an image ID, an instance state, a private DNS name, a DNS name, a key name, an instance type, and an availability zone. The parsing code should be able to pull out each of these elements.

The following examples don't bother to parse every single element from the XML. In fact, to maintain a clear and usable API, the client should extract and expose only the data that is necessary.

REXML

Ruby versions 1.8 and newer include REXML (http://www.germane-software.com/software/rexml/) as part of the standard library. It is a fully featured XML parsing library written in pure Ruby, with full support for XPath. XPath is a language for addressing elements within an XML document (see http://www.w3.org/TR/xpath). REXML also includes a simple API for traversing elements in a document. This example shows use of the basic REXML API.

The code for parsing the EC2 DescribeInstancesResponse can be broken down into three classes: one class for the entire response, another class for a reservation set, and another class to store information about specific EC2 instances. The following code example shows the class for parsing the response to a describe instances request:

```
require 'rexml/document'

class DescribeInstancesResponse
  attr_reader :reservation_sets
```

```
    def initialize(reservation_sets)
      @reservation_sets = reservation_sets
    end

    def self.parse(xml_string)
      doc = REXML::Document.new xml_string

      reservation_sets = []
      doc.elements.
        each("DescribeInstancesResponse/reservationSet/item"
          ) do |element|
          reservation_sets << ReservationSet.from_xml(element)
      end

      new(reservation_sets)
    end
  end
```

The `DescribeInstancesResponse` class acts as the wrapper for the entire response from EC2. The data that this class contains can be determined quickly by looking at the top of the class and noticing the attribute reader for `reservation_sets`. Other than the initialization, this class contains only one method: a class method for parsing an XML string into an instance of this class.

The parse method first creates a REXML document. It then sets up the reservation sets by looping through the items in the `reservationSet` element. Each `item` element is passed to a new class called `ReservationSet`, which is covered in a moment. Once the reservation sets are built, a new instance of the `DescribeInstancesResponse` class is returned from the `parse` method.

Having a separate class for the reservation set makes the code simpler to read and keep organized. Generally, it's a good idea to create a class for each logical grouping of data that you parse. This is usually a collection of XML elements that are the children of a common ancestor. The class for wrapping reservation sets continues the building of objects that represent the response, shown here:

```
class ReservationSet
  attr_reader :security_group, :instances, :reservation_id
```

```
def initialize(attributes)
  @security_group = attributes[:security_group]
  @reservation_id = attributes[:reservation_id]
  @instances      = attributes[:instances]
end

def self.from_xml(xml)
  elements  = xml.elements
  instances = []

  elements.each("instancesSet/item") do |item|
    instances << Instance.from_xml(item)
  end

  new(
    :security_group => elements["groupSet/item/groupId"].text,
    :reservation_id => elements["reservationId"].text,
    :instances      => instances)
  end
end
```

As with the class for parsing the describe instances response, this class shows the data that is exposed through the attribute readers and the initialization method. The security group, the reservation ID, and the instances that represent the set are accessible through this class.

The `from_xml` method takes an XML node. The use of the name `from_xml` rather than `parse` is intentional, as this method expects an already parsed XML node object. The method loops through the `item` elements in the `instancesSet` within this node. Each of those nodes is passed to the `Instance.from_xml` method to create an instance of `Instance`.

Finally, a new instance of `ReservationSet` is created. The constructor is passed the instances previously built and the extracted text from the appropriate elements for the security group and the reservation ID.

The class for each instance is the last part of code necessary to parse all of the elements required from the describe instances response:

```
class Instance
  attr_reader :id, :image_id, :state, :private_dns_name,
              :dns_name, :key_name, :type, :launch_time,
              :availability_zone
```

```ruby
    def initialize(attributes)
      @id = attributes[:id]
      @image_id = attributes[:image_id]
      @state = attributes[:state]
      @private_dns_name = attributes[:private_dns_name]
      @dns_name = attributes[:dns_name]
      @key_name = attributes[:key_name]
      @type = attributes[:type]
      @launch_time = attributes[:launch_time]
      @availability_zone = attributes[:availability_zone]
    end

    def self.from_xml(xml)
      elements = xml.elements
      new(
        :id => elements["instanceId"].text,
        :image_id => elements["imageId"].text,
        :state => elements["instanceState/name"].text,
        :private_dns_name => elements["privateDnsName"].text,
        :dns_name => elements["dnsName"].text,
        :key_name => elements["keyName"].text,
        :type => elements["instanceType"].text,
        :launch_time => elements["launchTime"].text,
        :availability_zone =>
           elements["placement/availabilityZone"].text)
    end
  end
```

The `Instance` class holds most of the important data for the call to describe instances. The attributes of the instance are all contained within this class. The attribute readers and constructor continue the examples for the previous two classes, showing clearly what data the `Instance` class holds.

The `from_xml` method takes an XML node. It calls the constructor and pulls out the required data from the elements within the passed-in node. One thing to notice about all three of these classes is that the XML parsing logic is all contained within a single public method. This makes it easier to get an immediate sense for where parsing occurs.

The constructors of all three classes expect attribute hashes. This is useful when creating test version of these objects later. It is much easier to pass in an attribute hash than sample XML.

Nokogiri

Nokogiri is an HTML and XML parser backed by the libxml and libxslt C libraries. It is compatible with versions of Ruby including 1.8, 1.9, JRuby, and Rubinius. Because of its use of underlying C libraries, Nokogiri is very fast. The results of benchmarks have varied, but Nokogiri has been shown to be consistently faster than other parsers, particularly REXML. Hpricot and LibXml-Ruby have parsing speeds that are either on par, a little faster, or sometimes slower. Your mileage may vary with each benchmark setup.

However, speed isn't the only reason to use Nokogiri, as it also includes support for powerful CSS3 selectors. Selectors are patterns that match against elements in an HTML or XML document tree. In addition to CSS selectors, Nokogiri has built-in support for XPath and a few other methods for traversing the document tree.

To install Nokogiri, you must have the libxml2, libxml2-dev, libxslt, and libxslt-dev packages installed. Once these prerequisites have been set up, installation is as simple as the following command:

```
gem install nokogiri
```

The following example using Nokogiri looks very similar to the REXML example:

```
require 'rubygems'
require 'nokogiri'

class DescribeInstancesResponse
  attr_reader :reservation_sets

  def initialize(reservation_sets)
    @reservation_sets = reservation_sets
  end

  def self.parse(xml)
    doc = Nokogiri::XML(xml)
```

```
      sets = doc.css("reservationSet > item").map do |item|
        ReservationSet.from_xml(item)
      end

      new(sets)
    end
  end
```

Because all parsing logic is contained within a single method in each class, those methods are the only ones that must be modified. The object interface looks identical whether you use Nokogiri or REXML. The start of the `DescribeInstansesResponse` class is the same as for the REXML example. The attribute readers and constructor show what data this class stores. The `parse` method contains the real changes.

First, there is a call to create a Nokogiri document from the XML string. The reservation sets are then extracted from the document. This is an example of a CSS selector. In this case, the selector is looking for `item` elements that are direct children of the `reservationSet` element. The selector returns a `NodeSet` that can be iterated through. This makes for a slightly cleaner notation because of the use of `map` instead of `each`, as in the REXML example. Each of the nodes is passed to the `from_xml` method on the reservation set:

```
class ReservationSet
  attr_reader :security_group, :instances, :reservation_id

  def initialize(attributes)
    @security_group = attributes[:security_group]
    @reservation_id = attributes[:reservation_id]
    @instances      = attributes[:instances]
  end

  def self.from_xml(xml)
    instances = xml.css("instancesSet > item").map do |item|
      Instance.from_xml(item)
    end

    new(
      :security_group => xml.css("groupId").text,
```

```
      :instances => instances,
      :reservation_id => xml.css("reservationId").text)
  end
end
```

The `ReservationSet` class keeps the same structure as in the previous example. The `from_xml` method contains the updates to this class.

First, the `Instance` objects are created by looping through the XML nodes with a CSS selector. This selector looks for nodes named `item` that are direct children of the `instancesSet` element. These nodes are then passed to the `Instance` constructor. When the instances have been built, the security group and reservation ID are passed out and handed to the reservation set constructor:

```
class Instance
  attr_reader :id, :image_id, :state, :private_dns_name,
              :dns_name, :key_name, :type, :launch_time,
              :availability_zone

  def initialize(attributes)
    @id = attributes[:id]
    @image_id = attributes[:image_id]
    @state = attributes[:state]
    @private_dns_name = attributes[:private_dns_name]
    @dns_name = attributes[:dns_name]
    @key_name = attributes[:key_name]
    @type = attributes[:type]
    @launch_time = attributes[:launch_time]
    @availability_zone = attributes[:availability_zone]
  end

  def self.from_xml(xml)
    new(
      :id => xml.css("instanceId").text,
      :image_id => xml.css("imageId").text,
      :state => xml.css("instanceState > name").text,
      :private_dns_name => xml.css("privateDnsName").text,
```

```
            :dns_name => xml.css("dnsName").text,
            :key_name => xml.css("keyName").text,
            :type => xml.css("instanceType").text,
            :launch_time => xml.css("launchTime").text,
            :availability_zone => xml.css("availabilityZone").text)
    end
  end
```

The Instance class is no different from the three others. The attribute readers and constructor look the same as before, while the changes in parsing are in the from_xml method.

The XML parsing logic consists of single calls with various CSS selectors. Each of the attributes can be parsed with this simple logic. With regard to parsing the individual attributes, the CSS selectors don't provide any particular advantage or disadvantage over the XPath-based selectors.

When you use Nokogiri for parsing, the choice of whether to use XPath or CSS is mainly one of familiarity. While the XPath selectors have been shown to be slightly faster than CSS, both are still faster than using REXML. You should use whatever you're most comfortable with.

SOAP

Simple Object Access Protocol (SOAP) is a specification for implementing web services using XML. Full coverage of SOAP is beyond the scope of this book. However, this section goes over a few basics and shows examples for working with SOAP-based services. There are multiple libraries for working with SOAP in Ruby. The most popular libraries are soap4r (http://dev.ctor.org/soap4r), Savon (http://github.com/rubiii/ savon), and Handsoap (http://github.com/unwire/handsoap). The examples in this chapter focus on using Savon because of its popularity and ease of use. soap4r is the oldest of the bunch, but it is slower and difficult to use; Handsoap is a framework for writing SOAP clients.

Exploring Web Services with a WSDL File

SOAP services expose their interface through a Web Services Description Language (WSDL) file. This is an XML file that describes the interface for a web service. The easiest method for exploring the interface of a SOAP service is to take a look at its

WSDL file. Amazon's Product Advertising API (http://docs.amazonwebservices
.com/AWSECommerceService/latest/DG/) is a useful real-world example. The
WSDL file, found at http://webservices.amazon.com/AWSECommerceService/
AWSECommerceService.wsdl, describes the API methods and the arguments they
take.

Savon includes methods for loading a WSDL file and looking at the output:

```
require 'savon'
client =
Savon::Client.new("http://webservices.amazon.com/
  AWSECommerceService/AWSECommerceService.wsdl")
puts "SOAP Endpoint: #{client.wsdl.soap_endpoint}"
puts "Namespace: #{client.wsdl.namespace_uri}"
puts "Actions: #{client.wsdl.soap_actions.join(', ')}"
```

In this example, the client is pointed to the API WSDL file. Then the client's wsdl
object is output, and the SOAP endpoint and namespace URI are output. (These two
will be useful later, when you create a client that doesn't need to use the WSDL file.)
Finally, the actions are output.

The Savon WSDL class doesn't expose the arguments that the operations take or the
results that the API calls return. For this information, the best resource is either the
API documentation or the WSDL file itself. It is a fairly readable XML file. For example, the following snippet shows the XML for making a search request for items in the
Amazon store:

```
<xs:complexType name="ItemSearchRequest">
  <xs:sequence>
    <xs:element name="Author" type="xs:string"
      minOccurs="0"/>
    <xs:element name="BrowseNode" type="xs:string"
      minOccurs="0"/>
    <xs:element name="Keywords" type="xs:string"
      minOccurs="0"/>
    <xs:element name="Manufacturer" type="xs:string"
      minOccurs="0"/>
    <xs:element name="MaximumPrice"
      type="xs:nonNegativeInteger" minOccurs="0"/>
```

```
    <xs:element name="Publisher" type="xs:string"
      minOccurs="0"/>
    <xs:element name="SearchIndex" type="xs:string"
      minOccurs="0"/>
    <xs:element name="Title" type="xs:string"
      minOccurs="0"/>
  </xs:sequence>
</xs:complexType>
```

In the Amazon API, each operation consists of the request and response complex types. This example shows only a subset of the possible arguments for the ItemSearch operation. Each of the elements has a type associated with it. The response contains many nested and complex types. Here is a snippet of the associated XML:

```
<xs:element name="ItemSearchResponse">
  <xs:complexType>
    <xs:sequence>
      <xs:element ref="tns:OperationRequest"
        minOccurs="0"/>
      <xs:element ref="tns:Items" minOccurs="0"
        maxOccurs="unbounded"/>
    </xs:sequence>
  </xs:complexType>
</xs:element>

<xs:element name="Items">
  <xs:complexType>
    <xs:sequence>
      <xs:element name="TotalResults"
        type="xs:nonNegativeInteger" minOccurs="0"/>
      <xs:element name="TotalPages"
        type="xs:nonNegativeInteger" minOccurs="0"/>
      <xs:element ref="tns:Item" minOccurs="0"
        maxOccurs="unbounded"/>
    </xs:sequence>
  </xs:complexType>
</xs:element>
```

```
<xs:element name="Item">
  <xs:complexType>
    <xs:sequence>
      <xs:element name="DetailPageURL" type="xs:string"
        minOccurs="0"/>
      <xs:element name="SalesRank" type="xs:string"
        minOccurs="0"/>
      <xs:element name="SmallImage" type="tns:Image"
        minOccurs="0"/>
      <xs:element ref="tns:ItemAttributes"
        minOccurs="0"/>
    </xs:sequence>
  </xs:complexType>
</xs:element>
```

At the top is `ItemSearchResponse`. This is the basic object that contains the results. Below `ItemSearchResponse` is the `Items` object. This represents a collection of items and includes the number of results, number of pages, and 0 or more occurrences of the `Item` object. Next is a part of the `Item` object. It contains some of the metadata about the returned results, such as their sales rank, a URI for their web page, images, and the item attributes.

Making Requests

After exploring the WSDL file of a SOAP service, the next thing to do is make requests against the API. The easiest way to get going is by loading up the WSDL file and making requests from there.

> ### Securing Requests
>
> There are multiple methods for making secure SOAP requests. Savon supports WS-Security (also known as WSSE). The Amazon API implements a method known as HMAC signing. HMAC uses a secret key to sign a message. Chapter 10, "Security," provides more coverage of HMAC security. WS-Security is beyond the scope of the book.

The following example makes a request to the Amazon API to complete a search for products:

```ruby
require 'rubygems'
require 'savon'
require 'hmac'
require 'hmac-sha2'
require 'base64'
require 'pp'

class AmazonProductAdvertisingAPI
  def initialize(aws_access_key_id, aws_secret_key)
    @aws_access_key_id = aws_access_key_id
    @aws_secret_key = aws_secret_key
    @client =

Savon::Client.new("http://webservices.amazon.com/
  AWSECommerceService/AWSECommerceService.wsdl")
  end

  def timestamp_and_signature(operation)
    timestamp = Time.now.gmtime.iso8601

    hmac = HMAC::SHA256.new(@aws_secret_key)
    hmac.update("#{operation}#{timestamp}")
    # chomp to get rid of the newline
    signature = Base64.encode64(hmac.digest).chomp

    [timestamp, signature]
  end

  def search(query)
    operation = "ItemSearch"
    timestamp, signature = timestamp_and_signature
      (operation)
```

```
  @client.item_search do |soap|
    soap.body     = {
      "SearchIndex" => "Books",
      "Keywords" => query,
      "Timestamp" => timestamp,
      "AWSAccessKeyId" => @aws_access_key_id,
      "Signature" => signature
    }
  end
 end
end


aws_access_key_id = ENV["AWS_ACCESS_KEY_ID"]
aws_secret_key = ENV["AWS_SECRET_KEY"]

Savon::Request.log = false
api = AmazonProductAdvertisingAPI.new
  (aws_access_key_id, aws_secret_key)
results = api.search("service oriented design with ruby")
pp results.to_hash
```

This example contains a file for making requests to the Amazon Product Advertising API. The class takes the Amazon access key ID and the shared secret key. The timestamp_and_signature method does the HMAC signing of the operation. The important parts of the SOAP request are all contained inside the search method.

The operation is the API method that will get called, namely ItemSearch. That is passed to the method to get a timestamp and an HMAC signature. The request is then made with the @client.item_search block. Within that block, the body of the SOAP request must be set. Amazon requires the access key, timestamp, and signature. The SearchIndex and Keywords options are arguments made to the ItemSearch method. The Savon::Result object is returned from that method.

While the WSDL method of using the API is slightly easier, it isn't suitable for production use. This is because it actually has to request the WSDL file and parse options. A more efficient method is to point the client directly to the SOAP endpoint.

Remember that this was an output from the first WSDL code example. The following changes make the same SOAP request without using the WSDL file:

```
# in the initialize method use this line
  @client =

Savon::Client.new("https://ecs.amazonaws.com/onca/
  soap?Service=AWSECommerceService")

# the search method has the other changes
  def search(query)
    operation = "ItemSearch"
    timestamp, signature = timestamp_and_signature(operation)

    @client.ItemSearch! do |soap|
      soap.namespace = "http://webservices.amazon.com/
        AWSECommerceService/2009-11-01"
      soap.input      = operation
      soap.body       = {
        "SearchIndex" => "Books",
        "Keywords" => query,
        "Timestamp" => timestamp,
        "AWSAccessKeyId" => @aws_access_key_id,
        "Signature" => signature
      }
    end
  end
```

This example shows two modifications from the previous WSDL example. First, the Savon::Client initialization points directly to the SOAP endpoint. Second, the search method must provide the client with a little more information. The method call on the client object is ItemSearch! instead of the WSDL example item_search. The reason is that when the WSDL file is used, Savon knows how to modify that method call into its SOAP equivalent. Without the WSDL file, the method call must have exactly the same casing as in SOAP.

There are two additions inside the code block passed to the ItemSearch call. First, the namespace must be set on the SOAP object. This was pulled earlier, using the

WSDL file. Second, the input must be set to the `ItemSearch` operation. Now the search method can make calls without downloading and parsing the WSDL file.

Sometimes constructing requests without the WSDL file can be a little tricky. A useful troubleshooting method is to write a WSDL-based version of the request and keep the Savon logging on. Both of the previous examples disable logging by using the line `Savon::Request.log = false`. The debug output shows the XML that is being sent in the request. You can run the WSDL version and the regular version and compare the XML. This will help you determine which additional parameters must be set on the SOAP object.

Conclusion

Parsing service responses can range from an easy task to a difficult task, depending on how much data is returned. While there are multiple options for parsing XML in Ruby, Nokogiri is currently the leading option in terms of speed and ease of use. When writing classes to parse service responses, there are a some key points to follow in designing classes:

- Keep parsing logic separate from object logic, preferably within a single method.
- Use multiple classes for data. Don't try to put everything into a single class.
- Make object constructors that take standard Ruby objects and not unparsed strings.

Following these guidelines when designing classes to wrap service responses results it more readable and maintainable code. These guidelines also apply to writing classes that make SOAP calls. Parsing, request, and SOAP logic should be handled within the class. Data objects should be returned from the class that show through a clear API what data a response contains.

CHAPTER 10

Security

There are three main areas of focus when securing services: authentication, authorization, and encryption. *Authentication* refers to verifying that the user is who she says she is and that no one has tampered with her message. *Authorization* refers to determining what a given user is allowed to do on the system. *Encryption* is a technique to keep people in the middle from being able to know what data is being sent back and forth. All three are important to properly securing a system, but each is approached in a different way. This chapter covers how to approach each of these facets of security to ensure that your services are not compromised.

Authentication

There are two main components to authentication. The first is validating a user's identity. The second is ensuring that the message the server received is the same message the client sent. The simplest form of user authentication is to require the user to provide a user name and password. This ensures that the user knows at least a valid login and its associated password, but it does little to guarantee that the message body the server received is the same as the one that the client sent. Message signing provides a more foolproof mechanism for validating that message contents have arrived unmodified. In addition, message signing can be used to validate a user's identity because the signing mechanism can also be used to uniquely identify a user.

This section starts with simple HTTP authentication to validate a user's identity and then moves on to two forms of message signing: shared secrets and public/private key pairs. It finishes with a quick look at using SSL certificates to validate the identity of a server. While reading this section, remember that passwords and message signing do not have to be used exclusively, and greater security can be attained by requiring both HTTP authentication and a signed message.

HTTP Authentication

One of the simplest ways of verifying the identity of a user is to use HTTP basic authentication, which is a simple challenge-and-response method that requires the user to provide a user name and password. On the client side, basic authentication is usually very easy to implement. In Typhoeus, it's as easy as adding an authorization header, like so:

```
require 'base64'
credentials = Base64.encode64("#{username}:#{password}")
response = Typhoeus::Request.get(
  "http://example.com/cool.json",
  :headers => {"Authorization" => "Basic #{credentials}"})
```

Thankfully, the work on the server side is nearly as simple. Rack ships with the `Rack::Auth::Basic` class, which is Rack middleware that you initialize with an authentication realm and authentication block, like so:

```
Filename: lib/protected_app.ru

require 'protected_app'
use Rack::Auth::Basic, "Protected Realm" do |username,
  password|
  # You could make a request to a user service here to
  # see if the user is correct.
  # For apps that are not externally accessible,
  # it's sometimes easier (though not quite as secure)
  # to just have a standard user/pass:
  username == "bobs_protection" && password =
    "bobs_sekret_pass"
end
run ProtectedApp.new
```

This `rackup` file ensures that only requests with a basic authentication header including the user name `bobs_protection` and the password `bobs_sekret_pass` are passed to the application. As the file notes, a request to an authentication service could also be made at this time to determine whether the user name and password are correct.

Though basic authentication is easy to set up and use, it is not the most secure approach. In particular, the user name and password are sent as clear text. For this reason, it is inadvisable to use basic authentication over anything other than SSL. If SSL is unavailable, HTTP Digest Authentication is also an option. Setup on the server side is accomplished with a Rack adapter similar to `Rack::Auth::Basic`. Unfortunately, usage on the client side is usually slightly more difficult, as it requires a handling of nonces and hashing of the user credentials.

Signing Requests

Request signing can serve two purposes. First and foremost, it is often used to verify that the contents of a message have not been modified. An unsigned message can be intercepted and modified by a malicious third party and then routed on to the intended recipient. To the recipient, it appears that the message has come directly from the client, but in reality, someone in the middle has changed it to convey false information. (This is referred to as a *man-in-the-middle attack*.) When a message has been signed, a unique cryptographic hash is appended to the message. The server uses this hash to validate the message contents. This prevents man-in-the-middle attacks because it is quite difficult for a man in the middle to generate the correct signature.

Second, request signing can be used to validate a user's identity. By assigning a unique signature key to each client, a server can be assured that only that client could have possibly signed the message. In this way, the signature serves as a validator both of the message contents and of the user.

Shared Secrets with HMAC

Using Hash-based Message Authentication Code (HMAC) is one of the easiest ways to sign a request. It requires the use of a shared secret and can be performed using the ruby-hmac gem (http://ruby-hmac.rubyforge.org). When using HMAC, the requester signs the message using a shared key and appends his or her signature to the message. It is usually best to include the signature as part of a header because it makes it easy for the server to pull it back out. However, you will see it appended to the query string or to the POST body in some APIs. Upon receiving the message, the server signs the message using the same key and verifies that the signature matches the one sent by the client.

For the implementation, an HMAC signature class is first needed to standardize signature generation. Encapsulating the signature algorithm in a single class makes it easier to reuse on both the client and server sides:

```ruby
require 'hmac'
require 'hmac-sha2'
require 'base64'

class HmacSignature
  def initialize(key)
    @key = key
  end

  def sign(verb, host, path, query_params)
    # sort the params alphabetically by key and join
    # them with '='
    sorted_query_params =
      query_params.sort.map do |param|
        param.join("=")
      end # => ["user=mat", "tag=ruby"]

    # join the sorted params into one string
    canonicalized_params = sorted_query_params.join("&")
      # => "user=mat&tag=ruby"

    # Construct the string to sign by concatenating the
    # various parts of the request.
    string_to_sign = verb + host + path +
      canonicalized_params

    # Construct an hmac signer using our secret key
    hmac = HMAC::SHA256.new(@key)
    hmac.update(string_to_sign)
```

```
      # Encrypt the string and Base64 encode it (to
      # make it cleaner when putting it into the request).
      Base64.encode64(hmac.digest).chomp
    end
  end
```

The signature class signs a message with the HTTP verb (GET, PUT, POST, DELETE), the host, the path, and the query parameters. To ensure that the message to be signed is consistent on both ends, the query parameters are put in sorted order by their keys. The message containing all these pieces of information are put together and signed using a HMAC::SHA256 signer.

It's important to note that this method does not protect against replay attacks—that is, listening in on a request and then reissuing it later. To ensure some level of protection against a replay, you should include a time in the query parameters. This can be checked on the server side to make sure that the time at which the request was signed is close to the time the server receives the request. Amazon's API provides an example of where this method is used.

With a signature generator written, the next step is to write a sample client. The client uses HmacSignature to create the signature and then executes to curl requests. The first is done without the signature to verify that the server is indeed protected. The second is done with the signature in the X-Auth-Sig header, which should ensure that the request is processed by the server:

```
require 'rubygems'
require 'cgi'
require 'hmac_signature'

verb = "GET"
host = "localhost"
path = "/"
query_params = {"user" => "mat", "tag" => "ruby"}

# The signature is generated and then CGI escaped
# to ensure it travels appropriately over HTTP.
# The key used to sign the messages is "our-secret-key"
unescaped_sig = HmacSignature.new('our-secret-key'
```

```
).sign(verb, host, path, query_params)
sig = CGI.escape(unescaped_sig)

query_string = query_params.map do |k,v|
  [CGI.escape(k), CGI.escape(v)].join("=")
end.join("&")

puts "Without Signature:"
system %Q|curl -i "http://localhost:9292/?#{query_string}"|
sleep 2
puts "\n\nWith Signature:"
system %Q|curl -i -H "X-Auth-Sig: #{sig}" \
  "http://localhost:9292/?#{query_string}"|
```

The next step is to write a simple Rack adapter that will be used to protect the application. This adapter will be initialized with the same secret key used by the client, our-secret-key. If the signature is also being used to validate the client's identity, another header (such as X-Auth-User) should be added to the request by the client. Then in signature_is_valid? the header could be used to look up the appropriate secret to use when validating signatures from that client. Here is an example that shows a rack module for performing signature validation:

```
require 'hmac_signature'
require 'cgi'

module Rack
  class SignatureValidator
    def initialize(app, secret)
      @app = app
      @secret = secret
      @signer = HmacSignature.new('our-secret-key')
    end

    def call(env)
      if signature_is_valid?(env)
        @app.call(env)
```

```
          else
            [401, {"Content-Type" => "text/html"},
              "Bad Signature"]
          end
        end


      def signature_is_valid?(env)
        # Rack::Request will make it easier to pull
        # off the query params
        req  = Rack::Request.new(env)
        verb = env["REQUEST_METHOD"]
        host = env["REMOTE_HOST"]
        path = env["REQUEST_PATH"]
        time = req.params["time"]


        # Rack appends HTTP_ to the header, so we do too.
        sig  = env["HTTP_X_AUTH_SIG"]


        # Verify the signature
        sig == @signer.sign(verb, host, path, req.params) &&
          (Time.now - Time.at(time)) < 120
      end
    end
  end
```

The validator gets the HTTP verb, host, path, request time, and signature from the request. It uses the verb, host, and path to sign the message using the same signer as the client. It compares this generated signature with the signature that was passed in the request. Finally, it ensures that the `time` value in the query string is within 120 seconds of the current time. Note that the method assumes that the time query parameter is an integer—that is, a Unix time epoch value generated when calling `to_i` on a Ruby time object.

The final step is to use `Rack::SignatureValidator` in a `rackup` configuration to protect the server. The following example defines a simple "Hello, World" application and instantiates `Rack::SignatureValidator` with the key `our-secret-key` to protect it:

```
require 'hmac_sig_validator'

use Rack::SignatureValidator, 'our-secret-key'

run Proc.new { |env| [200,
  {"Content-Type" => "text/html"},
  "Hello World! From Signature\n"] }
```

This example assumes that all users will use the same key to sign requests. This approach is practical only in a controlled setting where there are few clients, and all are highly trusted. In many circumstances, it is better to give each client a unique key, which the server looks up on each request. Amazon does this with the combination of the AWS access key ID and the AWS secret. The server looks up the shared secret based on the access key ID and uses that to verify the request.

One of the problems with a shared secret is that the secret must actually be given to the client. The next section discusses public/private key pairs, which provide a way around this deficiency at the cost of a more difficult implementation.

Public/Private Key Pairs with RSA

If there is an attacker in the middle when the shared secret for HMAC signing is shared, the attacker can steal the secret and then sign requests as if he were the actual client. One option for safeguarding against this type of attack is to use a public/private key pair generated using the RSA algorithm. In this approach, the client creates a key pair and then sends the public portion to the server. When the client makes an API request, it uses the private key to encrypt a signature string. Upon receiving the request, the server looks up the client's public key and uses it to decrypt the signature. If the signature matches what is expected, the request is valid.[1]

---

[1] In practice, generating and validating a signature generated using public/private keys is very similar to generating and validating a signature made with a shared secret. For this reason, the example shows only the code related to signing and validating. A more complete running example can be found with the sample code for this chapter at http://github.com/pauldix/service-oriented-design-with-ruby/tree/master/chapter_10/.

To get started with public/private key pairs, the actual keys are needed. These can be generated in many ways, but because this is a Ruby book, the following example shows how to do it in pure Ruby. It is important to note that openssl is required, and it is not part of the default Ruby package on Ubuntu. If you're running on Ubuntu, be sure to install the ruby-openssl package first. That said, actually generating the keys takes only a few lines:

```ruby
require 'rubygems'
require 'openssl'

module GenerateKeys
  def self.generate
    if File.exist?("example_key.pem") ||
      File.exist?("example_key.pub")
      puts "Keys exist, not generating"
      return
    end

    # Use a 2048 bit key, 4096 can be used if
    # stronger security is desired.
    rsa_private_key = OpenSSL::PKey::RSA.generate(2048)

    # Write the private key
    File.open("example_key.pem", "w") do |f|
      f.write rsa_private_key.to_s
    end

    # Write the public key
    File.open("example_key.pub", "w") do |f|
      f.write rsa_private_key.public_key
    end
  end
end

# If this file is the one being executed, go ahead
# and create the keys
```

```
if $0 == __FILE__
  GenerateKeys.generate
end
```

Once both keys are generated, the private key must be given to the client and the public key to the server. A sample client that uses the private key to sign a request can then be written as follows. The signature is again placed in X-Auth-Sig, and X-Auth-User could be added to allow the server to look up the appropriate public key based on a user identifier, as shown in the following example:

```
require 'generate_keys'
require 'cgi'
require 'openssl'
require 'base64'

# Since this is an example, we'll go ahead and
# generate some keys
GenerateKeys.generate

verb = "GET"
host = "localhost"
path = "/"
params = {"user" => "topper", "tag" => "ruby"}

# Sort the query params and concat them with
# everything else again
sorted_params = params.sort.map do |param|
  param.join("=")
end

canonicalized_params = sorted_params.join("&")
string_to_sign = verb + host + path +
  canonicalized_params

# Get our private key
private_key = OpenSSL::PKey::RSA.new(File.read
  ("example_key.pem"))
```

```
# Create the signature and escape it
unescaped_sig = private_key.private_encrypt(string_to_sign)
sig = CGI.escape(Base64.encode64(unescaped_sig))

query_string = params.map {|k,v| [CGI.escape(k),
  CGI.escape(v)].join("=") }.join("&")

puts "Without Signature:"
system %Q|curl -i "http://localhost:9292/?#{query_string}"|
sleep 2

puts "\n\nWith Signature:"
system %Q|curl -i -H "X-Auth-Sig: #{sig}" \
  "http://localhost:9292/?#{query_string}"|
```

On the server side, a validator is once again needed. This time, the validator uses the public key to decrypt the signature and compare it to the unsigned canonicalized query parameters. This differs from the HMAC validator's approach because the public key cannot be used to generate the same signature as the private key for the canonicalized query parameters. However, it can be used to decrypt strings signed using the private key:

```
require 'cgi'
require 'openssl'
require 'base64'

module Rack
  class RsaSigValidator
    def initialize(app)
      @app = app
    end

    def call(env)
      if signature_is_valid?(env)
        @app.call(env)
      else
```

```
        [401, {"Content-Type" => "text/html"},
          "Bad Signature"]
      end
    end

  def signature_is_valid?(env)
    # On your server, you'd want to actually look up
    # the public key using something else in the
    # params (like a user_id)
    key = OpenSSL::PKey::RSA.new(IO.read(
      "example_key.pub"))

    req  = Rack::Request(env)
    verb = env["REQUEST_METHOD"]
    host = env["REMOTE_HOST"]
    path = env["REQUEST_PATH"]
    body = env["rack.input"].read
    sig  = Base64.decode64(CGI.unescape(
      env["HTTP_X_AUTH_SIG"] || ""))
    return false if sig == "" # Short circuit

    # Generate the string to compare against
    sorted_params = req.params.sort.map { |param|
      param.join("=")}
    canonicalized_params = sorted_params.join("&")
    expected_string = verb + host + path +
      canonicalized_params

    # Decrypt the string and compare it to the
    # expected string
    expected_string == key.public_decrypt(sig)
  end
 end
end
```

With the validator written, the only step left is to wire it into a rackup configuration, which is left as an exercise for you.

What to Sign

In the preceding examples, the client signs only a simple query string along with some information about the request. The real world is more complicated and requires that POST bodies consisting of XML or JSON also be signed. As it turns out, signing a POST body is even simpler than signing query strings or form-encoded POSTs because the client does not need to worry about ordering parameters. The problem with query strings and form-encoded POSTs is that many common HTTP clients do not guarantee the order in which parameters will be added to the query string or POST body. For this reason, the client and server must agree on the order. The preceding examples use simple alphabetic sorting.

When the POST body is an XML, JSON, or other BLOB, however, the client does not need to worry about sorting and can simply append it to the string to sign. In the case of a JSON request, generating the string to sign on the client might look something like the following:

```
verb = "POST"
host = "localhost"
path = "/"
body = %|{"name": "Jenn", "lifeGoal": "Be Awesome"}|

string_to_sign = verb + host + path + body
```

On the server, only a slight modification is made to extract the request body and append it to the string to be signed:

```
body = env["rack.input"].read
expected_string = verb + host + path +
  canonicalized_params + body
```

Even though there is no query string in this example, it's better to keep the server side as general as possible by continuing to include canonicalized_params. In this way, the server can handle incoming requests with either canonicalized params or a POST body. However, keep in mind that a more robust implementation would check the Content-Type of the POST and parse and sort the parameters in the body if it is application/form-url-encoded.

SSL for Authentication

Although SSL is often thought of as an encryption mechanism, it can also be used to verify identities. In the case of a web server, the certificate acts as proof to the client that the server really is the correct server because a third party (such as VeriSign) validates the certificate. Unfortunately, validating a server's certificate is not exactly straightforward in Ruby. Unlike a browser, Ruby does not inherently know how to trust the third party's validation of the certificate. It is up to the programmer to provide a certificate authority's file for Ruby to use. The following code example tells the story:

```ruby
require 'uri'
require 'net/https' # Use net/https, *not* net/http

uri = URI.parse(ARGV[0] || "https://mail.google.com")

http = Net::HTTP.new(uri.host, uri.port)

# Tell Net::HTTP that SSL is in use.
http.use_ssl = true

# Tell Net::HTTP that we want to validate certificates.
http.verify_mode = OpenSSL::SSL::VERIFY_PEER

# cacert.pem contains certificate authority information.
http.ca_file = File.join(File.dirname(__FILE__),
  "cacert.pem")
http.start do
  puts http.get("/")
end
```

As you can see, Net::HTTP must be told to use SSL and be given a list of valid certificate authorities in the form of cacert.pem. In the case of this example, the cacert.pem used is the one from Haxx, the creators of Curl (http://curl.haxx.se/ca/cacert.pem). If self-signed certificates rather than purchased certificates are being used, then it is necessary to use a cacert.pem that contains the self-signing authority.

As mentioned earlier, authentication covers verifying both the identity of an individual and the validity of the message being sent. This section has only scratched the surface of authentication. Other topics include authenticating that messages sent from the server to the client are valid and using signatures to verify identity. Authentication is an essential piece of the security puzzle. As you will see in the next section, authorization is sometimes quite useless if the user's identity is not verified.

Authentication for Rails Applications

The previous examples of authentication concern authenticating service clients with services. Service clients in these cases have been other programmers. These could be programmers within your organization accessing shared services or external programmers connecting to your service (for example, programmers connect to Amazon Web Services). However, web applications also have to concern themselves with authenticating regular users.

Authenticating users of a web application with regard to services can occur in two forms. First, the user can log into the application and perform actions that require authentication. Second, the user can allow a third-party service to connect to your service on his or her behalf. The latter scenario is covered in Chapter 12, "Web Hooks and External Services," in the section on OAuth. The former scenario can be handled without much difficulty.

Chapter 1, "Implementing and Consuming Your First Service," works through an example of creating a user service. This same service can be used for authenticating users within a Rails application. Figure 10.1 shows the communication among the web user, the Rails application, and services.

Figure 10.1 shows an example from the social feed reader application. The Rails application handles all requests coming from a user. The user (pauldix) provides his user name and password so he can then be authenticated against the user service. Once this has occurred, the Rails application can make requests to the reading list and entry services. Note that the reading list and entry services will probably have their own authentication, as detailed in previous sections. However, that layer of security is designed for service-to-service communication.

If services are exposed directly to end users of an application, the services need to authenticate users. An example of this would be JavaScript calls from the web browser directly to services. It's usually a good idea to have those requests all come into a central place, such as the Rails application. However, it's possible to route those requests to the services themselves. In those cases, the service will have to call out to the user service to authenticate the request.

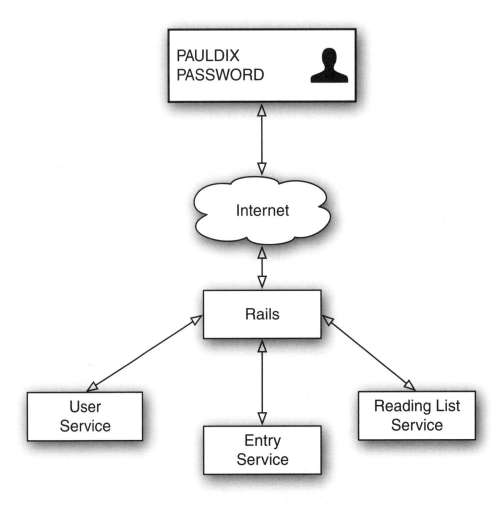

Figure 10.1   User authentication.

If the services handle authentication directly, they also have to concern themselves with session management. Coverage of user sessions is beyond the scope of this book. For more information, the Ruby on Rails guide to security is a useful resource (http://guides.rubyonrails.org/security.html#sessions). Note that each service that handles external requests directly from users has to deal with this. In this case, the best method is to write the user-based authentication as a Rack adapter, like the previously covered HMAC adapter. The important thing to keep in mind is that the user service must have very quick response times in order to ensure that request processing isn't held up.

Authorization

This section covers two major approaches to authorization. The first is a sort of blanket protection provided by software such as firewalls. In this approach, the user is not necessarily authenticated but is instead restricted from performing certain actions based merely on the fact that he is coming from outside the local machine. Sometimes a form of weak authentication is coupled with this when access is further restricted to coming in from only a few known IP addresses. The second approach leans more heavily on authentication to first verify the user and then determines whether this user is allowed to perform a certain action. It results in more fine-grained access control because it's easier to specify that a user can access only certain parts of a single application as opposed to the firewall approach of allowing users access to anything on a certain port. This section discusses role-based access control (RBAC) as one means of implementing this approach. It is important to keep in mind that these authorization mechanisms are not exclusive. In many applications, you will certainly want both.

Firewalls

One of the simplest and most effective ways to protect private services from unauthorized external access is with a simple firewall. A firewall can restrict access to only a few known IP addresses, which can be useful (though somewhat fragile, if dynamic IP addresses are in use) when you're limiting access to a ReaderList service to the web servers only. Because `iptables` is prevalent and easy to install on many Linux distributions, the following examples assume that it is being used. However, these concepts should generalize to other firewalls, so you should consult the documentation to translate these examples to your firewall of choice. To get started with `iptables`, you need to have it installed. On Ubuntu, you use a simple `apt-get` call:

```
sudo apt-get install iptables
```

Once `iptables` is installed, the rules must be set up. Gaining full mastery of `iptables` rules can take quite some time, so this section covers only turning on access to all but a couple external machines. The first step is to set up an `iptables` ruleset that restricts all traffic other than local (this machine) traffic, outbound requests, and SSH. You save this file to `/tmp/iptables.test.rules`:

```
*filter

# Allow local traffic
-A INPUT -i lo -j ACCEPT
-A INPUT -i ! lo -d 127.0.0.0/8 -j REJECT
```

```
# Allow a connection if it has already been accepted
-A INPUT -m state --state ESTABLISHED,RELATED -j ACCEPT

# Allow us to communicate out
-A OUTPUT -j ACCEPT

# Our rules for allowing traffic
# HOOK: INCOMING TRAFFIC (we'll replace this below)

# Enable ssh because we still want to get to the box
-A INPUT -p tcp -m state --state NEW --dport 22 -j ACCEPT

# log denied calls so that you can monitor them
-A INPUT -m limit --limit 5/min -j LOG \
   --log-prefix "iptables denied:" --log-level 7

-A INPUT -j REJECT
-A FORWARD -j REJECT
```

This ruleset blocks nearly all incoming traffic to this machine, which is more than ultimately desired.

The next step is to lock incoming TCP requests to specific ports. Assuming that an HTTP service is being protected, this involves opening ports 80 and 443 to all clients. You replace HOOK: INCOMING TRAFFIC in the preceding file with the following:

```
iptables -A INPUT -p tcp --destination-port 80 -j ACCEPT
iptables -A INPUT -p tcp --destination-port 443 -j ACCEPT
```

The next step is to restrict these ports even further by applying an iprange filter. This filter ensures that only requests from a certain IP range—in this case, 192.168.1.100 to 192.168.1.200—are allowed to connect. Typically, an iprange filter is applied only when restricting access to a few internal machines. If the service needs to be accessible over the Internet, an iprange filter is not practical. The filter looks like this:

```
iptables -A INPUT -p tcp --destination-port 80 -m iprange \
   --src-range 192.168.1.100-192.168.1.200 -j ACCEPT
iptables -A INPUT -p tcp --destination-port 443 -m iprange \
   --src-range 192.168.1.100-192.168.1.200 -j ACCEPT
```

Access to the server is now restricted to ports 80 and 443 from clients with an IP address in the 192.168.1.100 to 192.168.1.200 range. Any attackers coming from outside this range are immediately prevented from gaining access once these rules are actually loaded. Loading them involves a simple `iptables-restore` command. It is typically good practice to also execute an `iptables-save` to store the new configuration permanently:

```
sudo iptables-restore < /tmp/iptables.test.rules
sudo iptables-save > /tmp/iptables.up.rules
```

Using a firewall as a means of authorization is a very powerful tool, but it cannot distinguish one valid user of a web service from another. If the service needs to be publicly exposed as part of a broader API, a firewall protects other ports on the machine from unauthorized access but not the service itself. In these cases, an authorization service like the one described in the next section helps immensely.

An RBAC Authorization Service

An RBAC authorization service provides the kind of fine-grained authorization that a firewall is unable to provide. With RBAC, a user is assigned one or more roles, and protected resources are set as accessible by one or more roles. When a user requests access to a resource, access is granted only if one of the user's roles is also in the set of allowed roles.

There are a number of Rails plugins for RBAC, but they're usable only from within a Rails app. A more general RBAC solution is necessary for use with Sinatra or other Rack-based services. This section covers implementing RBAC as a Rack adapter and associated service. It allows for all access rules to exist in a single service, which can be scaled independently of the other services. In addition, it provides a write-once, implement-everywhere approach to RBAC security. If RBAC does not fit your particular need, this form of Rack adapter and associated service could also be used to implement other authorization mechanisms such as user-based access control.

RBAC Service

At its core, an RBAC authorization service consists of three main resources. First, it needs a way to create users and associate them with roles. Second, it needs a way to create resources and authorize roles to act on them. Third, it needs a way to query

whether a given user can access a given resource. The simplified server that follows
uses ActiveRecord data objects to store users (which map user identifiers to roles) and
resources (which match resources to roles). There are three actions for the server: create a user, create a resource, and query. To remove roles from a user or resource, the
user or resource is created again with no roles, which overrides the previous roles. This
RBAC server relies on two ActiveRecord models and utilizes a Sinatra front end to
serve the three URLs.

The RBAC model layer is relatively simple and consists of two classes, User and
Resource. Each has a name and a comma-separated list of roles associated with it.
In the case of User, roles denotes the roles the user belongs to. In the case of
Resource, roles denotes the roles that are allowed access. In a more full-fledged
system, the roles themselves may be broken off into a separate model. In this case,
however, a comma-separated list is sufficient. The following example shows a class
called RoleBased that provides an inheritable interface for adding roles to the User
and Resource models:

```
require 'rubygems'
require 'sinatra'
require 'json'
require 'active_record'

# Establish the ActiveRecord connection
ActiveRecord::Base.establish_connection(
  :adapter => 'sqlite3',
  :database => File.dirname(__FILE__) +
    "/../db/saint_peter_#{Sinatra::Application
      .environment}.sqlite3.db"
)

class RoleBased < ActiveRecord::Base
  # This class is an interface for the other two and
  # does not require a table.
  self.abstract_class = true

  # Either find an existing obj and update it or
  # create a new one.
```

```
  def self.find_and_update_or_create(attrs)
    obj = find_by_name(attrs[:name])
    if obj
      obj.update_attributes(attrs)
    else
      create(attrs)
    end
  end


  # We want to work with roles as an array.
  def roles
    str = read_attribute(:roles)
    str.split(/ *, */)
  end
end


class User < RoleBased; end
class Resource < RoleBased; end
```

The controller level exposes three URLs: /users, /resources, and /users/
:name/authorizations. The first allows a client to either create or update a user. To
simplify the example, both methods are handled through a POST. The second URL
allows a client to either create or update a resource, behaving nearly identically to the
first URL. The third URL is the one that is used most often. It allows a client to check
whether a user is authorized for a given resource by querying a URL in the form
/users/:name/authorizations?resource=%2Fadmin. If scaling were ever to
become an issue, caching this URL would be a good first step. The following is an
example of a Sinatra service for handling users and roles:

```
# Run on port 3333 to make it easier to test with the
# protected service
set :port, 3333


# Handle user creation and updating
post '/users' do
```

```
  user = User.find_and_update_or_create(params)
  user ? 'Created' : 'Failed'
end


# Handle resource creation and updating
post '/resources' do
  auth = Resource.find_and_update_or_create(params)
  auth ? 'Created' : 'Failed'
end


# Tell whether a user is authorized for a given resource
get '/users/:name/authorizations' do |name|
  user_roles = User.find_by_name(name).roles rescue []
  auth_roles = Resource.find_by_name(
    params[:resource]).roles rescue []

  # If subtracting auth_roles from user_roles results
  # in a shorter array, then at least one element in
  # auth_roles is in user_roles.
  authorized = (user_roles - auth_roles).length !=
    user_roles.length
  {:authorized => authorized}.to_json
end
```

The service is Sinatra based, so it can easily be started on its own or as part of a larger Rack application. At this point, it is accessible on port 3333, which is the port that the Rack adapter in the next section will use to talk to it.

The Rack Adapter

The RBAC service can be accessed from anywhere in the application stack via a simple HTTP call. However, the simplest method is to use a Rack adapter that sits in front of the protected application and checks whether the user can access the requested URL. This Rack adapter relies on a block to set the user name and resource that will be passed to the RBAC service to determine whether a user is authorized to act on that resource. In this way, the rackup configuration of the protected application can determine exactly how to identify users and resources. The following example shows a Rack adapter for RBAC:

```ruby
require 'json'
require 'cgi'

module Rack
  class RBAC
    # rbac_host:: The host for the RBAC server
    # block:: Extract the requested resource and
    # user and return as a two element hash
    # { :user, :resource }
    def initialize(app, rbac_host, &block) # :yields:
      env
      @app = app
      @rbac_host = rbac_host
      @rbac_port = 3333
      @extract_user_and_resource = block
    end

    def call(env)
      # Pull the user and resource from the provided block.
      user, resource = @extract_user_and_resource.call(env).
        values_at(:user, :resource)

      # If the GET fails or we are unable to parse the
      # response then they are unauthorized. Otherwise, we
      # use the value from the authorized key in the
      # response json.
      authorized =
        begin
          resp = Net::HTTP.get(
            @rbac_host,
            "/users/#{user}/authorizations?resource=#
              {resource}",
            @rbac_port)
```

```
          JSON.parse(resp)["authorized"]
        rescue
          false
        end

      if authorized
        # They're authorized, let them through.
        @app.call(env)
      else
        # Oh noes! Tell them to leave.
        [401, {'Content-Type' => 'text/html'},
          "Unauthorized\n"]
      end

    rescue => e
      # If we failed for any other reason, return a 500.
      [500,
        {'Content-Type' => 'text/html'},
        "Unable to authorize: #{e.message}\n"]
    end
  end
end
```

You can use `Rack::RBAC` to protect a simple application server with `config.ru`:

```
require 'rack_rbac'

use Rack::RBAC, "localhost" do |env|
  # We are taking the user from the X-User header.
  # This would ideally be set by an adapter higher in the
  # chain.
  {:user => CGI.escape(env["HTTP_X_USER"]),
    :resource => CGI.escape(env["PATH_INFO"])}
end

run Proc.new { |env| [200, {"Content-Type" => "text/html"},
                "Rack::RBAC gave you access\n"] }
```

This example relies on the X-User HTTP header being set, but alternate implementations could do a lookup of the user in a database, based on information stored in a cookie. If X-User is used, it should be set by another adapter higher in the chain, such as the HTTP basic authentication adapter.

In order to test the implementation, both servers need to be started, and the RBAC service needs to be populated with user and resource information. Because it is a simple HTTP server, this can be done with a few curl commands, as follows:

```
$ curl -X POST -d "name=pinot&roles=cat"
  http://localhost:3333/users
$ curl -X POST -d "name=/litterbox&roles=cat" \
  http://localhost:3333/resources
```

Now if the protected server is started with rackup config.ru, a few curl commands verify that only pinot can access /litterbox:

```
$ curl -H "X-User: trotter" "http://localhost:9292/litterbox"
  # => unauthorized
$ curl -H "X-User: pinot" "http://localhost:9292/litterbox"
  # => authorized
```

This is all there is to setting up a simple RBAC service that integrates with other applications via a Rack adapter. Users can be assigned to roles, and resources can be restricted to access only by specific roles through HTTP calls. Querying user authorization involves simply a single HTTP call to the service. As usage of the system grows, authorization lookups can be cached either on the service side or on the rack side. In addition, the system can be extended to support other means of user lookup or resource specification. In a RESTful Rails setup, the resource would likely be specified as a combination of the HTTP method and the request path.

Encryption

The final piece of the security puzzle is encryption. When sending any sensitive information over the wire, encryption is a necessity. Although authentication and authorization help ensure that information is sent by the correct client to the correct server, they cannot prevent a man in the middle from reading the traffic. Man-in-the-middle attacks are easier for would-be attackers when the victim is on a cloud solution such as Amazon's EC2. The lack of control over the networking hardware between machines enables the attacker to listen in on traffic between instances. For applications or situations where security is an important requirement, it is imperative that information between services be encrypted even when communicating with two "internal" services.

SSL for Encryption

When it comes to ease of implementation and knowing that it will "just work," SSL is the obvious solution for encryption. It easily integrates into most web servers, and RabbitMQ can even use it to encrypt traffic. Unfortunately, using SSL requires that you attain an SSL certificate, which can be costly. Thankfully, it is also possible to self-sign a certificate, and an Internet search reveals many resources that can show the best way to do so. Once a certificate is acquired, telling Apache or Nginx to use it is fairly trivial. For Apache, `mod_ssl` should be enabled, and the following three lines should be added to the virtual host:

```
SSLEngine on
SSLCertificateFile /path_to_your_crt/server.crt
SSLCertificateKeyFile /path_to_your_pem/server.pem
```

For Nginx, the following needs to be added to `nginx.conf`:

```
listen 443 ssl;
ssl_certificate        /path_to_your_cert/cert.crt;
ssl_certificate_key    /path_to_your_pem/cert.pem;
```

With an SSL certificate in place, all communication with the service will be encrypted. Most HTTP clients automatically detect that SSL is in use when given a URL that starts with https, so implementation on the client side takes no work. Using SSL really is just this easy.

Public/Private Key Pairs for Encryption

Public/private key pairs are used earlier in this chapter as an authentication mechanism. They can also be used to encrypt either the query string or the POST body of a request and the response body. This method does not provide as much security as SSL, but you use it as a form of encryption when SSL is not available or as extra encryption when it is.

In practice, using public/private key pairs for encryption is very similar to using them for signing. The only difference is that the unencrypted version of the query string or POST body is not included, and an encrypted version is put in its place. The client code once again uses GenerateKeys to create the keys. It then uses the key to encrypt the entire query string and places it on the request as q. If this code needs to encrypt the body instead, the encrypted body can be placed directly into the request body rather than in a parameter named q. When the request comes back from the server, it is also encrypted. The client can then use private_decrypt to decrypt the response body:

```ruby
require 'generate_keys'
require 'cgi'
require 'openssl'
require 'base64'


GenerateKeys.generate


verb = "GET"
host = "localhost"
path = "/"
query_params = {"user" => "topper", "tag" => "ruby"}


# Load the private key
private_key = OpenSSL::PKey::RSA.new(File.read
  ("example_key.pem"))


query_string = query_params.map { |k,v|
  [CGI.escape(k), CGI.escape(v)].join("=") }.join("&")


# Encrypt and escape the query string
encrypted_query_string =
  CGI.escape(Base64.encode64(
    private_key.private_encrypt(query_string)))
```

```
puts "Encrypted"
encrypted = 'curl "http://localhost:9292/
  ?q=#{encrypted_query_string}"'

# Decrypt the response
puts private_key.private_decrypt(encrypted)
```

The server now uses a Rack adapter that acts as an around filter rather than a before filter. It takes the incoming request, pulls off the q parameter, decrypts it, and passes the decrypted query string through to the application. Once the application has returned a response, the adapter encrypts the response body using the public key and passes it on:

```
require 'cgi'
require 'openssl'
require 'base64'

module Rack
  class RsaEncryption
    def initialize(app)
      @app = app
      @key = OpenSSL::PKey::RSA.new(IO.read
        ("example_key.pub"))
    end

    def call(env)
      # Decrypt the query string and place it back in
      # the ENV.
      env["QUERY_STRING"] = decrypt_query_string(env)

      # Pass the modified env to the application.
      resp = @app.call(env)

      # Take the body of the response and encrypt it.
      resp[-1] = @key.public_encrypt(resp[-1])
      resp
    end
```

```ruby
    def decrypt_query_string(env)
      req = Rack::Request.new(env)

      # Do lookup for user's key here if desired

      # Pull off the encrypted query param
      encrypted = req.params.delete("q")

      # Decrypt it and turn it into a hash
      decrypted = @key.public_decrypt(Base64.decode64
        (encrypted))
      as_query_hash = Hash[*decrypted.split("&").map { |p|
          p.split("=") }.flatten]

      # Turn the hash back into a query string.
      pairs = req.params.merge(as_query_hash).map { |k, v|
        [k,v].join("=") }
      pairs.join("&")
    end
  end
end
```

All that remains at this point is to link the Rack adapter to an application in a rackup configuration:

```ruby
require 'rack_rsa_encryption'

use Rack::RsaEncryption

run Proc.new { |env| [200, {"Content-Type" => "text/html"},
  "Here's your decrypted query string:
    #{env["QUERY_STRING"]}\n"] }
```

Encryption is a necessary piece of any security strategy. No level of authentication is truly secure if an attacker can intercept the message in transit and write down the user's credentials. Encryption helps prevent this form of attack and ensures users that their sensitive data is not left in the clear for anyone to see.

Conclusion

This chapter covers the basics of restricting access to services to authenticated and authorized individuals connecting over an encrypted channel. Many of the technologies covered can fit into more than just one form of security. SSL is used to both verify a server's identity and encrypt information. Other public/private key pairs can be used to verify the client's identity, to verify the integrity of a message, and to encrypt the message. Other tools, such as an authorization service, `iptables`, HMAC signing, and HTTP authentication, are also used as means to protect a service. With all these technologies, it is important to remember that choosing only one of them is not enough. Effective security involves using many means of authenticating, authorizing, and encrypting access to services.

CHAPTER 11

Messaging

Application architectures designed around services need to build methods for communicating between these services. While REST and HTTP and JSON enable quick synchronous communication, messaging systems enable the creation of more robust asynchronous communication between services. This chapter looks at how messaging systems can be used in place of HTTP for writing data between services. It also goes over parts of the AMQP messaging standard and RabbitMQ, an open source implementation of AMQP.

What Is Messaging?

Messaging is how services communicate with each other. Traditional service-oriented architecture (SOA) approaches use HTTP as the message transport protocol and SOAP as the message format. SOAP is an XML standard for exchanging structured information between web services. When a service wants to communicate with another service, it creates a SOAP XML message and sends it over HTTP to the other web service.

Most Rails applications opt for the more modern approach of using RESTful HTTP APIs. With REST, the URLs indicate which resource is being accessed, while the message can be XML, JSON, or some other format. The example in Chapter 1, "Implementing and Consuming Your First Service," uses a RESTful approach with JSON-formatted messages.

While communication between services often occurs in the form of HTTP-based methods, messaging in general isn't limited to HTTP. In fact, Ruby has a built-in method of communicating between processes, which could be separate services, called Distributed Ruby (or DRb for short). Another messaging standard is the more recent BERT-RPC (http://bert-rpc.org) and its associated implementation Ernie (http://github .com/mojombo/ernie), which power GitHub. Other HTTP-based methods include XML-RPC and JSON-RPC.

Synchronous Versus Asynchronous Messaging

Messaging can occur in the form of synchronous or asynchronous communication. When talking about messaging systems in this book, synchronous messaging refers to the following scenario:

1. Client makes a request (sending a message).

2. Server receives the request.

3. Server performs whatever task the message is requesting, during which time both the client and server are blocked and waiting.

4. Server sends response back to the waiting client.

5. Client is free to continue processing.

   Asynchronous messaging looks like this:

1. Client makes a request (sending a message).

2. Server receives the request.

3. Server queues the message to be processed by some other thread or process.

4. Server sends a response back to the waiting client.

5. Client is free to continue processing.

   There are a few important things to note about these two different flows. First, in the synchronous model, the actual processing occurs so that a response can be sent back to the client that contains the result of that work. Second, during the synchronous processing, the client and server are tied up waiting for responses. Most servers can handle multiple clients simultaneously, but the client is waiting.

In the asynchronous model, the server doesn't actually perform the work while the client waits. Instead, it tells someone else to process the message and instantly hands back a response to the client. The advantage is that the server can usually handle more messages per second, and the client is no longer tied up and waiting for the processing to occur. The disadvantage is that the client does not know the result of the processing. Thus, transactions are not possible in the asynchronous model of communication.

Synchronous and *asynchronous* can also refer to how clients or servers handle communication. Chapter 6, "Connecting to Services," touches on this. With respect to messaging, *synchronous* and *asynchronous* refer to whether the message is processed while the client waits or whether it gets put onto a queue for processing while a response is sent back to the client.

Queues

Queues are the simple first-in, first-out (FIFO) data structure. Messages go into a queue and are pulled out of the queue in the order in which they were inserted. Using queues is the standard method for creating an asynchronous messaging system. When the messaging server gets a message, it places it on a queue for processing.

Message Formats

When building a messaging-based application, a message format must be selected. There are many different formats. SOAP was mentioned earlier as a format popular with Java-based SOA. Some APIs use XML with schemas defined by the programmer. DRb uses Ruby's `Marshal` class to create its message format. BERT uses a message format pulled from the programming language Erlang.

The general goal of message formats is to serialize some object so that it can be deserialized and manipulated by the message processor. JSON offers a simple serialization standard that can be used across many languages. In addition to its ubiquity, its ease of use makes it ideal to work with. Further, the C-based Ruby libraries for working with JSON make it very fast to parse. For these reasons, this book uses JSON for all messages.

RabbitMQ and AMQP

RabbitMQ is an open source implementation of AMQP, short for Advanced Message Queuing Protocol. AMQP is an open standard for messaging middleware. There are multiple implementations of AMQP, but RabbitMQ is a mature and well-tested solution with regular improvements. The AMQP standard was developed at multiple financial firms that have very demanding messaging needs. It was designed from the ground up to be quick and flexible.

The following sections don't cover the full AMQP spec but only the parts that are important for designing messaging-based services. The major concepts covered are queues, exchanges and bindings, and durability. A fuller description of AMQP can be found in the published spec at http://www.amqp.org/confluence/display/AMQP/ AMQP+Specification.

Queues in RabbitMQ

Queues in RabbitMQ are very much like queues in other messaging systems. First, to create the queue, a call must be made from a client to the server. The call to create a queue is an idempotent operation, so it can be made many times. Once created, messages can be published to a queue, and workers can pull messages off the queue.

One area where AMQP diverges from normal server work queues is in how messages are pulled from the queue. The optimal mode of operation for reading messages from a queue is by creating a consumer. This equates to a process that reads messages from the queue. However, the process is different in AMQP in that the consumer calls out to the server and creates a subscription. Now, while the consumer is running, the server automatically pushes messages from the queue asynchronously to the process.

Exchanges and Bindings

Exchanges represent the layer of messaging that really starts to differentiate AMQP from more basic queuing systems. An exchange can be viewed as a kind of message router. Messages are published to the exchange, which forwards those messages to queues based on the exchange type and bindings. Further, each message has a routing key. This key is matched against the bindings. Queues can have multiple bindings to one or more exchanges.

Exchanges are a little different than a typical router. A router directs a packet through a system. An exchange copies messages to all queues that have bindings that match up.

With the basics out of the way, it's time to go over the different types of exchanges. The three primary exchange types are the direct, fanout, and topic exchanges.

Direct Exchanges

The direct exchange routes messages based on a simple rule: Does the routing key of the message match exactly the routing key in the binding? Figure 11.1 shows an example of what that might look like.

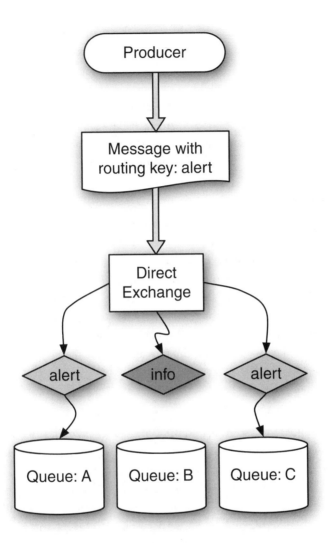

Figure 11.1   A direct exchange sends messages to exact matches.

In Figure 11.1, a producer publishes a message to an exchange. *Producer* is the word in AMQP lingo that refers to the processes that publish messages to exchanges. The message published to the exchange has the routing key alert. The contents of the message are not important for the exchange or queue. Only the routing key and the exchange type matter.

A direct exchange looks at each queue bound to it and checks the routing key on the binding against the routing key of the message. In Figure 11.1, queues A and C are both bound to the exchange with the key `alert`. Copies of the message are put in each of those queues. Meanwhile, queue B does not get a copy because it is bound with the key `info`.

This simplified example shows how direct exchanges work when a queue has only a single binding. It's worth remembering that queues can have multiple bindings to one or more exchanges. For example, queue A could have a binding to the direct exchange for messages with the key `alert` and another binding for messages with the key `info`. Keys are defined by the producers of messages.

Fanout Exchanges

The fanout exchange has very simple rules for how to route messages. It sends messages to every queue bound to it, regardless of the key. Thus, when a producer publishes a message to a fanout exchange, no routing key should be attached to the message. Figure 11.2 shows the operation of a fanout exchange.

The example in Figure 11.2 shows that a message published to a fanout exchange is sent to every queue bound to that exchange. The advantage of a fanout exchange is that it is extremely fast. It doesn't need to compare routing keys; it simply has to go through each bound queue and send the message.

Topic Exchanges

The topic exchange offers the greatest power and flexibility. Its rules for routing messages add the ability to use wildcards in bindings. To see how these wildcards are used, a more formal definition of a binding must first be created. Formally, a binding key is defined as a routing key with zero or more tokens separated by a dot (.). A token, on the other hand, is simply a string of characters.

The wildcard operators introduced by the topic exchange are # and *, and they can be used in place of tokens. The # specifies a match with zero or more tokens. The * specifies a match of exactly one token. This is a little different from regular expressions, where * specifies zero or more characters and ? specifies exactly one character.

Queues binding to a topic exchange can use this functionality or mimic the behavior of direct and fanout exchanges. To bind a queue to a topic exchange and have it behave like a direct exchange, you simply specify a binding that has exactly the key you want to match. To mimic the behavior of a fanout exchange and get every message published to the exchange, you simply bind with #, which routes every message to the bound queue. Figure 11.3 shows some examples of the message routing that topic exchanges provide.

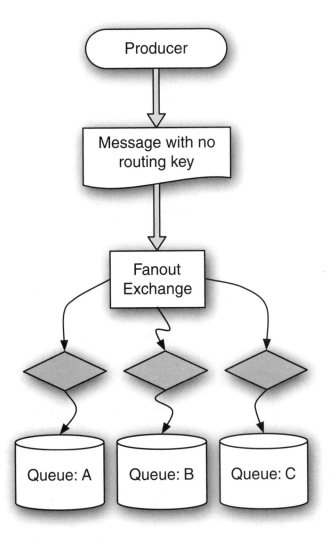

Figure 11.2 A fanout exchange sends messages to all bound queues.

Figure 11.3 shows some possible bindings that would match against a message with the routing key update.name.address. Queue A is bound with #, which gets every message published to the exchange. Queue B is bound with update.#, which states that it wants all messages that have update as the first token. Finally, Queue C is bound with *.name.*, which states that it wants all messages that have name as the second token.

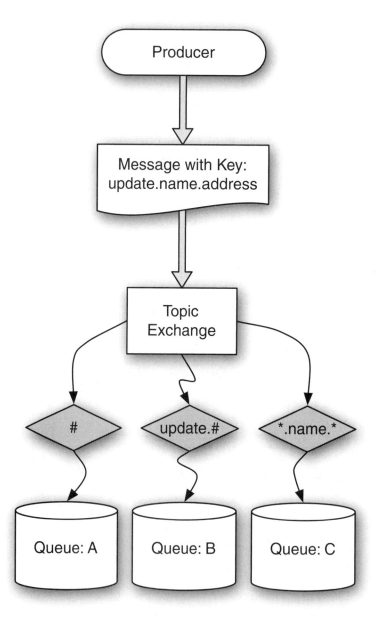

Figure 11.3 A topic exchange sends messages based on patterns.

Two more interesting examples can be drawn from this type of routing key. For example, say that the first token represents an operation such as update, create, or destroy. The tokens after the first can represent the fields that were included in the operation. The message would include the old and new values of the fields in the operation. Thus, if you wanted to get messages for any modification that includes the name field, you could bind with `#.name.#`, which means "zero or more tokens with a name token followed by zero or more tokens." To get messages only concerning updates to the name field, you bind with `update.#.name.#`.

The topic exchange is the most powerful of the three exchange types covered here. It could be used entirely in place of direct and fanout exchanges. However, the performance of direct and fanout exchanges is generally better. Which type of exchange is best depends on the setup. The smaller the number of bindings on an exchange, the less performance is an issue. As you add more bindings to an exchange, more checks must be performed for each incoming message. For this reason, it is sometimes a good idea to create multiple exchanges or one for each service that requires messaging capabilities.

Durability and Persistence

Durability refers to the ability for exchanges or queues to survive server restarts or crashes. *Persistence* refers to whether messages will be kept on disk and thus able to survive server restarts or crashes. In RabbitMQ, durability can be set on the queues and exchanges, while persistence can be set on the messages. In addition, consumers can be configured to tell the server that an acknowledgment for message processing is required. Which combination you want depends on the processing needs.

Durable Exchanges and Queues

Exchanges and queues that are marked as durable still exist after a restart. However, it is important to note that just because a queue is durable does not mean that the messages in the queue are also durable (or persistent). It is also worth noting that if an exchange is marked as durable, only durable queues can be bound to the exchange and vice versa.

Persistent Messages

Messages can be marked as persistent. This means that the messaging server writes a copy to disk and keeps it around until it is pushed off to a consumer. If a message is not persistent, it exists only in memory and disappears if there is a server restart before the message can be processed. Generally, persistence slows performance, so it is recommended only in situations where persistence is a requirement.

Message Acknowledgments

In AMQP, messages are pushed to consumers. These pushes generally happen asynchronously, so it is possible for a consumer to have multiple messages waiting to be processed. If the consumer process experiences a crash, the messages on the consumer can be lost. For this reason, it's a good idea to turn on acknowledgments. To do this, the consumer tells the AMQP server that each message sent must be acknowledged. If it is not acknowledged and the consumer dies, the AMQP server pushes the message to the next available consumer.

There are many different settings in AMQP, and it can be difficult to understand them all together. When you use the messaging server to convey data that has not been saved elsewhere, it is a good idea to have durable exchanges and queues, have persistent messages, and have acknowledgments turned on. If data is being stored elsewhere and the messages can be resent after a critical server failure, a good configuration may be to have durable exchanges and queues, memory-only messages, and acknowledgments. It's a good idea to have acknowledgments turned on at all times to guard against the possibility of a consumer having an unexpected restart or crash. The AMQP server will generally be more reliable than the consumers.

Client Libraries

In the Ruby world, there are two popular client libraries for interacting with AMQP and RabbitMQ: the AMQP Client and Bunny.

The AMQP Client

The AMQP client (http://github.com/tmm1/amqp) was written by Aman Gupta. It is an EventMachine-based client. EventMachine (http://rubyeventmachine.com/) enables asynchronous communication with the RabbitMQ server. This means that messages can be processed (in Ruby code) while messages are pushed from the server to the consumer.

This small example shows the basic usage of the AMQP library:

```
require 'rubygems'
require 'mq'

AMQP.start(:host => "localhost") do
  mq = MQ.new
  topic_exchange = mq.topic("logger", :durable => true)
```

```
mq.queue("logger some_host", :durable => true).bind(
  topic_exchange, :key => "some_host.*").subscribe(
  :ack => true) do |info, message|
    puts message
  end

topic_ exchange.publish("some exception message",
  :key => "some_host.some_service")
end
```

The call to AMQP.start starts the EventMachine reactor loop and opens a connection to the RabbitMQ server on the localhost. EventMachine is based on the reactor pattern, which processes I/O (such as network calls) asynchronously.

Once the connection is started, calls can be made to the RabbitMQ server. First, a new instance of MQ is instantiated. This is the primary interface to the API for the AMQP library. Next, a topic exchange named logger is created and set to be durable. Notice that exchanges have names. In this example, the exchange will be a place where error-logging messages are published.

After the exchange is created, a queue can be created and bound. Queues, like exchanges, also have names. In this case, the example uses a descriptive name, with the first term specifying what exchange it is primarily bound to and which messages it is processing. It is bound to the topic exchange that was just created with the key pattern some_host.*. The pattern in this logging example is that the first term represents the host name, and the second term is the process or server that is reporting a log message. Thus, this binding logs any errors from some_host.

subscribe is then called on that binding with a passed block. The block is called when messages come in from the RabbitMQ server. The block gets information including the routing key and the actual message body.

Finally, a test message is published to the logger exchange. Because the routing key matches the pattern for the subscription, the message is routed to the waiting consumer. This represents most of the basic functionality of the AMQP client library.

AMQP is a very performant library due to its use of EventMachine. However, it can be difficult to work with. This is especially true when you have a process such as a web application server that doesn't run EventMachine (for example, Unicorn) and needs to publish to an exchange from the application. This is a very common use case. When a user request comes in that requires background processing, a message would usually be published to an exchange. So while AMQP's performance makes it ideal for writing consumers, it is a little difficult to work with for producers that run inside a web application.

Bunny: An AMQP Client Library

Bunny (http://github.com/celldee/bunny) is a synchronous AMQP client library written by Chris Duncan. Much of the code for handling the actual AMQP protocol comes from the original AMQP client covered earlier. Due to Bunny's synchronous nature, many users may find it easier to work with than the AMQP client. When calls are made to the RabbitMQ server, the process blocks until a response comes back. While this may sound slow, it is actually quite fast in practice due to RabbitMQ's excellent performance. Response times are usually under a millisecond.

This Bunny example accomplishes the same things as the earlier AMQP example:

```
require 'rubygems'
require 'bunny'

client = Bunny.new(:host => "localhost")
client.start

exchange = client.exchange("logger", :type => :topic,
  :durable => true)
queue = Bunny::Queue.new(client, "logger some_host",
  :durable => true)

queue.bind(exchange, :key => "some_host.*")

exchange.publish("some error message",
  :key => "some_host.some_service")

queue.subscribe(:ack => true) do |msg|
  puts msg[:payload]
end
```

In this example, first a connection is made to the RabbitMQ server. With Bunny, a call must be made to start before any requests can be made to the server. Just as in the AMQP example, the exchange is declared, the queue is declared, the queue is bound to the exchange, and a message is published. Each of these calls is made synchronously, and the process blocks while waiting for a response from the server.

The final part of the script shows how a consumer is created. The call to `subscribe` blocks. Each time a message comes in, the block is called. When the block completes, an acknowledgment is sent to the server that the message has been processed. The process then blocks again until another message is pushed to the consumer, or the process calls the block with the next message if the message has already been pushed from the server to the consumer. Consumers can buffer a number of messages before the server stops pushing to them automatically.

Synchronous Reads, Asynchronous Writes

Using a flexible and powerful messaging system such as RabbitMQ along with HTTP-based services enables highly scalable architectures. The design pattern I call "synchronous reads, asynchronous writes" (SR/AW) refers to a system that routes all data writes through a messaging system while performing data reads through RESTful HTTP services. The advantages of building in this architecture are twofold. First, it is highly scalable due to the decoupling of the data store from user writes. Second, it enables event-based processing within an overall system.

HTTP-Based Reads

Data reads generally must be synchronous due to the fact that a user is waiting on a response. This also means that reads must occur quickly. The good news is that data reads are much easier to optimize than data writes. They are easily cached, which means that in a well-designed system, Ruby processes can be skipped entirely. (Caching is covered in greater detail in Chapter 8, "Load Balancing and Caching.")

The important part of the read portion of SR/AW is that data should reside in separate services. These services can then be optimized with individual caching strategies. With good caching, it is trivial to serve a few thousand requests per second.

Messaging-Based Writes

While data reads must be synchronous, data writes often do not have the same requirement. This is ideal because writes are often much more difficult to optimize than reads, due to their need to write to disk. Routing data writes through AMQP also enables event-based processing. Briefly, this is a system that can trigger events based on changes in data. This comes in handy when replicating data across services to make fully cached data reads easy. Before we dive in to an example, there are two exchanges the write system uses that should be mentioned: the write exchange and the notify exchange.

The Write Exchange

The write exchange is a fanout exchange through which all data writes are routed. At a minimum, there must be a single consumer that pulls data off a queue bound to the exchange and writes it to a data store of some kind. This data store represents the primary responsibility holder and canonical storage of the data being written in. This consumer is in turn responsible for sending out notifications to the notify exchange.

The Notify Exchange

The notify exchange is a topic exchange that receives published events that result from writes sent through the write exchange. A good convention is to use routing keys in the following pattern: `<create|update|destroy>.<field1>.<field2>.<field3>`. The first token represents the operation that was performed on the data. The following tokens indicate which fields were changed by the write. The message should have the following format:

```
{
  "id" : "...",
  <field1>    : {"old" : "...", "new" : "..."},
  <field2>    : {"old" : "...", "new" : "..."}
}
```

The message includes the ID of the written object and the new and old values for the fields. In the case of a previously null value, the `"old"` value would be omitted from the message. This section lays out the basic structure of the asynchronous writes system. The following section provides an example to help highlight a possible use of this notification system.

Receiving Notifications

In the social feed reader application, users can follow other users to get updates on their activities. This can include subscribing to a new feed, voting or commenting on an entry, or following another user. An activity service could be built that optimizes storage and reads of these different activity streams. This activity stream service would not be the primary holder of the data. It would simply act as an optimized data store for returning results for activity streams for specific users. The asynchronous writes system make the replication of the data fairly painless.

Figure 11.4 shows the full lifecycle of the asynchronous writes design. In the example, a user is following another user. The Rails application publishes a message to the `user.write` exchange. The message contains data with the "following" user ID and the "followed" user ID. The write exchange is a fanout, so that message has no associated routing key. The message is put into every connected queue, one of which is the queue for user data. The user data consumer is just a process running on a server that can write to the backend user data store.

The user data consumer saves the update and sends out a notification to the `user.notify` exchange. Remember, the notify exchange is a topic exchange, so the message should have a routing key. In this case, the routing key shows that it was an update operation to `follows`. The message includes the ID of the user that was updated and the new data. This case is a little special with regard to the notification. With other types of fields, it makes sense to include the old data. However, with `follows`, you probably wouldn't want to push out the full collection of IDs that a user is following each time. So this update includes only the new user.

Now it's time for the `user.notify` exchange to push out these changes to all the queues that are interested. The activity service that is responsible for keeping an optimized data store for retrieving activity has a binding to listen for `follows` updates. It has bindings for new comments, votes, and subscriptions as well. The exchange matches the key against the binding, and the queue now has the message. The activity service can consume the message and write the activity to its data store. During normal system operation, all this would happen in under a second. However, during times of unexpected load, it can take longer, but the overall system performance would look as though it is just as responsive as during low-traffic times.

The asynchronous writes design can be particularly useful when you're creating services that are responsible for optimizing specific portions of an application's data. The write exchange gives a system as a whole the flexibility to manage spikes in write traffic. The notify exchange enables replication to other services to occur without requiring an update to the primary data writer. The only requirement is that the primary data owner write notification messages. Another service can bind to that exchange and pull off whatever data it is interested in.

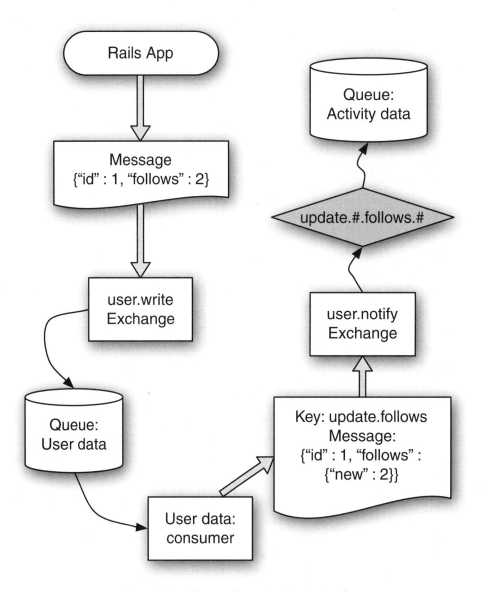

Figure 11.4   The asynchronous write event cycle.

The CAP Theorem

In 2000, Eric Brewer gave a talk on the trade-offs in designing distributed systems. He stated that the trade-offs occur between three primary design goals: consistency, availability, and partition tolerance. Brewer stated that in distributed systems, only two of these requirements can be strictly maintained. Two years later, this was proven as the CAP (consistency, availability, and partition tolerance) theorem.

Consistency refers to data consistency across replicated systems. To maintain a strongly consistent environment, all data stores must reflect the same state. Take, for example, two databases that are replicated together. To remain consistent, each must be able to replicate data writes to the other before a transaction (or a write) can be completed. A typical monolithic database such as MySQL or PostgreSQL resides on a single server and offers a strongly consistent data store.

Availability is a system's availability to serve requests. With a single server, the availability is entirely dependent on that server. This is known as the "single point of failure" problem. With multiple servers, availability can be maintained as long as one server continues to run. However, this assumes that every server is able to serve a request. This is sometimes the case, but not always. For example, large datasets may be sharded across multiple servers. *Sharding* refers to splitting up the data so different portions go to different servers. If each shard contains only one server, the single point of failure still exists.

Partition tolerance is a system's ability to tolerate breaks in network connectivity—that is, partitions in the network of distributed systems. This is important when looking at data replication. For example, consider two databases that are exact replicas of each other. They are said to be partition tolerant if connectivity between the two of them can be lost but each can continue to serve reads and writes to clients.

Together with partition tolerance, it can be seen that consistency and availability would be impossible to maintain. If a system is partition tolerant and consistent, it might not be available. Once a partition is made, writes can no longer be made to either database because the replica would be inconsistent with the database that took a write. If consistency is enforced, then neither database can take a write when a partition occurs.

Eventual Consistency

Werner Vogels, the CTO of Amazon, proposed a way around the limits of the CAP theorem, with the idea of eventual consistency. That is, it is possible to have partition tolerance and high availability if the consistency requirement is loosened from strongly consistent to eventually consistent.

A system that is eventually consistent can take data writes even when a partition is made. When a write is made to one database, data reads reflect this most recent write. Meanwhile, the replica reflects the older state of the data. When the partition is fixed and network connectivity is restored, the replica can be brought back in sync.

Put more succinctly, eventual consistency is a form of weak consistency that states that if no updates are made to an object, eventually all accesses to that object will return the same value.

Designing Around Consistency

Designing a system that supports eventual consistency takes some effort on the part of an application programmer. Eventually consistent systems do not support transactions. Further, they lack the ability to lock values, which makes it hard to support uniqueness constraints and avoid write collisions.

Field Value Checking

The following scenario is an example of a write collision in an asynchronous writes system. Consider the inventory of a specific book in a store. If one customer orders a book, the count of books in inventory must be reduced by one. In a regular database system, this would mean wrapping in a transaction a read of the book stock count and updating that to the count minus one.

In an SR/AW system, you might read the inventory count and write to the messaging system the count minus one. Meanwhile, another customer could order a book before the first write has gone through. If an update is made, the system would attempt to write the count minus one again. The inventory count at this point would reflect that the system has one more book than is actually in stock.

One method of designing around the transaction/update problem is to write the previous value of the field along with the new value into the write exchange. When the writer gets the message, it can check the previous value in a regular transaction. If an error occurs, the customer can be informed or another process can attempt the operation using current data.

The specific use case of incrementing or decrementing a count by a certain number can be designed around in another way: by including an increment or decrement operator in the write. The consumer specifies the number to increment or decrement by, and the writer that gets messages from the write exchange can perform that increment or decrement in a transaction inside its own system.

Value Uniqueness

Value uniqueness is another property that is difficult to account for in an eventually consistent system. One of the most common use cases for value uniqueness is for user profile paths or user names. For example, selecting a user name for Twitter maps the user name to http://twitter.com/<username>. A couple design strategies in the SR/AW system enable name uniqueness.

The first method for enabling name uniqueness is through a form of optimistic locking. It's not really a lock, but it is optimistic. When a user requests a user name, or some other unique value, the application can make a synchronous request to see if that name is available. If it is, the application publishes the write to the messaging system. When the message gets through the system and the writer attempts to make the write, it verifies uniqueness again. Most likely, the name is still unique. However, if a problem is encountered, the user must be notified to select a new name.

The process of requesting a name and either succeeding or failing can occur through the messaging system in under a few milliseconds. The timing is less important than designing around the possibility that there might be a failure that the user will have to be notified of. Most of the time this is successful, so it may be a strategy that works well.

The second method to enforce uniqueness is through a lock service. A synchronous HTTP-based service can be created to hand out locks. In the case of a user name, it would request a lock with the scope of a user name for the specific name requested. The lock would issue for some reasonable amount of time (such as less than 5 minutes). Once the lock has been granted, the write can go through. This ensures that no other writers can attempt to write the same name in that time frame. They are not able to obtain a lock.

Transactions

Transactions are a requirement that the asynchronous writes system does not support. The classic example for when a transaction is needed is when making a balance transfer from one account to another. Both modifications must be made within a single transaction, and the business rules usually stipulate that neither account can end the transaction with a negative amount.

One method of designing around this requirement is to implement an optimistic system. The write message should state what amount to move from one account to another. If both accounts end in a valid state, the transaction is successful. However, if one account ends up negative, the user must be notified that a failure has occurred. Note that this has to occur after the user has already left the site or has navigated on to another page. Remember that when the user made the request, the write was queued up, and a response was sent back before the actual write occurred.

The final method to deal with transactions is to bypass the asynchronous writes system for only the updates that absolutely require transactions. A synchronous service (either a database or an HTTP service) can perform the operation that requires a transaction while the user waits for the transaction to complete. This amounts to a service partition strategy where the transactions are partitioned into their own area. Meanwhile, more flexible data can be put into asynchronous writes–based services.

Data Is the API

When you design distributed systems that communicate through messaging queues such as AMQP, the data that passes through becomes a focal point. That is, every service that subscribes to updates from another service gets messages with the raw data. Field names and schema take on greater importance. The data itself becomes the API through which services interact. Specific fields can be expected to behave in a certain way. It is important when building a distributed system to document these design decisions so that they can be programmed against.

The notify exchange example earlier in the chapter shows one example of using the data as an API. The messages in the notify exchange contain the ID and the new and old values of fields. For other services and consumers to interact with this data, the messages should be consistent and known. For example, if there was no previous value (or it was null), the "old" section of the notification would be omitted for that field. The data in the notification messages takes on the importance of being the agreed-upon interface through which other services are notified of data updates.

"Data is the API" is meant to point out the importance of schemas. By nature, an API is something that should not be changed very frequently. Changes in an API force all clients dependent on it to make updates. The data that gets routed through the messaging system should be thought about with a little more care than a standard ActiveRecord model that has very flexible and quickly changing schemas.

Operations on Fields

The earlier section on designing around consistency hinted at one possibility of having the data behave as an API. An example mentions providing an increment or decrement operator. Here is an example of what a message published to the write exchange requesting an increment would look like:

```
{
  "id" : 23,
  "balance.inc" : 678
}
```

The message includes only the ID of the item to be incremented and the amount of the increment. This schema has the increment as a `.inc` addition to the field name. The type of data being incremented is already known because it has its own AMQP exchange. Another option is to create a message that looks like this:

```
{
  "id" : 23,
  "balance" : {"inc" : 678}
}
```

In this message, the operation is specified in the JSON object that is the value for the field. This method provides a little more flexibility and power (for instance, if the old field value was provided to make sure that the new value isn't writing with stale data). This could be accomplished easily with just "old" and "new" keys and values in the object. Ultimately, neither of these situations is more correct than the other. The important thing is to choose one and remain consistent across all services and write exchanges.

Modifications to Field Operations

There are many different ways to specify field operations. One option is to turn the write exchange into a topic exchange and use the routing key to identify field operations. This method cleanly separates the actual data from the operation, but it has the limitation that only one operation can be performed per message.

More operations that might be supported are `add to set`, `delete from set`, `push onto list`, `pop from list`, `queue`, and `dequeue`. The write exchange and the data that passes through it truly becomes an API. All these can be built using whatever code and backend data store makes the most sense. The writer that gets messages from the exchange must be able to handle them, and the HTTP-based interface needs to pull from the data store. The specifics of what powers those can be improved over time.

> **Minimal Writes**
>
> The writes that go into the write exchange should be minimal. That is, they should include only the data that needs to be updated and no more. This saves on overall network traffic and reduces the likelihood of overwriting data from another process.

Conclusion

Messaging provides more than a simple method for performing long-running tasks. With a highly performant messaging system, messaging can be used to achieve a number of goals. The main advantage is that messaging-based writes are able to maintain high performance under bursts of traffic and load. In addition, decoupling the client from the data store enables independent iterations on both the client and server. Finally, the notification system enables event-based processing, which makes it easy to create additional optimized data stores and services as the need arises.

CHAPTER 12

Web Hooks and External Services

Applications that send and receive requests from external services have been such a key factor in the boom of web applications, APIs, and innovation over the past few years that a term has even been coined for this network: the Programmable Web. Applications that rely on resources that are outside a project's or an organization's control bring a level of dynamism with unique challenges for development teams. Some of these traits can change various aspects of how an application should be designed or the level of attention that needs to be paid to how the application performs and behaves if these services are unavailable or otherwise limited.

This chapter provides a broad overview of some of the most important ways to think about solving the challenges associated with external web services. This chapter provides a definition and overview of web hooks, along with examples for implementing both web hook providers and consumers. The chapter also discusses strategies for dealing with external services, queuing systems, and OAuth-delegated authentication. This includes how to manage the effects that the availability or performance (or lack thereof) of an external service may have on the way an application behaves. Where possible, representative projects, libraries, and resources are referenced so that readers can dig deeper into the concepts that may specifically affect their applications and projects.

Web Hooks

Web hooks are essentially callbacks for services. When speaking of callbacks, developers are typically talking about methods or messages that are automatically "fired" on completion of some other process or event. Most web developers are familiar with the typical case of using JavaScript in the browser to handle click, mouse, and other user-initiated events, such as `onClick` and `onMouseOver`.

In the Ruby world, a similar concept is built into ActiveRecord objects. A series of callbacks are fired during the lifecycle events of ActiveRecord objects, including `before_save`, `before_validation`, and `after_validation`, `after_save`.

Suppose there is a resource in an application called `Car`, and the application requires some work to be done after every `Car` is created. These tasks could be initiated using the following code:

```
class Car < ActiveRecord::Base
  after_create :do_work
  def do_work
    # do some work here
  end
end
```

The `after_create` line tells the `Car` class to call the `do_work` method after the create occurs. Web hooks take this concept of callbacks, or event-based programming, and move it into the sphere of web services.

Let's look at an example that highlights the motivation for the use of web hooks. Say that an organization requires that an event be created in its calendar system every time a new milestone is added to a separate project management system. The typical way to accomplish this is to build a client plugin for the calendar system that polls the project management system for new milestones. This process could run nightly, hourly, or every five minutes. It could pull new milestones into the calendar as they are found. When it comes time to scale this model to thousands of calendars or hundreds of project management systems, the polling method quickly becomes unmanageable. Massive amounts of wasted resources will be used when the calendar system polls the project management system and finds no updates. Further, the updated data will always lag a little bit behind, based on the polling interval.

Web hooks represent a different way of thinking about the problem of exposing data to clients. By focusing on the events that would trigger a client's interest, web hooks turn the model on its head. In the web hooks model, the project management system implements a web hook callback that posts data to a predetermined URI whenever new milestones are entered. The calendar system implements a service endpoint specified by a URI that receives these callbacks and takes the appropriate action (in this case, entering a new event in the calendar). When no action is taking place, both systems are idle, and no resources are wasted on unnecessary polling.

PubSubHubbub

PubSubHubbub (http://code.google.com/p/pubsubhubbub/) is a decentralized protocol that extends the Atom and RSS protocols to include support for web hooks. The general idea behind PubSubHubbub is that Atom/RSS feed servers can direct potential subscribers to "hubs." Instead of continually polling the feed, clients can subscribe to the hub and be notified via web callback when updates are published. The following sequence shows how PubSubHubbub operates:

1. A client makes a request to the Atom feed at http://pauldix.net/atom.xml.

2. The client parses Atom XML and finds the URI for the hub.

3. The client makes a request to the hub (at http://pauldix.net/hub) to be subscribed to the Atom feed (http://pauldix.net/atom.xml), with notifications sent to http://trottercashion.com/notify.

4. When the Atom feed is updated, the server (or publisher) sends a notification to the hub.

5. The hub gets the Atom feed and sends the update to all the the subscribed clients.

6. The subscriber (http://trottercashion.com/notify) gets the notification from the hub.

This example shows one client subscribing to an Atom feed to be notified of updates. PubsubHubbub uses the word *topic* to refer to the Atom feed URL. What occurs in step 4 is referred to as a *ping* sent to the hub by the server. Note that anyone can host a hub. There is no requirement that the hub for http://pauldix.net/atom.xml be hosted at the same domain. There is a competing standard in RSS called rssCloud (http://rsscloud.org) that does nearly the same thing.

Receiving Web Hooks

A continuous integration server is a good example of where web hooks can be used. A continuous integration server runs an application's test or build suite whenever changes are made to the code base. Thus, a web hook can be used to notify the integration server of an update to the code.

Following is an example of how this works with the post-receive hooks web callbacks provided by Github (http://help.github.com/post-receive-hooks/) and the continuous integration server Integrity (http://integrityapp.com). Post-receive hooks can be enabled in Github by going to the project home page as a logged-in user, clicking Admin, and then setting the URL. In Integrity, the post-receive hooks callback URL should be set to `http://yourserver/github/token`, where `yourserver` is the public host name of the server Integrity is running on, and `token` is a string that has been set in Integrity's configuration options.

Once this URL is set in the repository's options, Github POSTs a web hook in the form of a JSON payload to the Integrity server after every changeset is pushed. As of this writing, the payload contains details about the repository and a list of the commits in the changeset that is being pushed. The following is an example of a payload provided in Github's documentation:

```
{
  "before": "5aef35982fb2d34e9d9d4502f6ede1072793222d",
  "repository": {
    "url": "http://github.com/defunkt/github",
    "name": "github",
    "description": "You're lookin' at it.",
    "watchers": 5,
    "forks": 2,
    "private": 1,
    "owner": {
      "email": "chris@ozmm.org",
      "name": "defunkt"
    }
  },
  "commits": [
    {
      "id": "41a212ee83ca127e3c8cf465891ab7216a705f59",
```

```json
      "url": "http://github.com/defunkt/github/commit/41a212",
      "author": {
        "email": "chris@ozmm.org",
        "name": "Chris Wanstrath"
      },
      "message": "okay i give in",
      "timestamp": "2008-02-15T14:57:17-08:00",
      "added": ["filepath.rb"]
    },
    {
      "id": "de8251ff97ee194a289832576287d6f8ad74e3d0",
      "url": "http://github.com/defunkt/github/commit/de8251",
      "author": {
        "email": "chris@ozmm.org",
        "name": "Chris Wanstrath"
      },
      "message": "update pricing a tad",
      "timestamp": "2008-02-15T14:36:34-08:00"
    }
  ],
  "after": "de8251ff97ee194a289832576287d6f8ad74e3d0",
  "ref": "refs/heads/master"
}
```

The body of the callback is essentially a JSON-formatted payload of what was once a Ruby object. This data can be marshaled back into a Ruby object or parsed into a hash by any application that needs to act on it.

Integrity is a lightweight Sinatra application. The following code matches incoming post-receive hooks callback requests:

```ruby
post "/:endpoint/:token" do |endpoint, token|
  pass unless endpoint_enabled?
  halt 403 unless token   == endpoint_token
  halt 400 unless payload =  endpoint_payload

  BuildableProject.call(payload).each do |b|
    b.build
```

```
      end.size.to_s
  end
```

When Integrity receives the POST request from Github, it does a quick check to make sure the endpoint (Github) is enabled and that the token matches the configuration. Then it passes the payload information to the class responsible for running the build.

Using web hooks to notify an integration server shows how simple and powerful web hooks are. Having just one push done in a day triggers only a single call instead of the hundreds that a poll-based method would use. For event-driven interactions, using web hooks is much more efficient than constantly polling another server to look for changes. The number of web hook implementations out in the wild is still relatively small, but services that are providing them as part of their applications are providing their customers with another powerful tool to implement innovative applications.

Providing Web Hooks

To show an example of providing web hooks in an application, let's jump back to the hypothetical example of a project management tool that needs to send milestone dates to a calendar. Because ActiveRecord already has built-in callbacks around the object lifecycle, this provides a simple place to hook in and provide the behavior the application needs:

```ruby
class Project < ActiveRecord::Base
  has_many :milestones
end

class Milestone < ActiveRecord::Base
  belongs_to :project
  after_save :send_callback

  def send_callback
    if project.callback_uri
      Typhoeus::Request.post(callback_uri,
        :body => self.to_json)
    end
  end
end
```

This implementation has a few issues that need to be dealt with at some point in the near future. First, the project has only one potential callback URI. Second, the web hook POST happens within the request lifecycle when a milestone is created. Adding multiple callback URIs is a simple modification that can be accomplished with the addition of a WebhookCallback model and some slight changes to the existing models:

```
class Project < ActiveRecord::Base
  has_many :milestones
  has_many :webhook_callbacks
end

class WebhookCallback < ActiveRecord::Base
  belongs_to :project

  def post(payload)
    Typhoeus::Request.post(callback_uri,
      :body => payload)
  end
end

class Milestone < ActiveRecord::Base
  belongs_to :project
  after_save :send_callbacks

  def send_callbacks
    project.webhook_callbacks.each do |callback|
      callback.post(self.to_json)
    end
  end
end
```

Posting callbacks within the normal request lifecycle (that is, while the user is waiting for the application to respond) is not desirable in most production applications. The method for moving work outside the request lifecycle is to use a queue or messaging system to communicate with a background worker.

Next we'll build on the introduction in Chapter 11, "Messaging." A few simple modifications to the WebhookCallback class allow the application to write data to a queue on a RabbitMQ server, using the Bunny library discussed in Chapter 11.

Anything that is written into the queue is picked up by workers. Workers can be run on any machine that has access to the queue, and multiple workers can be run and can consume messages out of the queue:

```ruby
class WebhookCallback < ActiveRecord::Base
  belongs_to :project

  def queue
    # we should already have an open connection to the AMQP
    # server so that the overhead of connecting is not felt
    # within the request life-cycle
    BUNNY_INSTANCE.queue('milestone_callbacks' )
  end

  def post(payload)
    message = {
                :callback_uri => callback_uri,
                :payload => payload
              }
    queue.publish(message.to_json)
  end
end
```

Enough information is pushed into the queue (in this case, the destination URI for the callback and the payload that should be sent) that a generic worker can pick the message off the queue and accomplish the task. Applications can marshal or serialize Ruby objects directly into the queue as YAML or JSON, but the more generic the message is, the better.

Strategies for Dealing with Failure

A couple of basics need to be dealt with when implementing a delayed work and queuing strategy in an application. It is sometimes prudent to track the number of attempts for any job, when a job is run, when a job has failed, when a job is locked (being executed), or which worker is running a job.

Retry logic is vital when working with external services. If the third-party service that data is being posted to is unreliable, or if the network in between the two applications is unreliable, a retry mechanism can ensure that a single failure does not prevent the web hook callback from being issued. When designing retry logic, it's best to have an exponential back off on the time. For instance, when a failure occurs, the worker should retry two seconds later, then four, then eight, and so on until some threshold has been reached. If the remote server has still not responded after a reasonable number of retries, an error should be logged or the job should be placed into an error state so that it can be addressed again later.

Web hook callback receivers should be idempotent. That is, if a callback is called once and done again, the second call does not have a different effect. This is common in the RESTful design paradigm and an important aspect of web API design. Remember that the HTTP verbs GET, PUT, DELETE, and HEAD are all idempotent actions. Designing callback receivers to be idempotent ensures that if a worker attempts to run a callback and fails partway through, another worker can run the callback again without adverse consequences.

Job deletion should be the last action a worker takes on an item. This assumes that the jobs are idempotent, but a worker should be able to fail until the last possible moment without hindering the ability of another worker to retry the job. Tangentially, recording failures (perhaps in an independent queue, database table, or log file) can provide a level of forensic insight into why jobs are failing and may allow some of those failures to be worked around. AMQP-based queues have the concept of acknowledgment built in. Messages are deleted from the queue when they are read but are reinserted directly back into the queue if acknowledgment is on and the client does not acknowledge receipt of the message.

OAuth

While web hooks provide a method for services to communicate with each other quickly about updates in their data, OAuth provides a method for users to give services access to their data. OAuth is an open protocol that allows API authorization for desktop and web applications. More specifically, OAuth enables users of one service to allow other applications to access their data without the need to reveal or store their account credentials. OAuth accomplishes this by sending the user to the service to authenticate while the service creates an authorization token for each consumer application. The user or data provider can then revoke the token at any future point.

Implementing an OAuth Consumer

Following is a brief tutorial that steps through the OAuth flow, with some sample code for using the OAuth gem to connect to the Twitter OAuth service. It shows how to connect to an OAuth-protected API from your web application on behalf of a user.

First, the new consumer application needs to be registered with the service that is going to be connected to, in this case Twitter, and a consumer key must be obtained. Go to http://twitter.com/oauth_clients to start this process. Figure 12.1 shows the application registration page.

The important things here are setting the application type to Browser to ensure that users are redirected back to the application after authorization at Twitter, and the callback URL, which is where users will be sent.

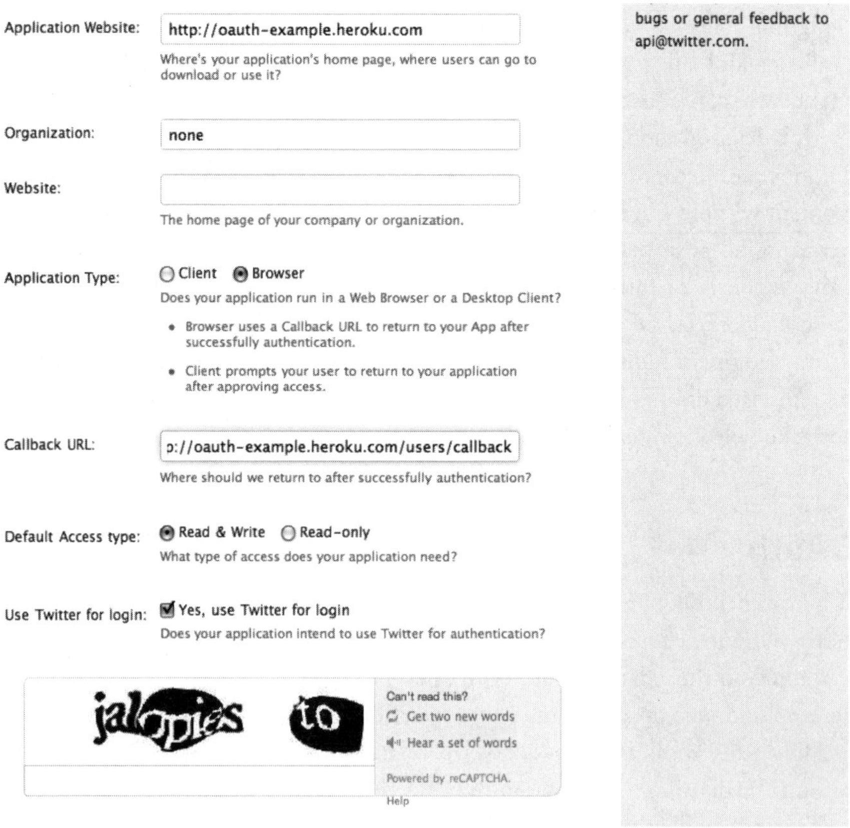

Figure 12.1   The Twitter OAuth consumer application registration.

After you create the application, a confirmation page appears, as in Figure 12.2. The confirmation page shows the consumer token and secret that will be used later.

Now you set up the OAuth gem and client. The official fork can be found at http://github.com/mojodna/oauth:

```
gem install oauth

# In the app. Use the key and secret obtained
# when registering the application
@consumer = OAuth::Consumer.new(APP_KEY,APP_SECRET,
   :site => "http://twitter.com")
```

Application Details

OAuth Book Example by none

This is an example implementation to show usage of the Twitter OAuth service.

created by Jake Howerton - **read and write access by default – 0 users**

Edit Application Settings   Reset Consumer Key/Secret

Consumer key

9VzoUvAWSZSyirOf7D4miw

Consumer secret

4qp98DWZs7EBDfbLj7LuhER9lovmcxjKXwCWKeO2c

Request token URL

http://twitter.com/oauth/request_token

Access token URL

http://twitter.com/oauth/access_token

Authorize URL

http://twitter.com/oauth/authorize

*We support hmac-sha1 signatures. We do not support the plaintext signature method.

Welcome to the Developer Beta of the Twitter Application Platform! We're just getting started, but we thought we'd start releasing components that will help you, the developers, connect your users with the world, right now.

For starters, we're allowing you to both register your application here, as well as providing an improved Authentication System, OAuth. To read more about how this help both you and your users, please visit http://oauth.net.

Enjoy! And please report any bugs or general feedback to api@twitter.com.

Figure 12.2   Twitter OAuth consumer application registration confirmation and credentials.

The first step in the process is retrieving what OAuth calls the request token from the provider (Twitter). This token is sent along with the user as the user authenticates so that the provider can identify the application that is being authorized:

```
@request_token = @consumer.get_request_token(
  :auth_callback => APP_CALLBACK_URL)

session[:request_token] = @request_token
```

This request token will be exchanged later for an authorization token. Be sure to set the callback URL in place of APP_CALLBACK_URL. The request token needs to be stored somewhere while the user leaves the site to authorize. In this example, it is being stored in the user's session.

Next, you redirect the user to http://twitter.com to authorize the connection:

```
redirect_to @request_token.authorize_url
```

The authorize URL that the user is redirected to looks something like http://twitter .com/oauth/authorize?oauth_token=fkmutXA.

The user needs to authenticate with Twitter and agree to authorize the app, as shown in Figure 12.3.

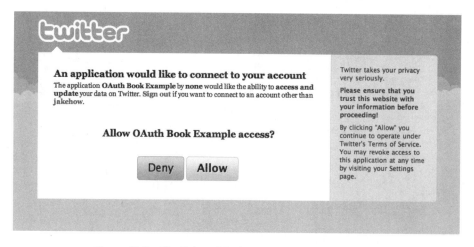

Figure 12.3   The Twitter OAuth access authorization screen.

After authorization, the user is redirected back to the application through the callback URL that was set. The application should then trade the request token for an access token and store it for future use:

```
@request_token = session[:request_token]
@access_token = @request_token.get_access_token(
  :oauth_verifier => params[:oauth_verifier])

# store it for the current user
@user.update (:twitter_token => @access_token.token,
  :twitter_secret => @access_token.secret)
```

In the future, the access token will need to be reconstructed to perform other actions:

```
consumer = Oauth::Consumer.new(APP_KEY, APP_SECRET,
  :site => "http://twitter.com")

access_token = OAuth::AccessToken.new(consumer,
  @user.twitter_token, @user.twitter_secret)
```

Using the access token, the application can now retrieve data or write data to the user's Twitter account as long as the token and account are valid.

Implementing an OAuth Provider

An application needs to implement a few features in order to provide access to its resources via OAuth:

- Developers need to be able to register new applications to receive consumer key/secret pairs.
- Users need to be able to approve, manage, and revoke tokens that have been issued against their account.
- The application needs to be able to authorize access to resources when presented with a token.

Luckily, there is a full implementation that provides these basic features out of the box for Rails applications. The plugin is compatible only with Rails 2.x as of this writing,

but it should be adaptable to newer versions relatively easily. The code is available at
http://github.com/pelle/oauth-plugin:

```
# Install the gem

gem install oauth-plugin

# Add it to the Rails environment
config.gem 'oauth-plugin'
# Run the bundled generator
script/generate oauth_provider
```

The generator spits out several models, most importantly ConsumerToken,
ClientApplication, OAuthToken, and OAuthNonce, along with a migration for these
new tables, some default views, and the following routes:

```
map.resources :oauth_clients

map.test_request '/oauth/test_request',
  :controller => 'oauth',
  :action => 'test_request'
map.access_token '/oauth/access_token',
  :controller => 'oauth',
  :action => 'access_token'
map.request_token '/oauth/request_token',
  :controller => 'oauth',
  :action => 'request_token'
map.authorize '/oauth/authorize',
  :controller => 'oauth',
  :action => 'authorize'
map.oauth '/oauth', :controller => 'oauth', :action =>
  'index'
```

You need to add the following two lines to the user model in the application:

```
has_many :client_applications
has_many :tokens, :class_name=>"OauthToken",
```

```
:order=>"authorized_at desc",
:include=>[:client_application]
```

And then you need to run the database migration:

```
# Run the migration
rake db:migrate
```

At this point, the plugin is completely set up. The current implementation assumes that the application uses a RESTful authentication–style authentication plugin and provides filters for allowing OAuth authorization to restricted resources:

```
before_filter :login_or_oauth_required
before_filter :oauth_required
```

These methods authorize and populate `current_user` and other expected conventions from `restful_authentication`, making integration relatively seamless. The views need to be customized to look like they belong in your application, but otherwise, the application is now ready to provide access to consumers as described in the previous section.

Integrating with External Services

Integrating with external services involves consuming data from or sending data to another service. Twitter is one of the best examples of a platform that provides relatively open access as a service to individual developers, other services, and users. Allowing access in this fashion has let these third parties iterate and innovate on Twitter's core platform by providing additional services, features, and applications that are built around and into the various core features that Twitter itself provides. Thus, the Twitter services provide for the examples in the following sections.

Consuming Data

With the background understanding built around using OAuth to authenticate with Twitter, the next logical thing that an application needs to do is grab some data from this service. Consuming data from external services can present unique challenges, but

let's take a look at a basic case in which the application needs to fetch the friend's timeline of the authenticated user:

```
# Reconstructing the AccessToken
consumer = OAuth::Consumer.new(APP_KEY,APP_SECRET,
  :site => "http://twitter.com")
access_token = OAuth::AccessToken.new(consumer,
  @user.twitter_token, @user.twitter_secret)

oauth_params = {:consumer => oauth_consumer,
  :token => access_token}

hydra = Typhoeus::Hydra.new

# Get the user's friends timeline
uri = "http://api.twitter.com/1/statuses/friends_timeline.json"
req = Typhoeus::Request.new(uri, options)
oauth_helper = OAuth::Client::Helper.new(req,
  oauth_params.merge(:request_uri => uri))

# Sign the request
req.headers.merge!({"Authorization" => oauth_helper.header})

# Queue it up and fire it off
hydra.queue(req)
hydra.run

@response = req.response
@response.body # json of timeline
```

This example creates the access token from the user's token and secret. A request
points to the friends timeline of the user. The OAuth parameters are merged into the
request, and it is sent to Twitter. The response is a Typhoeus response object. The
body contains the user's friends timeline in JSON format.

Pushing Data

The quintessential example of pushing data into Twitter is the status update, or tweet. Much of the tool chain necessary to accomplish this action has been dealt with at this point. The only difference is that this request is going to be a POST, with the status message sent along in the params hash:

```
# Reconstructing the AccessToken
consumer = OAuth::Consumer.new(APP_KEY,APP_SECRET,
  :site => "http://twitter.com")
access_token = OAuth::AccessToken.new(consumer,
  @user.twitter_token, @user.twitter_secret)

oauth_params = {:consumer => oauth_consumer,
  :token => access_token}

hydra = Typhoeus::Hydra.new

# Let's send a status update.
uri = "http://twitter.com/statuses/update.json"
req = Typhoeus::Request.new(uri,
  :method => :post,
  :params => {:status => "nyc.rb rocks the party"})

oauth_helper = OAuth::Client::Helper.new(req,
  oauth_params.merge(:request_uri => uri))

# Sign the request
req.headers.merge! ({"Authorization" =>
  oauth_helper.header})

# Queue it up and fire it off
hydra.queue(req)
hydra.run

@response = req.response
@resonse.code # => 200
```

This example sets up the access token, builds a request, and sends it through `hydra`. The response should indicate a 200 code.

The Request Lifecycle

As with web hooks, the examples of consuming and publishing data to external services must take into consideration the issues of failover and performance. Requests to these services should almost never happen within the request lifecycle of a user. However, data from third-party services may not have an immediate time sensitivity like the normal data in an application. Perhaps the application can rely on a `cron` job that runs once an hour and caches data in the application's own database. This would allow all work to be done outside the request, and it would allow results to be pulled directly from the cache instead of being fetched across a public network on every request.

If real-time results are necessary for an application, one strategy is to load the main page content first and have an AJAX widget that checks whether the data is ready. In the background, the application sends a job to a queue that assembles the results. When the data is ready, it can be loaded onto the page through the embedded AJAX widget. If there is a failure, a message can be displayed to the user, or the job can be retried in the background. These strategies are used heavily in complex web applications such as Google's Gmail.

Worker Processes

In order to push interactions with external services outside the request lifecycle, a new piece of infrastructure comes in to play: the worker process. Ideally, worker processes are always-on daemons that monitor the queue and process jobs as required by the application. The following example of building a simple worker daemon uses the Servolux library from Tim Pease. Code for this library is available at http://github.com/TwP/servolux, and it is also available as a gem. This library provides generic wrappers to do many of the common tasks necessary for managing long-running jobs. In the case of building a worker process, Servolux helps manage a pool of child processors that actually do the work.

The worker that you are building here takes the example from the earlier section on pushing data and accomplishes the same task within a worker. This assumes that the application is now pushing JSON with the authorization header and body of the tweet into a RabbitMQ queue called `tweet_callbacks`:

```ruby
module WorkerPool
  # Before we start the server run loop, allocate our pool of
  # child workers and prefork two JobProcessors to execute work.
  def before_starting
    @pool = Servolux::Prefork.new(:module => Worker,
                                  :timeout=> 10)
    @pool.start 2
  end


  # This run loop will be called at a fixed interval by the
  # server thread. If the pool has any child processes that have
  # died or restarted, then the expired PIDs are read from the
  # proc table. If any workers in the pool have reported an
  # error, then display those errors on STDOUT; these are errors
  # raised from the child process that caused the child to
  # terminate. Logic for restarting workers could be implemented
  # here depending on requirements.
  def run
    @pool.reap
    @pool.each_worker do |worker|
      if worker.error
        err = "#{Process.pid} error: #{worker.error.inspect}"
        $stdout.puts err
      end
    end
  end


  # After the server run loop exits, stop all children in pool
  def after_stopping
    @pool.stop
  end
end
```

The WorkerPool module manages a simple pool of workers. In this case, you have set the pool size to two workers in the body of the built-in setup method before_starting. Servolux executes the run method at a specified interval in order to manage the workers and report on any errors that may have occurred in the pool. The specific worker implementation is encapsulated in a module called TweetSender, and the details are shown here:

```
module TweetSender
  # Implement any setup logic here, will be run once
  def before_executing
    @client = Bunny.new(:host => "localhost")
    @client.start
    @queue = @client.queue("tweet_callbacks")
  end



  def after_executing
    # Implement any teardown logic here
    @client.stop
  end

  def hup
    # Cleanup for when the process receives SIGHUP or
    # SIGTERM
    @client.stop if @client
    @thread.wakeup
  end
  alias :term :hup

  # Work goes here, Servolux automatically runs this
  # in a loop
  def execute
    # The :ack => true option tells RabbitMQ to
    # reinsert the message if we do not acknowledge
    # receipt
    msg = @queue.pop(:ack => true)
```

```ruby
    if msg[:payload] && msg[:payload] != :queue_empty
      tweet = JSON.parse(msg[:payload])
      begin
        hydra = Typhoeus::Hydra.new
        uri = "http://twitter.com/statuses/update.json"
        req = Typhoeus::Request.new(uri,
          :method => :post,
          :params => {:status => tweet[:status]})

        # Sign the request
        req.headers.merge!({"Authorization" =>
          tweet[:authorization]})

        # Queue it up and fire it off
        hydra.queue(req)
        hydra.run

        # Send acknowledgment to RabbitMQ on success
        # which will permanently delete message from
        # the queue
        if req.response.code == 200
          delivery_tag = msg[:delivery_details]
            [:delivery_tag]
          @queue.ack(:delivery_tag => delivery_tag)
        end
      end
    end
  end
end
```

The worker has built-in hooks for setup and teardown as well, with the addition of methods that can respond to signals sent to the process. For our purposes, SIGHUP and SIGTERM should be dealt with in the same fashion, but individual implementations can be made for each. The real crux of what happens here occurs in the body of the execute method. Servolux runs this code in a loop until an exception is thrown.

The code pulls one message at a time off the queue and ships it over to the Twitter API, using the method described in the previous section. If it is successful, the queue is sent an acknowledgment, which permanently removes the message from the queue:

```
# Create a new Servolux::Server and augment it with the
# WorkerPool methods. The run loop will be executed every
# 30 seconds by this server.
server = Servolux::Server.new('WorkerPool',
                                   :logger => Logger.new($stdout),
                                   :interval => 30)
server.extend WorkerPool

# Startup the server. The "before_starting" method will be
# called and the run loop will begin executing. This method
# will not return until a SIGINT or SIGTERM is sent to the
# server process.
server.startup
```

Here you are simply loading your custom `WorkerPool` module, setting the interval at which the `run` method will be executed, and starting up the server.

As you might imagine, implementing queues and worker pools to support scaling an application and taking slow writes out of the user's request lifecycle is a significant change and addition to the infrastructure that a team is supporting. These worker pools should be managed and instrumented in much the same way as the actual application servers in order to ensure that they are running and healthy at all times. The example here is relatively generic and would require that additional considerations be dealt with in a live application. This is left for you as an exercise because the actual requirements are unique to the project at hand.

Ensuring Performance and Reliability

Using messaging and work queues to bring external services into in an application is a necessary step in increasing performance and bringing a service-oriented design to fruition. You need to give some thought to how the connections to external services are managed. They should be isolated to ensure that the performance of one service does not have a negative impact on others. For your own APIs that are exposed to the public, you should be careful to ensure their reliable operation. The following sections cover some of the factors you need to take into account when working with and exposing services to the public.

Segregating Queues

Imagine that there is a shipping company that has one warehouse. All trucks deliver packages to this warehouse and pick them up there for delivery elsewhere in a hub-and-spoke system. One day a hurricane destroys the warehouse. All shipping is halted. Queuing systems operate in much the same way as this warehouse and shipping system. Therefore, queues should be segregated to prevent failure. Some common ways that queues can be separated are by feature, by current state of the work, by region, and by customer. When integrating with multiple external services, queues should always be segregated by service. Segregating queues by service allows work to continue even if one service is down. For example, if an application pushes status updates to both Facebook and Twitter, and the work for these tasks both go through the same queue and worker pool, an outage at Twitter will affect the application's ability to send messages to Facebook. Maintaining separate queues for each service ensures that a single failure does not cascade to the rest.

Metrics

Metrics are a window into the operational health of a system. Basic metrics that are important in queuing systems include the size of each queue, the length of time any item spends in the queue before being picked up by a worker, and the rates of ingress and egress. Because queues can sometimes abstract away pain points that customers would normally feel immediately, knowing these simple metrics can put an operations team ahead of issues that may be happening in the system but that customers have not yet noticed. For instance, if the queue of status updates going to Twitter is growing, it may be because the marketing plan is finally working, and users are joining en masse. But a quick comparison with the total time that messages are staying in the queue can help a team instantly distinguish between this situation and something being broken.

Having metrics for services that are exposed within an application is just as important. However, the determination of what to measure is likely to be quite unique. Some API metrics that may matter in an application are usage by geography, usage by customer, usage by time of day, usage by application feature, and internal usage versus external usage. Performance in any of these cases is also important, as is general usage. Keeping track of these metrics can help determine when one part of an application is degrading performance of another unrelated feature or whether a new customer is bringing more load onto the system than capacity can currently support.

Throttling and Quotas

Throttling and quotas refers to the limiting of API access by the number of times the API can be hit by an external consumer. This could come in the form of requests per second/hour/day or number of connections per IP address. Throttling and quotas can be used for preventing abuse (whether intentional or from inept client implementers) that may degrade more legitimate use of services. Or they can be used for providing different classes of service to users and customers.

There are a few Rack middleware–based implementations of throttling, but these examples are from `Rack::Throttle` (http://github.com/datagraph/rack-throttle). `Rack::Throttle` has three strategies built in for throttling client requests.

- **`Rack::Throttle::Interval`**—Sets a specific minimum interval between requests
- **`Rack::Throttle::Hourly`**—Sets a maximum hourly rate
- **`Rack::Throttle::Daily`**—Sets a maximum daily rate

The interval strategy is one of the most useful methods for regular applications. Hours and days are large intervals that may not be able to prevent potential abuse. For instance, an out-of-control client may be able to affect availability of resources in a shorter time period (a couple minutes) without ever hitting the hourly quota.

Because `Rack::Throttle` is a Rack middleware–based implementation, implementing it in a Rack-based application such as Rails or Sinatra is simple:

```
# Setup in config.ru
use Rack::Throttle::Interval,
   :min => 3.0 # seconds required between requests
```

This single directive in your application's `config.ru` file forces every request to go through the throttler to verify that the client can make the request. In a small Sinatra service that serves only a web service API, this is ideal. But this isn't something that you would do for an entire Rails application.

`Rack::Throttle` allows customized choices for counter storage and response codes. *Counter storage* refers to where the counters for a client are kept. For instance, if you set a limit of one request every two seconds, the throttler needs to store the counts of when the client making the request last made a request. Counter storage is usually done in Memcached or some other fast in-memory data store. A customized response code can be given after a user has hit his or her request limit. `Rack::Throttle` can be further customized by subclassing the various throttlers provided.

Conclusion

This chapter provides a whirlwind tour through some of the most important concepts and pitfalls involved in implementing and integrating with external services in real applications. Developers working with and exposing external services have unique needs based on an application's traffic and the complexity of the API. Providing web hooks to other developers enables developers to create highly responsive and performant applications that integrate with others. Authenticating with other external services via OAuth enables an application to request data on behalf of the user while maintaining the user's trust. Finally, when exposing your own APIs, it is important to take into consideration the performance, metrics, and possible throttling that should be done to ensure reliable operation.

Overall, this book discusses a number of tools and techniques for building Ruby and Rails applications that are built from multiple services. Splitting a large application into services can lead to improved performance, scalability, and reliability. It also provides the ability to manage complexity and creates a more robust infrastructure. As an application matures, there are many advantages to pulling functionality out of the main Rails code base and into discrete services. You can use messaging systems and web services, and you can package your own code into libraries to make a large project more manageable.

Appendix

RESTful Primer

Roy Fielding described Representational State Transfer (REST) in 2000, in his doctoral dissertation (http://www.ics.uci.edu/~fielding/pubs/dissertation/rest_arch_style .htm), as an architectural style for distributed hypermedia systems. His work wasn't tied specifically to HTTP and web services, but it has often been applied to the problem of web services design. This appendix takes a quick look at Fielding's paper, reviews the basics of HTTP, and outlines how these map to the concepts of REST.

Roy Fielding's REST

REST is an often-invoked and often-misunderstood concept. To help clear up some of the confusion, let's look at the original source, Fielding's paper. In the summary of the section on REST, Fielding states:

> REST provides a set of architectural constraints that, when applied as a whole, emphasizes scalability of component interactions, generality of interfaces, independent deployment of components, and intermediary components to reduce interaction latency, enforce security, and encapsulate legacy systems.[1]

---

[1] Fielding, Roy Thomas. *Architectural Styles and the Design of Network-Based Software Architectures*. Irvine: University of California, 2000. http://www.ics.uci.edu/~fielding/pubs/dissertation/rest_arch_style .htm#sec_5_5.

The key component in this summary is that REST is merely a set of architectural constraints. There's nothing in there about HTTP, naming conventions for resources, or how to properly use the HTTP verbs. However, it does mention a few of the goals of service-oriented design mentioned in Chapter 1, "Implementing and Consuming Your First Service." Most notably, it mentions scalability, agility, isolation, and interoperability. The rest of Fielding's paper describes how REST helps achieve those goals.

Constraints

One of the primary characteristics of REST is the set of design constraints it proposes. Here's the list of constraints, with brief descriptions:

- **Client/server**—REST applies to client/server architecture.
- **Stateless**—This is one of the most commonly mentioned constraints. Each request from the client to the server must contain all the information necessary to service the request.
- **Cache**—The cache constraint states that each response from the server must be implicitly or explicitly labeled as cacheable or not cacheable. This often-overlooked feature provides a key part of the scalability of the RESTful style.
- **Uniform interface**—Interactions between the client and server must conform to a uniform interface. In the context of HTTP, this maps to the commonly understood verbs GET, PUT, POST, DELETE, OPTIONS, and HEAD.
- **Layered system**—This constraint states that the architecture can be composed of multiple layers. Further, each layer cannot see beyond the next layer it communicates with. With regard to our service-oriented design, this is analogous to the consumers of web services not having direct knowledge of a database behind a service.
- **Code-on-demand**—This constraint states that the functionality of a client can be extended by downloading additional code. With respect to the web, this refers to technologies such as JavaScript, Flash, or Java applets. However, it is listed as an optional constraint.

Architectural Elements

REST focuses on the architectural elements of a system. This means bringing a focus on the components of a system and their interactions as opposed to the implementation-level details or protocol syntax. Fielding outlines the following elements in his paper:

- **Data elements**—The data elements piece of a RESTful architecture are often an area of focus for design purists. This includes resources, resource identifiers, representations, representation metadata, resource metadata, and control data.
- **Connectors**—Connectors are interfaces for communication between components. The primary types defined are client, server, cache, resolver, and tunnel. For the purposes of our RESTful web services design, the connectors element doesn't really come into the picture.
- **Components**—REST components are separated by their roles within the architecture. These include the origin server (Apache, Nginx, and so on), the gateway (HAProxy, Squid, CGI, reverse proxy, and so on), the proxy (a client chosen proxy server), and the user agent (Firefox, Safari, Internet Explorer, and so on).

Connectors and components are important, but they are relatively well defined through third-party applications that you usually don't have to modify. The architectural components are an implementation detail that can be chosen after a service has already been written and is ready for deployment. The only concern going forward for RESTful web services is how these components take advantage of data elements.

Architectural Views

Fielding's description of REST defines three architectural views that help illuminate how the pieces of a system work together:

- **Process view**—This view shows the interactions between components as data flows through the system.
- **Connector view**—The focus for this view is on the details of network communication between components.
- **Data view**—The data view reveals application state as data flows through the components of the architecture. Because REST specifies a constraint of statelessness, this is most applicable when looking at caching layers. The data view shows where cached responses can come from.

REST and Resources

Now that we've taken a fairly detailed look at Fielding's definition of REST, we're ready to tie it all together with the goal of designing RESTful web services. Resources are at the heart of the design of services.

The concept of resources lies at the core of a RESTful design. At its most basic level, a resource is simply a stream of bits representing something. This could map to a record in a database, a text file, an image, or a set of search results.

Here are some examples of resources that you might use in the social feed reader example:

- The profile information for a user
- A comment
- An entire comment thread
- A user's activity stream
- A list of a user's friends
- The last 100 activities of a user's friends

Notice that some of the listed resources are actually collections of other resources.

URIs and Addressability

All resources must be addressable. A uniform resource identifier (URI) provides the address for each resource. A resource must have at least one unique URI by which it can be accessed. Note that it is possible to access the same resource through multiple URIs. A good example of this is a specific version of a software release. The following two resources could point to the same thing:

- http://ruby-lang.org/pub/ruby/1.9/ruby-1.9.1-p129.tar.gz
- http://ruby-lang.org/pub/ruby/1.9/current-release.tar.gz

The two resources point to a release of the Ruby programming language. While these two URIs may reference the same resource at one point in time, this could change. When a newer version of Ruby comes out, the current-release URI points to that. The first URI here represents the canonical address for that resource and should not change.

A final important thing to point out about URIs is that they don't specify any naming convention. Rail imposes certain conventions through controllers and actions, and many developers think of this as part of REST. It isn't. While it's generally good practice to use naming conventions in your URIs, there's nothing in the constraints of REST that limits URI style.

Representations

Representations are the sequence of bytes and metadata for a resource. In lay terms, a representation is the format that a resource can take. This could be HTML, text, XML, JSON, JPG, TIFF, GIF, or any custom format you can dream up. For Rails developers, this looks most familiar when looking at the actions in a RESTful controller. Take a `comment show` action from the social feed reader as an example:

```
def show
  @comment = Comment.find(params[:id])

  respond_to do |format|
    format.html # show.html.erb
    format.xml  { render :xml  => @comment }
    format.json { render :json => @comment }
  end
end
```

From this controller action, you can see that each comment resource has three possible representations that can be requested. These are the relative URIs for the three representations of the comment resource:

- **/comments/2.html**—Gets the HTML representation of the comment with ID 2.
- **/comments/2.xml**—Gets the XML representation of the comment with ID 2. Note that Rails automatically calls to_xml on the comment object.
- **/comments/2.json**—Gets the JSON representation of the comment with ID 2. Note that Rails automatically calls to_json on the comment object.

Rails uses a file system–style naming convention in the URI to specify the representation of the requested resource. This is the .html, .json, and .xml at the end of the URI. While these three URIs are different, it is entirely possible for all three to point to the same resource (as you saw earlier with the Ruby software release example). Other methods for specifying which representation you're requesting are covered in the next section of this chapter.

Yet another resource detail that could be considered part of the representation is the language. From our example, a comment could be represented in English, Spanish, Japanese, Farsi, or any other language. Most of the time, this isn't an issue because a comment is available in only a single language. Further, automatic translators lack the ability to reliably convert to other languages with any level of quality. However, HTTP provides a method for specifying languages as well.

HTTP and the Uniform Interface

One of the key constraints of REST is the uniform interface. The goal of the uniform interface is to make the interaction between components as simple to understand as possible. This means that components should use the same methods to communicate between each other. Resources and their addresses are part of this uniformity. The uniformity of component interaction is the fixed set of operations that can be performed on resources. HTTP provides a small set of methods to enable simpler APIs along with gateway and caching servers.

HTTP Methods

The HTTP methods are the verbs for the uniform interface. You use them to communicate your needs against resources. The methods in HTTP are GET, POST, PUT, DELETE, HEAD, OPTIONS, TRACE, and CONNECT. For the purposes of RESTful interfaces, we'll pay attention primarily to the first four methods. OPTIONS and HEAD come into play in special cases, while TRACE and CONNECT don't concern our services designs. Before we dig into the specifics of each method, it's worth mentioning two concepts that are important to HTTP and services design: safe and idempotent methods.

Safe and Idempotent Methods

Safe methods are those that do not request any server-side effects. That is, they are methods that only request information. They do not modify resources in any way. GET and HEAD methods are considered safe. This means that programs such as web crawlers can perform GET and HEAD operations without concern for what may happen on the server. An example is following hyperlinks on a page. Because POST is not considered a safe operation, well-behaved crawlers do not submit HTML forms.

Idempotent methods are those that can be replayed any number of times without a change from the first one. In more mathematical terms, these are methods for which the result of running them $N > 0$ times will always be the same. GET, HEAD, PUT, and DELETE are idempotent. GET and HEAD are idempotent because they have no side effects. PUT is idempotent because putting the same resource at the same URI again results in no change from the first time the PUT was run. DELETE is idempotent because once a resource is deleted, deleting it again doesn't have any effect.

GET

The GET method is a read request for a specific resource. It retrieves information, which is identified by the URI. This could be a request that simply returns a static asset from disk (such as an image or a regular HTML file), or it could be a request that requires processing to return the result (for example, a search results page). So the GET method does literally what it says: It gets a resource. Further, it should produce no side effects. So it's safe and idempotent.

POST

At its most basic level, a POST is appended to an existing resource. It is a request that includes an entity (some data) that the server should accept. It can be used to annotate an existing resource (such as adding a comment to a list of comments), appending data, or simply providing data to some backend process.

Rails applications commonly use POST as a create or insert for a record. This is very much like an append to a collection. Consider comments from the social feed reader application, for example. A POST to /comments would create a new comment. Thus, the request can be viewed as an append to the collection of comments. Further, it assigns an ID and creates a whole new resource at /comments/:id.

One final thing about POST is that it is neither safe nor idempotent. Running POST multiple times results in multiple resources being created. In some cases, you might want to take more care in creating a resource on a POST. This could be a way to hack around the fact that POST is not idempotent. In the earlier comments example, before doing an insert, you could check the database first to see if the comment body is the same as the last comment posted by the user. Of course, that's beyond the realm of what HTTP cares about. It doesn't specify exactly what the server-side behavior should be.

PUT

The PUT method places a resource at a specific URI. The request includes data and specifies that the server should store that data under the request URI. If there is already a resource at that URI, the data should be viewed as a modified version of the preexisting resource. Otherwise, that URI should become a reference to the data supplied in the request.

In simpler terms, this means that PUT can be either an insert with a client-supplied URI or an update. For most Rails programs, PUT isn't used for inserts at all. This is because the server is usually responsible for supplying the full URI for created resources. For creating a comment in the social feed reader, it would look like this:

- **POST to /comments**—Here the body of the POST would supply the information for the comment. The server would then do an insert in a database to create the resource.
- **PUT to /comments/2**—With Rails, this would be an update to the comment with an ID of 2. In a standard Rails application, this would never indicate an insert. However, HTTP specifies that this could indeed be an insert.

Some HTTP purists will tell you that a PUT should always be an insert or a complete replace of the resource at the specified URI. This means that you wouldn't be able to do partial updates as you commonly do in Rails. Instead, you'd have to do something like this:

```
PUT to /comments/2/body
```

In this case, the body of the request would be the replacement of the body of the comment. So to update any two attributes, you would have to make multiple requests to the specific attribute resources. Obviously, doing things this way would be completely maddening. Indeed, Roy Fielding has stated that PUT doesn't adhere to a strict definition of "store at this URI." Here's what he had to say on the subject on a mailing list in 2006:

> *FWIW, PUT does not mean store. I must have repeated that a million times in webdav and related lists. HTTP defines the intended semantics of the communication—the expectations of each party. The protocol does not define how either side fulfills those expectations, and it makes damn sure it doesn't prevent a server from having absolute authority over its own resources. Also, resources are known to change over time, so if a server accepts an invalid Atom entry via PUT one second and then immediately thereafter decides to change it to a valid entry for later GETs, life is grand.*[2]

---

[2]Fielding, Roy T. Re: *Meaning of PUT, with (gasp) evidence*, June 15, 2006. http://www.imc.org/atom-protocol/mail-archive/msg05425.html.

So the next time a REST or HTTP zealot tells you that partial updates aren't allowed with the formal definition of PUT, you can point the person to Roy's own words.

We still need to make sure that the server-side results of a PUT request remain idempotent. If a partial update happens with a PUT, the result of running that multiple times should not be any different from running it once.

DELETE

The DELETE method is fairly simple and straightforward. It deletes the resource at a specified URI. However, the operation can be overridden on the server.

HEAD and OPTIONS

The HEAD and OPTIONS methods are the final two methods worth mentioning for the RESTful services design. These two lesser-used methods provide information about resources.

HEAD works exactly like GET, with one difference. It doesn't return the actual resource. Instead, it returns only the header information for a resource. This includes things like content-size, last-modified, content-type, and ETag headers. This can be useful when you're determining whether a cached resource should be considered stale.

OPTIONS is a method for getting information about what operations can be performed on a resource. As an example, if you wanted the comments API to conform more closely to HTTP conventions, an OPTIONS request on /comments/2 might return the following header:

```
Allow: GET, HEAD, PUT, DELETE
```

The response contained in the header tells you that you can perform any on of those HTTP methods on the specific comments resource.

HTTP Headers

HTTP headers work on both sides of client/server communication. Clients issue request headers, and the server issues response headers. Together, these help the two parties agree on and convey information about resources.

Request Headers

Request headers let the client specify additional information to the server about the requested representation of a resource. This list is by no means complete, but here are some common request headers, with examples that a client may specify:

- `Accept: text/plain, text/html`—This tells the server that the client is looking for a plain-text or HTML representation of the resource. Other options could be `application/json`, `text/javascript`, `application/xml`, `text/xml`, `image/jpeg`, and countless others.

- `Accept-Encoding: compress, gzip`—This header tells the server whether the client can take a gzip or compressed response.

- `User-Agent: pauldix-service-client/1.0`—In most cases, the user agent field isn't required. However, some servers reject requests that don't specify a user agent of some kind. It's generally part of being a good Internet citizen to specify a user agent that server administrators can find information on.

- `Accept-Language: en`—This header tells the server what language the resource should be returned in. This example requests English.

- `If-Modified-Since: Tue, 30 Jun 2009 08:30:31 GMT`—This header tells the server that the client has a version of the resource that was last generated at 8:30 AM on June 30. If the server has a newer version, it should return that in the response. If that version is the latest, then the server should return an empty response body with a 304 Not Modified response code. This is one piece of the caching mechanisms that is built into HTTP.

- `If-None-Match: "sdfzlkjsd"`—This header is another way for the client to tell the server that it has a cached version of a resource. The supplied string matches up with an ETag in the response header. If the client-supplied ETag matches that of the most current version of the requested resource, the server should return an empty response body with a 304 Not Modified response code. Otherwise, the server should return the latest version of the requested resource.

- `Content-Type: application/x-www-form-urlencoded`—The content type field is used in POST and PUT requests to specify to the server the format of the request body. The example here is for a form POST. Two other common examples are `application/json` and `application/xml`.

- `Content-Length: 1274`—This tells the server the length of the request body, in bytes.

- `Cookie: user_id=PaulDix; sort=date`—Cookies are set in the request header. This is a list of name/value pairs separated by semicolons.

- **`Authorization: Basic QWxhZGRpbjpvcGVuIHNlc2FtZQ==`**—This header is for specifying client credentials for a request. This example uses basic authentication and passes the user name and password as a base 64–encoded string.

> **Complete List of Request Headers**
>
> A more complete list of request headers can be found at the W3 definition site, at http://www.w3.org/Protocols/HTTP/HTRQ_Headers.html.

Representation Headers

RESTful purists argue that the representation of a resource should be specified by the client in the request headers. This includes the format (JSON, XML, HTML, and so on) and the language. Obviously, Rails doesn't follow this exactly. You specify to Rails the format you want with the end part of the URI. For example, `/comments/2.json` tells Rails that you want the JSON-formatted representation of the comment with ID 2. When it comes to languages, Rails leaves application developers on their own.

There are three arguments against taking the HTTP purist's approach of specifying representation in headers. First, it's easier for most client-side developers to deal with specifying the format in the URI rather than in the header. Seeing a `.json` or `.xml` extension on the end of the URI is understandable almost immediately. While using the URI to specify format may not be exactly technically correct, it often results in more accessible APIs.

Second, some cache servers, such as those at Akamai, cache only based on the URI. So if you specify which representation you want in the request header, your caching layer may end up broken. This is a definite reason to keep this information in the URI.

Finally, language representations may not map to exactly the same resource. When using the request headers to specify representation, you are always asking for the same resource each time, but with different options. With formatting such as XML and JSON, this is a direct machine representation of the same thing. With languages, machine translation is rarely the best way to go from one language to another. It's often better if you have human translators create the different language versions. In that case, the translated versions represent distinct resources and should be specified with different URIs.

Response Headers

Response headers from the server give the client metadata about the resource being returned. Often, the response headers have matching corollaries in the request headers. Here is a list of response headers that you will most often be concerned with:

- **`Age: 30`**—This gives the time the resource has been in proxy cache, in seconds.
- **`Allow: GET, HEAD, PUT, DELETE`**—This lists the HTTP methods allowed on the resource. You saw this earlier, in the response to an `OPTIONS` request.
- **`Cache-Control: max-age=120`**—This header allows either the client or server more control over caching than the default mechanisms. These commands are intended for proxy caches that lie between the client and server. Chapter 8, "Load Balancing and Caching," covers this in greater detail.
- **`Content-Encoding: gzip`**—This tells the client the encoding of the response. It is used for compression and gzip.
- **`Content-Length: 234`**—This gives the length of the response body, in bytes.
- **`Content-Type: application/json; charset=utf-8`**—This tells the client the MIME type of the response. This should match up with one of the types in the `Accept` header from the request.
- **`ETag: sdlkf234`**—The `ETag` gives a unique identifier of some sort for the resource. This identifier should match up with the version of the resource in some way. This could be an ID combined with a `last_updated` field or a hash of the 2 or some other value. This is used for caching purposes and matches with the `If-None-Match` request header.
- **`Expires: Wed, 01 Jul 2009 09:02:12 GMT`**—This tells the client or a proxy cache when a response should be considered stale. Either of these can verify whether the resource is up-to-date for a later request.
- **`Last-Modified: Wed, 01 Jul 2009 09:03:45 GMT`**—This is another caching mechanism. This matches up with the client-side header `If-Modified-Since`. Thus, with later requests for the same resource, the client can use the `Last-Modified` value for `If-Modified-Since`.
- **`Set-Cookie: user_id=paul`**—This sets the client-side cookie.

HTTP Status Codes

Status codes are three-digit integers that specify the status of a response. With regard to our RESTful services, status codes should be used as part of the API and the uniform interface. While REST doesn't state a specific need for the use of status codes, it is generally considered good design practice to conform to the definitions of HTTP.

The first digit of the status code indicates the general nature of the response. Here are the classes of responses from the W3 definition:

- 1xx—Informational status which states that the request has been received and is continuing
- 2xx—Success status which states that the request was received and accepted
- 3xx—Redirection status which states that to complete the request, further action must be taken at another URI
- 4xx—Client error status which states that the request is either improperly formatted or cannot be completed for some reason
- 5xx—Server error status which states that the server failed to complete the request despite it being valid

One thing to note about status codes is that the HTTP methods often define which specific code should be taken on certain actions.

Conclusion

REST and HTTP provide basic guidelines for building services. While the exact definition of REST is debatable, we can focus on the set of constraints that make for a RESTful architecture. Four constraints often resurface while you're designing services:

- **Client/server**—REST is a client/server architecture.
- **Stateless**—The server contains no state between requests.
- **Cache**—Responses are labeled as cacheable or not cacheable.
- **Uniform interface**—Interactions between a client and a server should conform to a uniform interface.

At the center of RESTful design lies the concept of resources. Resources are the objects that requests can be performed against. They are addressable through URIs and have representations (format and language).

The HTTP verbs are the building blocks of the uniform interface. They can be roughly mapped to database actions and CRUD. Here they are again:

- **GET**—Maps to SQL SELECT.
- **PUT**—Maps to SQL UPDATE or INSERT with a specified key.

- **POST**—Maps to SQL INSERT. The key is generated by the database.
- **DELETE**—Maps to SQL DELETE.

Ultimately, the important thing to remember about REST is that it is merely a set of constraints and guidelines for designing and architecting scalable client/server systems. Many developers like to get embroiled in arguments about what represents REST and what doesn't, but often the distinctions aren't that strong. The best approach usually involves a number of trade-offs and compromises.

Index

Numbers

X

Y

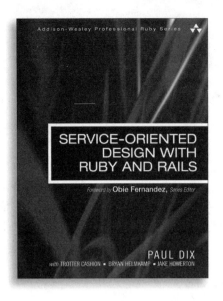

FREE Online Edition

Your purchase of **Service-Oriented Design with Ruby and Rails** includes access to a free online edition for 45 days through the Safari Books Online subscription service. Nearly every Addison-Wesley Professional book is available online through Safari Books Online, along with more than 5,000 other technical books and videos from publishers such as Cisco Press, Exam Cram, IBM Press, O'Reilly, Prentice Hall, Que, and Sams.

SAFARI BOOKS ONLINE allows you to search for a specific answer, cut and paste code, download chapters, and stay current with emerging technologies.

Activate your FREE Online Edition at www.informit.com/safarifree

R.C.L.

AVR. 2011

> **STEP 1:**

G

> **STEP 2:**
> Safari subscribers, just log in.

I.

If you have difficulty registering on Safari or accessing the online edition, please e-mail customer-service@safaribooksonline.com